THE COMPLETE
CLOUD OF UNKNOWING

PARACLETE
GIANTS

ABOUT THIS SERIES:

Each Paraclete Giant presents collected works of one of Christianity's greatest writers—"giants" of the faith. These essential volumes share the pivotal teachings of leading Christian figures throughout history with today's theological students and all people seeking spiritual wisdom.

Also in this Series...

THE COMPLETE FÉNELON
Edited with translations by Robert J. Edmonson, CJ
and Hal M. Helms

THE COMPLETE JULIAN OF NORWICH
Translation and commentary by Father John-Julian, OJN

THE COMPLETE THÉRÈSE OF LISIEUX
Edited with translations by Robert J. Edmonson, CJ

THE COMPLETE MADAME GUYON
Edited with translations by the Rev. Nancy C. James, PhD

THE COMPLETE IMITATION OF CHRIST
Translation and commentary by Father John-Julian, OJN

THE COMPLETE FRANCIS OF ASSISI
Edited, translated, and introduced by Jon M. Sweeney

For more information, visit www.paracletepress.com.

PARACLETE
GIANTS

The COMPLETE

Cloud

OF

Unknowing

with *The Letter of*
Privy Counsel

Translation and Commentary by
Father John-Julian, OJN

PARACLETE PRESS BREWSTER, MASSACHUSETTS

For John Patrick Hedley Clark,
who best knows The Cloud,
and for James Hogg,
who has told the rest of the world.

2015 First Printing

The Complete Cloud of Unknowing: *with* The Letter of Privy Counsel

Copyright © 2015 by The Order of Julian of Norwich

ISBN 978-1-61261-620-9

The Paraclete Press name and logo (dove on cross) are trademarks of Paraclete Press, Inc.

Library of Congress Cataloging-in-Publication Data

The complete Cloud of unknowing : with the Letter of privy counsel / translation and commentary by Father John-Julian, OJN.
     pages cm
  Translated from the Middle English.
  ISBN 978-1-61261-620-9 (paperback)
  1. Mysticism—Early works to 1800. I. John-Julian, Father, O.J.N. II. Cloud of unknowing. III. Letter of privy counsel.
  BV5082.3.C58 2015
  248.2'2—dc23   2014042297

10 9 8 7 6 5 4 3 2 1

Published by Paraclete Press
Brewster, Massachusetts
www.paracletepress.com
Printed in the United States of America

CONTENTS

TRANSLATOR'S INTRODUCTION   *vii*

NOTES ON THE TRANSLATION   *xxxix*

The Cloud of Unknowing   1

The Letter of Privy Counsel   189

NOTES FOR THE TRANSLATOR'S INTRODUCTION   257

APPENDICES   263

BIBLIOGRAPHY   271

As it is now here in this book: where we enter into the darkness that is above mind, we shall not only find the inadequacy of words, but, as it were, a madness and a total irrationality in all that we say. And in all the other books our composition descends from the highest things to the lowest; and after the amount of descending, it spreads out to a great number. But now [our composition] ascends in this book from the lowest things to the highest; and after the movement of the ascension—which is sometimes more rapid than others—it is focused. And above all such ascension, it shall all be without voice and it shall be all knitted to a thing that is unspeakable.

—DEONISE HID DIUINIE
by the author of
The Clowde of Vnknowyng

TRANSLATOR'S INTRODUCTION

Devout friend in God (as our author would put it): When you open this book, you are opening the door on a profound mystery and on the deep struggle this devout author has undertaken to try to share that mystery with a younger, contemplative protégé. His efforts necessarily stretch and strain the language as he strives to explain what is virtually inexplicable and can only be "known" by being experienced—but he is a serious and devout mystical guide who knows the territory from his own experience, and he provides hints, suggestions, and warnings that will serve any devout Christian sincerely committed to the development of a serious ascetical life of prayer.

This unknown monk is, preeminently and inescapably, a mystic. Dom Cuthbert Butler wrote in the early twentieth century:

> There is probably no more misused word in these days than "mysticism." It has come to be applied to many things of many kinds: to theosophy and Christian Science; to spiritualism and clairvoyance; to demonology and witchcraft; to occultism and magic; to weird psychical experiences and visions; to other-worldliness, or even mere dreaminess and impracticability in the affairs of life; to poetry and painting and music of which the motif is unobvious and vague. It has been identified also with a certain outlook on the world—seeing God in Nature, and recognizing that the material creation in various ways symbolizes spiritual realities: a beautiful and true conception . . . but which is not mysticism according to its historical meaning. And, on the other side, the meaning of the term has been watered down: it has been said that the love of God is mysticism; or that mysticism is only the Christian life lived on a high level; or that it is Roman Catholic piety in extreme form. Against all of this stands the perfectly clear traditional historical meaning, handed down in the Christian Church throughout the centuries, not subject to confusion of thought until recent times.[1]

A mystic is one who is not satisfied with limiting reality to only what can be seen as visible, or comprehended as rational, or experienced as sensory. The mystic lives, in a sense, "beyond the dictionary," beyond systematic theology, beyond legalistic morality, and beyond creedal simplicity. (Please note, however, that here "beyond" must also be understood to be *inclusive* and not taken to suggest "opposition." Christian mysticism should be thought of as "all of ordinary Christianity *plus....*") The world in which a mystic lives is—for her or him—alive with God, pulsing with divinity, and overflowing with spiritual reality. God is no mere abstract concept but is present in all dimensions of life—in every breath, every movement, every object, every thought. A mystic is unwilling to live life at a level acceptable to most others—not in derision of their commitments and concerns, but simply in dissatisfaction with less than the heart-stirrings of grace that press one into the heart of the Divine Mystery itself.

Consequently, the mystic often moves along the knife-edge of metaphor, paradox, poetry, and enigma—aware of the contradictions of theodicy, the ambiguity of biblical incongruities, and the challenges of theological conundrums, but recognizing a divine reality deeper and more profound than all these matters. It was once put simply that a mystic is one who lives as though God actually existed—unsatisfied with anything less than Godself— "one who seeks by contemplation and self-surrender to obtain union with or absorption into the Deity, or who believes in spiritual apprehension of truths beyond the understanding."[2]

It is important to recognize that although a true Christian mystic may be discovering dimensions of faith and reality not commonly or universally discerned, these intuitive insights are not "secret" or "covert" as were the teachings of the heretical Gnostics of the early centuries. They are not *withheld* from any Christian, but they often involve a deeper spiritual insight than most Christians take the trouble to seek, and also a dimension of vocation in which some are led by God's grace to pursue a life of deeper contemplative prayer than others.[3]

The four notable identities that tend to be characteristic of the mystical way are (a) the repudiation of literalism; (b) the development and practice of some form of contemplation; (c) engagement with apophatic theology, known as the *via negativa*, focusing on what God is *not* rather than what God is; and (d) the goal of absolute identity and total union of the soul with God. These are so close that what was called mysticism (or hesychasm[4]) in the Eastern Orthodox traditions could be thought of as almost identical to what in the West came to be called simply "contemplation"—a solitary, eremitical prayer, dedicated to liberation of the soul from its ties to the world, and whose goal was perfect willed union with God.

This desire most often steered one toward the apophatic *via negativa* ("the negative way") that declared that nothing we can say in earthly speech about what/who God is can ever be exhaustively true, unqualifiedly accurate, or pragmatically meaningful. As Giles Fraser recently put it: "all religion exists to make raids into what is unsayable."[5] The Divine Nature is so far beyond us, so far beyond our culture, our world, our imagination, and our understanding that all of our language fails to describe God, and the only thing we can say with any truth or accuracy about God is what God is *not*—for example, God is *not* created, *not* multiple, *not* evil, does *not* take up space, is *not* bound to time, does *not* change.[6] Apophatic prayer is a way of praying that makes no reference to earthly or material realities but is only concerned with purity of heart and total detachment from worldly thought and language as one seeks a fleeting experience of God.[7]

The final goal for a mystic is immersion in God—the abandonment of ego in a perfect union of one's will with God's will in love. The operative human dynamic is neither intellect nor emotion, but the vision of the intuition and the action of the will—which is the agent of love/charity.[8]

The author's comprehension of the human process of understanding basically describes the imagination and sensuality (the action of the five senses) as producing the raw material—that is, the senses give us information about the physical world around us, and the imagination produces information about what *could* be. Both of these feed into the reason/intellect, which in turn "organizes" the input from the imagination and the senses and "passes it on" to the mind, which then acts by way of the will to make choices and decisions. And the act of the will that is central to the author's purposes here is the willful act of love—the choice to love unsentimentally, unselfishly, and sacrificially.

In that act of love, one utterly *chooses* God above and beyond all else—and thus one's own will comes into union with the Divine Will. "The exercise of the will directed solely to God pleases God more than any other exercise."[9] For the mystic this union may be brief—even ephemeral—occasional, and rare. It is the transient momentary experience on earth of the ultimate eternal union of heaven. This process is often referred to as "divinization" (or "deification" or *theosis*) as the soul takes on itself a more and more celestial nature and shares more intimately with God's very Self. (It must be pointed out that a proper contemplative's practice *may* aim less high and may aspire to opening the self to God simply in order to be silently available and vulnerable to spiritual insights, intuitions, or discernments short of divinization—and this less "strenuous" approach to contemplation is not to be discredited: it is entirely mystically valid and spiritually beneficial.)

In our author's fourteenth-century church, mysticism was endemic and extensive—especially in England and the German Rhineland—but it had its roots in much earlier ages—indeed, to some degree, in Scripture itself. None of the following passages, for instance, can be interpreted simply in literal terms; they must all lend themselves to an allegorical, metaphorical, or mystical sense and carry meanings beyond the merely denotative designations of their words.[10]

"We look not to things that are seen, but the things that are not seen. For the things that are seen are transitory: but the things that are not seen are eternal" (2 Cor. 4:18). (And one may reverse the tautology: "Things that are eternal are invisible.")

"He has granted to us his precious and very great promises, so that through them you may become sharers in the divine nature, having escaped from the carnal corruption that is in the world" (2 Pet. 1:4). Note: Humans will share in God's own Divine Nature—a common notion of the Christian mystic.

"For you are dead, and your life has been swallowed up with Christ in God" (Col. 3:3). Note: A living human is declared to be dead, but spiritually "consumed" by Christ within God! Here the human is mystically made one with the risen Christ who is in perfect union with God the Father—hence it is in union with Christ that a Christian is one-ed to God.

"While I live, it is no longer I: but, in truth, Christ lives within me" (Gal. 2:20). A person who has died (Christ) now lives inside a live human—a typical mystical paradox!

"He who believes in me, as the scripture said, out of his belly will flow rivers of fresh water" (Jn. 7:38). Certainly this verse cannot be read in any literal way but must be interpreted allegorically and mystically.

"But whoever is joined to the Lord becomes one spirit with him" (1 Cor. 6:17). Union with God means that one shares the divine spirit.

It is likely that the very early emphasis on the importance of allegorical and mystical interpretation of the Scriptures may, in a way, be the initial expression of Christian mysticism and the agent for the application of the same dynamic to ascetical and speculative theology itself.

And among the early Fathers of the Church, we find many expressing strongly mystical concepts and insights. In many cases they reveal what came to be called "Christian gnosticism" (Greek *gnosis* translates as "knowledge"), which suggests a particular knowledge that was not broadly available to non-Christians.[11] Here is only a collection of samples to demonstrate the breadth of mystical and speculative theology among the early Church Fathers. (All translations are mine.)

- Justin Martyr († 165): "But pray that, above all things, the gates of light may be opened to you; for these things cannot be perceived or understood by all, but only by the one to whom God and His Christ have imparted wisdom" (*Dialogue with Trypho*, ch. 7).
- Theophilus of Antioch († 190): "[By] keeping the commandment of God, [one] should receive immortality as a reward from [God], and should become God" (*To Autolycus*, bk. 2, ch. 27).
- Irenaeus of Lyons († 200): "… the Word of God, our Lord Jesus Christ, who became what we are … that he might cause us to become even what he is himself" (*Against Heresies*, bk. 5, preface).
- Clement of Alexandria († 215): "I say, the Word of God became human so that you could learn from a human how a human can become God" (*Exhortation to the Heathen*, ch. 1); and "We, then, are those who are believers in what is not believed, and who know what is unknown" (*Stromata* 5, ch. 1).
- Origen of Alexandria († 254): "If one considers that the richness of what there is in God to contemplate and know is incomprehensible

to human nature and perhaps to all beings which are born, apart
from Christ and the Spirit, one will understand how God is enveloped in darkness, for no one can formulate any conception rich
enough to do him justice. It is then in darkness that he has made
his hiding-place; he has made it thus because no one can know all
concerning him who is infinite" (*Commentary on John* 2.28).

• Gregory of Nazianzus († 390):
  "How can words sing praise to you
  when no word can even speak of you?
  How can the mind think about you
  when no mind can ever grasp you?
  You alone are indescribable
  since you created all things that can be described.
  You alone are unknowable
  since you created all things that can be known"
  (*Hymn* 1.1.2 "On the Incarnation of Christ").

• Gregory of Nyssa († 395): "For abandoning everything that can
  be seen ... [the soul] keeps on penetrating deeper until by intelligence's longing for comprehension it gains access to the invisible
  and the incomprehensible and there it sees God. This is the true
  knowledge of what is sought: this is the seeing that consists in not
  seeing, because what is sought passes beyond all knowledge, being
  separated on every side by incomprehensibility as by a kind of
  darkness" (*Life of Moses* 163).

• Augustine of Hippo († 430): "Under your guidance I entered the
  depths of my soul ... and with the eye of my soul ... I saw the Light
  that never changes casting its rays ... over my mind.... What I saw
  was something very, very different from any light we know on
  earth. It shined above my mind, but not as oil floats above water or
  the sky hangs over the earth. It was above me because it was itself
  the Light that made me, and I was below because I was made by
  it. Everyone who knows the truth knows this Light, and all who
  know this Light know eternity.... And, far off, I heard your voice
  saying *I am the God who IS* ..." (*Confessions* 147).

• Maximus the Confessor († 662): "For God is not only beyond
  knowledge, but also beyond unknowing; His revelation itself is

also truly a mystery of a most divine and extraordinary kind, since the divine manifestations, even if symbolic, remain unknowable by reason of their transcendence" (*The Triads* 1.3.4, trans. Nicholas Gendle).

- Symeon the New Theologian († 1022): "Be aware also how those men are changed who leave behind all things out of love for Him who has loved us ... how those who are darkness become light in marvelous fashion as they draw near to the Great Light; how those who come from below . . . become gods as they are united to things above" (*Discourse* 17.4).

- Bernard of Clairvaux († 1153): "And yet, 'he who is united to the Lord becomes one spirit with him,' his whole being somehow transformed into a movement of divine love. He no longer has the power to experience or savor anything except God and whatever Godself experiences and relishes, because he is filled with God. But God is love, and the deeper one's union with God, the more full one is of love" (*On the Song of Songs*, Sermon 26.5).

- Thomas Aquinas († 1274): "Furthermore, everything infinite, as such, is unknown. And, indeed, God is infinite ... therefore, he is unknown" (*Summa Theologica* 3.1.12 [Cambridge: Cambridge Univ. Press, 2006]).

- Meister Eckhart († 1327): "A man should not have, or be satisfied with, an imagined God, for then, when the idea vanishes, God vanishes! Rather, one should have an essential God, who far transcends the thought of man and all creatures" (*The Tasks of Instruction*, sect. 6).

- Johann Tauler († 1361): "And in this way all our conditions are transformed into God so that we neither notice nor enjoy anything nor know anything more truly than God, though in a way that transcends the powers of reason and rational knowledge" (*Sermon* 50).

- Henry Suso († 1366): "[Christ speaks in the person of Wisdom]: 'Although I give myself to be felt by men in their inmost hearts, yet no tongue can ever declare or explain in words what I am. For verily all the beauty, grace, and adornment that can be conceived by you or by others exists in me far more excellently, more copiously,

xiv | *The Complete* Cloud of Unknowing

than anyone could say in words.... By no other way can you know the certainty of my presence better than when I hide myself from you and withdraw what is mine from your soul. Then at last you know by experience what I am and what you are'" ("A Meditation on the Passion of Christ" in Inge, William Ralph, trans., *Light, Life, and Love: Selections from the German Mystics of the Middle Ages* [Methuen; London; 1904], 91).

- Walter Hilton († 1396): "After being reformed by virtues to the likeness of God, we see the face of our soul uncovered by the opening of our spiritual eye, and behold as in a mirror the heavenly joy, completely conformed and one-ed to the image of our Lord, from brightness of faith into brightness of understanding, or else from clarity of desire into clarity of blessed love. And all this is wrought in a person's soul by the spirit of our Lord" (*The Scale of Perfection*, Clark, J.P.H. and Dorward, Rosemary, eds. [Paulist Press, New York; 1991], ch. 9).

As Saint Edith Stein wrote: "The mystical stream, which flows through the centuries, is not a meandering side-stream that has separated from the prayer life of the Church; it is her very lifeblood. If it breaks with traditional forms, it does so because the Spirit is living in it, a Spirit that blows where it wills. He created all the old forms and he has to create new ones."[12]

It should be clear that the mystical way is not something invented in the late medieval Church but has been a quiet undercurrent in Christianity from the very beginning. There were Christian eras when almost nothing was heard of it, and other periods when it seemed to blossom—and, up to that time, no such period or place more than fourteenth-century England.

In our day some lament the supposed departure of modern Christianity from its orthodox theological roots, or from its mandate to serve the poor, or for its own accumulation of wealth and comfort, or for its narrow and exclusive character. But perhaps the most pervasive and most critical deviation had been the tendency for the early modern Church to abandon its mystical roots. Fortunately contemporary efforts have been made recently to try to reclaim the mystical heritage and the contemplative way by people such as the Benedictines John Main and Laurence Freeman with their "World Community for Christian Meditation," the Trappist Thomas Merton (who at one point seriously considered leaving the Trappists for a Carthusian Charterhouse),[13] and Cistercians William Meninger, Basil Pennington, and Thomas Keating with their "Centering Prayer" movement. And, indeed, the recent comment by Pope Francis is notable: "A religion without mystics is a philosophy. . . . The mystic manages to strip himself of action, of facts, objectives and even the pastoral mission and rises until he reaches communion with Beatitude. Brief moments but which fill an entire life."[14] Evelyn Underhill wrote that mystics are "the great pioneers of humanity."[15]

But the mystical way has also been seen as dangerous and either discounted or condemned by ecclesiastical authority because it challenges the neatness of reason-based theology, the orderly operation of the institutional church, and the superficiality of much ordinary Christian practice and belief. A contemplative who in the height of ecstatic experience encounters the very Self of God makes an awkward and uncomfortable fellow traveler for a regimented and disciplined monsignor or a passionately enthusiastic evangelical pastor. So the movement has not been without its critics. And we are reminded of Cardinal Newman's old saw: "Mysticism begins in mist and ends in schism."[16]

To these criticisms, I can only add Karl Rahner's wise words: "The devout Christian of the future will be a 'mystic,' one who has 'experienced' something, or he will cease to be anything at all."[17] And I especially appreciate Ann Fontaine's remark, "Even the word 'God' is like a pronoun without antecedents."[18]

THE AUTHOR

Certainly the first mystery we encounter in taking up *The Cloud* is the identity of its anonymous author.[19] And let it be said at the outset that no one—no expert, no commentator, no analyst, no translator—has ever been able to make a firm, indisputable identification of the person who wrote this book. There are practically as many proposals and opinions as there are translators[20]—and I shall offer my own—but none are or can be wholly certain unless some new evidence turns up in the future.

It does seem a virtual certainty that the author was a priest: he uses a vesting prayer that only a priest would ordinarily know[21] and he offers a clear priestly blessing.[22] The literary quality of the text also gives evidence that he is a highly educated person—another suggestion of his ordained status since relatively few laity in the fourteenth century would have had access to the level of literacy he manifests. His reference to communal and liturgical prayer is quite probably good evidence of his own base in monasticism.[23]

For some years, he was identified by authorities as Walter Hilton—a fellow English fourteenth-century mystic—but that identification has been virtually expunged in later scholarship,[24] although our author and Walter Hilton do remain closely associated, possibly even knew each other personally, and were certainly acquainted with each other's works[25] (which may suggest that they lived not far apart geographically, as well).

Our priestly author also seems to be a serious contemplative and a solitary in his own right. He does not discuss the contemplative experience as an objective observer, but as one who has "been there" himself and knows the experience firsthand. And this opens doors to several possibilities: the Benedictines, the Cistercians, the Dominicans, the Carmelites, and the Augustinian Hermits all have provisions in their rules and statutes for derivative solitaries and hermits—and most of them could involve the practice of meditation of one kind or another. And certainly the Carthusians' entire monastic model is eremitic (although within a community of other hermit-monks) and contemplative. It is *possible* that our author could have spent communal time with any one of these orders and then, under that aegis, have become a solitary/hermit. The fact that at the time of his writing he is living as a solitary is plainly evident from his writings.[26]

But what one may call the severity, rigorousness, and strictures of the style of contemplative practice promulgated by the author gives extremely great weight to his engagement with the Carthusian tradition. No other monastic tradition promoted and practiced so thorough and scrupulous an eremitic and contemplative lifestyle as did the Carthusians—what might almost be called "immoderate contemplation" was, indeed, the very heart of their tradition. And it is inconceivable to me that the author should have made up his complicated mystical system by himself without reference to a broader precedent contemplative tradition.

The Carthusian Order was founded by Saint Bruno of Cologne in 1084.[27] His first hermitage was built in the Chartreuse Mountains in the French Alps, from which the name "Carthusian" is derived. (*Chartreuse* became "Charterhouse" in English—the name given to all Carthusian monasteries in England.) Eventually, after an avalanche killed seven of the brothers, the monastery was relocated and enlarged and became the famous *Grande Chartreuse*—the motherhouse for all Carthusians.

In the beginning the order was simply a small group of hermit priests living separately, independently, and privately but geographically together in one community, sharing in liturgy and occasional festal meals. Saint Bruno wrote no formal rule, but in 1129 Guido I, the fifth prior of the order, compiled the first *Consuetudines* ("Customs"), which described the life of a Carthusian and with a few later additions came to serve as the Statutes of the order. The prologue to the Statutes begins:

> To the praise of the glory of God, Christ, the Father's Word, has, through the Holy Spirit, from the beginning chosen certain men, whom he willed to lead into solitude and unite to himself in intimate love. In obedience to such a call, Master Bruno and six companions entered the desert of Chartreuse in the year of our Lord 1084 and settled there; under the guidance of the Holy Spirit, they and their successors, learning from experience, gradually evolved a special form of hermit life, which was handed on to succeeding generations, not by the written word, but by example.[28]

The Charterhouse was unlike any other monastery in that it was comprised (ideally) of either twelve, twenty-four, or thirty-six individual and separate cells or cottages arranged around a common cloister, a church, a refectory, a chapter room, and a *courery* or separate settlement for lay brothers. Each monk's cell consisted of a small two-level cottage with a high-walled garden where the monk could grow flowers for himself or vegetables for the community. On the ground floor was a workshop with workbench or loom or lathe, since each monk engaged in manual crafts work of some kind, and a store of lumber as well as firewood for the hearth. In the loft above was a narrow entryway, and a room with a wooden box bed (with a straw mattress and woolen blankets), a small table for meals, a study desk, a bookcase, a wood stove, and a prayer niche with stall and kneeler.[29] Next to the door of the cell was the *guichet*—called a "turn" or a "hatch"—a small revolving compartment through which food and other items could be passed into or out of the cell without a monk's direct contact with anyone from the outside world—including the lay brother who delivered his food. There was also usually a covered ambulatory in the garden where the monk could take private exercise. A fairly modern piping system brought fresh water to each of the cells and carried away waste from their outhouses.

According to the Statutes a Carthusian monk was also supplied for writing with "pens, chalk, two pumice-stones, two inkwells, a small knife, two razors for leveling the surface of the parchment, a *punctorium* [a small compass used to mark the parchment for drawing lines], an awl, a lead pencil, a ruler, writing tablets, and a stylus."[30]

The Carthusian spent most of his day in the cell, praying, working on his craft, studying, writing, or cultivating his garden. He left the cell only three times a day (and always in silence) for the Office of Matins, for Mass, and for the Office of Vespers. On Sundays and feast days all the monks would eat a meal together (in silence), and once a week the whole community would take a three-hour *spacia* (communal walk) together around the monastic property during which talking was allowed. But the monastery's isolation and seclusion was so complete that even the bishop of the diocese was not allowed a visit.[31] Twice a year on appointed days, a monk's family was allowed to call on him. As the Statutes put it plainly: "Our special study and intention is to spend time in silence and the solitude of the cell."[32]

The Carthusian priories—unlike many other monastic establishments— were inevitably extremely poor and often on the brink of dissolution. A story is told that on one occasion a nobleman visited the monastery and was so moved by the monks' poverty that he sent them some silver plate "of great price." The monks sent back the silver, saying that they had no need for it, but they could use some parchment for writing books.[33]

Unlike all other monastic orders in fourteenth- and fifteenth-century England, the Carthusians were universally praised and respected for their devout sincerity, their freedom from scandal and abuse, their unswerving commitment to their vows, and the unvarying strictness of their lifestyle.[34] Indeed, there is an adage applied to the Carthusians: *Nunquam reformata quia nunquam deformata*—"Never reformed because never deformed."[35]

The Carthusian Order alone was committed to precisely the radical contemplative model described in *The Cloud*. Other monastic traditions practiced meditation and contemplation, but none fits so well with the exactitude, extremity, and specificity of *The Cloud*. Indeed, many of the surviving manuscripts of *The Cloud* were found to have been in Carthusian hands.

It is also true that it has long been part of the ascetical Carthusian tradition to write and publish *anonymously*, and it may well be that the author seriously took trouble to remain nameless.[36] A simple conclusion would certainly be that the author was, indeed, a Carthusian monk, but the matter is not entirely that simple. And we need first to consider the recipient of the book.

THE PROTÉGÉ

The Cloud is addressed to a young man[37] of twenty-four, who has just come (or was just about to come) into a "singular" or "solitary form of living," but who had previously been "a servant of His Special servants [of God, where he had] learned to live more specially and more spiritually in his service."[38] This phrase, if it is an accurate description, would perfectly depict the class of Carthusian affiliates called *redditi* or *conversi*.[39] These lay brothers were, in fact, retainers for the monks and lived under somewhat less stringent vows in a *courery*—a separate community building usually attached to the gate house of the monastery, with facilities for worship and domestic accommodation.[40] They prepared and delivered food to the cells, chopped wood for heating, repaired and maintained the monastery buildings, managed the properties, saw to the planting and harvesting of crops, and served under the direction of the Procurator or Steward, who, although he was a regular monk, had responsibility for the administration of the monastery, serving as a liaison between the monks and the *conversi* and *redditi*—usually with living quarters beside or outside the monks' cloister.[41]

It seems likely that the protégé was at the brink of becoming one of the Cloister Monks himself. It is also possible—since all Carthusian monks were ordained priests or were preparing for ordination—that he may have been approaching ordination to the priesthood as well.[42]

THE PLACE

Before anything can be said about the location, we must understand that "the basis of the language in all the manuscripts is that of an East Midland Dialect … written in the north part of the central East Midlands."[43] That is to say, the writer had quite certainly been brought up and lived a significant period of time in that area of Nottinghamshire and Lincolnshire where he was raised and learned that dialect.[44]

It is also held by all the linguists and historians who have studied *The Cloud* that the writing can be reliably dated to the late second half of the fourteenth century—in most cases between 1380 and 1400.

There was only one regular Carthusian priory in the East Midlands: Beauvale,[45] which was founded in 1343.[46] It is likely that if our author was a Carthusian (as we believe), he began his monastic life there at Beauvale Charterhouse.

In 1381, the new Charterhouse in Coventry was in unusual difficulty even before it was fully established. Its intended founder—William, Lord Zouch—had given fourteen acres of land for the Charterhouse and had just arranged for the seconding of three monks from the London Charterhouse to Coventry when his intended further endowment and engagement was lost by his unexpected death. These three monks, in turn, arranged for three more to come from the Beauvale Charterhouse and added four newly professed monks for Coventry. In 1382, King Richard granted the Coventry community a license, although there were as yet no proper buildings. They built each cell/cottage as they found funding, but it was seven years before the monastic structures at Coventry were completed.[47]

However, there was also one curious Carthusian establishment in the East Midlands, which no modern commentator seems to have noticed: in 1080, land in Haugham, Lincolnshire, had been given to the French Benedictine abbey of St. Severus in Coutances, Normandy, by Hugh of Chester (one of the Norman knights who came with William the Conqueror), and it functioned as a Benedictine grange (i.e., a farm and barns separate from the monastery itself) ever since. Although not properly a priory, it was locally called "Haugham Priory," and it was maintained by one or two French monks who oversaw the lands, the laborers, and the harvest. During the Hundred Years' War with France, King Richard II began to seize alien monastic foundations, and in 1397 the French Haugham property was granted to the struggling Coventry Charterhouse.[48] It would have been necessary, then, that a Carthusian Procurator (or Rector) be sent to oversee that Haugham property, its lay brothers, and its laborers.[49]

THE CONNECTION

Against that background, it might be productive to consider possible connections between the author and his protégé.

1. I maintain that the English author's strenuous, demanding, and radical model of contemplative prayer could only have been the product of Carthusian training and practice. Although several other monastic traditions included provisions for solitary contemplative life, none, to my knowledge, promoted a practice as intense and severe as that promulgated in *The Cloud*.

2. I recognize, based on that premise, that since the author certainly had been personally experienced in the strenuous model of contemplative prayer that he presents, it is extremely probable that he was a professed Carthusian monk. It is extremely improbable that he had actually *left* a Carthusian Charterhouse and *still* continued the strenuous contemplative practice. Carthusians were seldom released from their vows.[50]

3. Since all Carthusian monks were ordained priests (or in preparation for ordination), our author, if a longtime Carthusian, was assuredly a priest. There are also two evidences of priesthood in the text.

4. Since his language indicates that he was native to the northern East Midlands, it is likely that when he sought out a Carthusian

Charterhouse to join, it would have been Beauvale—the only
Charterhouse in the East Midlands.

5. In 1381–82 when the Coventry Charterhouse was new and
in trouble and three monks were sent from Beauvale to help
shore up the community, it is likely that those would have been
monks whose experience and leadership abilities would benefit
the struggling Coventry Charterhouse. It is therefore entirely
possible that the author was sent from Beauvale to Coventry,
where he served in a leadership position. Since we know that
John Netherbury (who had been Procurator of the London
Charterhouse) became prior at Coventry and Robert Palmer
followed him as second prior, it is possible (even likely) that
our author could have been named Procurator at Coventry and
thus would have had oversight over the lay brethren, *redditi*, and
other laborers there. Note: The spiritual advisor of a *professed*
Carthusian monk was always the prior himself; but the spiritual
director of a *redditus* or *conversus* would have been the Procurator.

6. When Coventry Charterhouse was given the property of Haugham
Priory in Lincolnshire, the monk who was sent to Haugham as
Rector[51] to oversee the property and laborers would need to
have been experienced in leadership and management—and the
author's native familiarity with the northern East Midlands (where
Haugham was located) would have made his selection a strong
possibility.

7. At Haugham he would have been a solitary, contemplative
monk—over a hundred miles from Coventry—writing back to
a young *redditus* or *conversus* who had in the recent past been
under his direction (in the Coventry Charterhouse). Note: The
author and protégé would not reasonably have been in the *same*
monastery when *The Cloud* was written. No Carthusian could
have afforded to use precious and very expensive parchment for
in-house notes and advice.[52] The two must have been separated,
but also must have had a *previous* close association of director-to-
directee—that is, before the author left Coventry and went to live
alone at Haugham.

8. One more purely personal view: the writing in *The Cloud* seems to include some fairly intimate autobiographical references, some harsh criticism of another spiritual writer (Richard Rolle), some strong personal approval of others (e.g., Walter Hilton), and even humor.[53] All of this suggests a liaison between author and protégé that is more personal than that of merely a formal director-directee relationship. There is a "paternal" feeling to much of the writing in *The Cloud* (and even more in *The Letter of Privy Counsel*), and while it is unlikely there is a natural father-son relationship here, I sense a kinship of some kind—perhaps uncle to nephew.

All of this would lead to a simple conceivable timeline:

13??—Author joins Beauvale Charterhouse, possibly becoming Procurator.

1382—Author is moved to Coventry Charterhouse and made Procurator in charge of lay brothers—one of whom becomes his protégé.

1397—Author is sent to be solitary Rector of the Haugham Grange.

1397–98—Author writes *The Cloud* to send back to his erstwhile protégé at Coventry and later writes *The Letter of Privy Counsel* as a follow-up.

Of course, all of the above is ultimately a conjecture and cannot be substantiated, but it provides a scenario that seems to meet the criteria we know about the author, his protégé, and their relationship. In the barren facts alone, there are only seven things we can reasonably be sure of: we have an (a) experienced, (b) educated, (c) solitary, (d) contemplative (e) priest, addressing a (f) young (g) novice contemplative. That's all we can certify as incontrovertibly true.

THE BOOK

In her definitive volume on *The Cloud*, Phyllis Hodgson provides ninety-two pages of meticulous and exhaustive word-by-word analysis and comparison among the various early manuscripts of *The Cloud* and

The Letter of Privy Counsel, and John Clark offers three entire volumes of profound further analysis.[54] The recounting of the intricacies of these analyses would be of little value here, since they cannot be improved upon and are of significant interest only to the most serious scholar. With deep gratitude for the superb work, I refer my readers to those volumes should they be interested in a more detailed textual and philological analysis.

As the basis for this translation, I have followed the conclusions of Hodgson, Clark, and Gallacher[55] in using British Library MS Harleian 674—in the handsome and meticulous Middle English transcription made by Patrick Gallacher—as the basis for my translation of *The Cloud* (Gallacher 21ff.), and Phyllis Hodgson's transcription of *A Letter of Privy Counsel*—which she titled *The Book of Privy Counselling* (Hodgson 135ff.).

Many *Cloud* scholars (notably Clark, James Walsh, and Hodgson) have provided extensive information regarding influences and other sources which may have affected and influenced the author's work—Hugo de Balma, Thomas Gallus, Richard of St. Victor, John Cassian, Ludolph of Saxony. These references are of value and I respect them greatly, but, once again, they have worth primarily for scholars and academics, and the intricate details do little to help us understand the author's own work, so I have chosen not to include them (except specific instances in which they may actually affect a translation). Since the author purposely chose *not* to give scholarly or authoritative references within his work, I have followed his lead. In his own words: "You do not need it and therefore I do not do it."[56]

But special mention must be made of one major influence: somewhere around the year AD 500—give or take twenty years—a highly literate Christian philosopher and theologian, probably in what is now Syria, wrote a series of works that took the philosophical insights of the neo-Platonists Plotinus, Proclus, and the Platonic Academy of Athens and transposed them into a entirely unique pattern of Christian mystical thought. He wrote under the pseudonym of "Dionysius the Areopagite"—that is, the Athenian who was converted by Saint Paul[57]—thereby virtually guaranteeing himself an audience. His known works include *The Divine Names, Mystical Theology, The Celestial Hierarchy, Ecclesiastical Hierarchy,* and some ten letters.

Dionysius's use of the pseudonym was not considered a "forgery" in the modern sense and was a common practice in his day in that the writer intended to convey not a unique personal idea, but a tradition older than himself. It seems to have worked well, and his writings took on enormous importance in Europe in the Middle Ages and Renaissance. There were occasional doubters (e.g., Hypatius of Ephesus and Nicholas of Cusa), but by and large his work was accepted and several Latin translations were made of it. By the thirteenth century his thought became widely popular—indeed, he is quoted by the great Saint Thomas Aquinas over 1,700 times.

The Latin version of his treatise *Mystical Theology* was a groundbreaker— the first serious proposal that Christian theology had a dimension that was "hidden" and not apparent to all. It was an idea that had significant impact on our author, who translated a Latin version into Middle English as *Dionese Hid Divinite*.

The principal theological feature stressed by Dionysius and embraced by our author was the concept of the *via negativa*, the negative way. As we have said above, this perception implied that God was so transcendent, so immeasurably unique, and so incalculably beyond our human experience that there were literally no human words that could accurately describe God or any human concepts that could include God. God was entirely a *Deus Absconditus*, a hidden God, and could only be described accurately by reference to what God was *not*—hence the *negativa*. Our author embraced this understanding wholeheartedly in *The Cloud*.

In general, I hope to leave the understanding of the author's specific message to the reader, assisted (I hope) by the parallel commentary to the text. However, there are some generic concepts and understandings that underlie all the work, and since these are often radically difficult to grasp, I think it wise to deal in a broad and introductory way with some of those basic notions and tenets.

First, be aware of considerable repetition; with careful reading one will come to realize that each recurrence of any particular matter will be a bit clearer, a bit more detailed, or a bit richer. The structure is more like a spiraling gyre than a mere repetitious circle.

As the author explains, he proposes a four-part division of the Christian spiritual life: Common, Special, Singular, and Perfect. The "Common" life is that which was lived by most ordinary Christians: attending Mass on Sundays and Holy Days, fasting during Lent, paying one's annual tithe, praying before meals and at bedtime, avoiding mortal sins, and making formal confession and receiving Holy Communion once a year on Easter. Indeed, this pattern is continued fairly closely in ordinary Christian lives today. It describes what might be called the fundamental, basic minimum of a "good Christian life" in the Catholic tradition.

The "Special" Christian life assumes all the above and then adds extra efforts and activities: perhaps the recitation of the Offices from a Book of Hours, attendance at Mass on weekdays, intentionally striving to practice the Seven Virtues, providing aid to the poor and needy, caring for those who are ill, and making confession regularly. Once again, this is a pattern of life a seriously devout Christian of either the fourteenth or the twenty-first century might well choose to live. It is certainly above the minimum and involves a more resolute commitment and dedication.

Beyond this point in spiritual growth, one crosses a line: it might be described as "turning toward heaven"—that is, in addition to all the above (which involve regular earthly activities) a person at the "Singular" level begins to seek a palpable nearness to God and will in all likelihood undertake some form of meditation—perhaps pondering one's own sinful life, or meditating on the life and miracles of Jesus, or on the details of Christ's passion, or on the virtuous lives of the saints. And there is a good likelihood that at this point one might also seek entry into a religious order as a way of making a more perfect offering of oneself. The previous activities and degrees of devout life continue, but the balance of one's commitment now begins to tip more thoroughly toward God and one's relationship with God. It is also likely that in entering this stage, one may enter the monastic life. Note: It is this "Singular" state that our author's protégé is apparently about to enter.

And the final and "Perfect" level of spiritual development is demonstrated when one chooses to detach entirely from any and all earthly things, to repudiate even the outward characteristics of one's own self, and to direct one's entire attention and consideration to an intimate bonding with God's very Self. It is almost impossible to imagine this life in any other configuration than eremitic solitude. It is for those who may be approaching this final level of ascetical and mystical life that this book has been specifically written. It is, as it were, the deepest, most serious, and most profound level of Christian ascetical spirituality possible during earthly life.

It must be said, however, that this ladder of spiritual development is not merely a convenient way for a Christian to decide to approach God. Each of the four levels requires what the author calls a "stirring" of the soul by God—an inexplicable sense of desire for a deeper union with divinity—what Julian of Norwich called a "longing" or "yearning"[58] that God implants in a soul to draw it onward. This calling or vocation has its source in God, and the serious Christian must commit to vulnerability and openness to this divine "stirring" if she or he is to receive it. The primary action of the contemplative soul is passivity, vulnerability, and the willing submersion of one's ego—none of which is easy even for the most devout among us.

But it must be clear that the author does not intend to *discount* any of the earlier stages. Indeed, living at any of these levels is creditable in itself, and surely the vast majority of very good and devout Christians seldom move beyond the Special stage. Very few are "stirred" or called to the Singular level, and still less to the Perfect stage, so that as a complete guide to Perfection, *The Cloud* and *Privy Counsel* are aimed at a tiny quota of Christians. However, before the author writes a word, he has bought into the theology, ecclesiology, Christology, and soteriology of late medieval Catholic England (although he doesn't hesitate to criticize it). That means there is relatively little of what we would call "ordinary Christianity" in the book—but the thoughts, insights, and basic teachings are still entirely relevant to any seriously devout Christian.

The author is further clear that one does not move to the next higher level without (1) acceptance of the move by one's own clear conscience, and (2) approval of one's spiritual advisor. There is not a do-it-yourself project—because if one senses a true "stirring" or a calling to a further level of growth, one will also be provided with the divine grace to make the next step possible. Without that peculiar grace, spiritual advancement in this particular mode is impossible, and without significant reference to a spiritual advisor, one can easily stray into serious spiritual and mental trouble.

There is much talk of "grace" in this book—and it is a word whose meaning in our day has been almost entirely worn away by overfamiliarity. The Middle English word means not only a "gift from God," but also "an attribute of God." For our purposes here, we need to recognize it clearly as the actual life or vitality of Godself imparted to a human being. When our author speaks of "grace," he means a sharing out of the Divine Life itself—that is, in "receiving grace" one is given a free and unmerited share of the divine *Élan Vital*, the grant of a sliver of God's own essence, a "spilling out," as it were, of divinity into the human soul—a manifestation of the divine created nature of human beings who in that creation were made so like God, so much in God's image, that they were open and receptive to sheer Divinity itself. It is an extremely powerful aspect of the mystic way to comprehend this apportioned divinity—still manifested in our Eucharistic prayer, "that he may dwell in us and we in him,"[59] and in our Bible: "If we love one another, God remains in us and his love is brought to full measure in us. By this we know that *we remain in him and he in us* because of his spirit he has delivered to us."[60] In his book *The Descent of Man*, Charles Darwin wrote the famous line: "Man still bears in his bodily frame the indelible stamp of his lowly origin."[61] And as a Christian mystic might have it: "We still bear in our souls the indelible stamp of our heavenly origin."

There are, for our author, six preconditions for entry into the author's "Perfect" state: (1) God's "stirring" in one's soul—the call or vocation; (2) the authenticating intuition of one's conscience—the morality; (3) the consonance with Holy Scripture—the compatibility; (4) full sacramental confession of all one's sins—the absolution; (5) the support and approval of one's spiritual advisor—the validation; and (6) the gift of God's grace without which any spiritual step forward would be impossible—the faculty. It is also clear that in this complicated and extensive process, it is virtually essential that one undertake an eremitic life of solitude with little, if any, spiritual commerce with the rest of the world—at least the life of a hermit, if not an anchorite.

The theology and metaphysics of Aquinas and the Scholastics of the previous century are embraced, especially the distinction between substance and accidents, between essence and attributes, that is so central to his contemplative pattern. For our author, reason and intellect are incapable of finally bringing one into union with the Divine Presence; that can only be achieved by an act of love, or charity. In the process of "knowing," one takes the known object into one's mind (of course, an impossibility if the object is God); but in "loving" oneself goes out to the other (as one does to God). The intellect may be part of the preparatory activity that precedes the Work, but it is the "lance of longing love" alone that finally pierces the spiritual density of the cloud of unknowing. That is to say, the cloud of unknowing is not of our making, but exists as an obstacle for us because of our earthbound spiritual inadequacy, and that cloud can be pierced only when one has stripped oneself (and has been stripped by God's grace) of all that is earthly, leaving only the spiritual core of one's soul alone—that is, that spiritual dimension of the human being which is "divine" in its created nature as the "image of God."

However we must clearly understand that in calling for "love," the author is not speaking of sentimental warm feelings toward God—rather, for him (as for the Scholastics) love is an unselfish, sacrificial act of the will—it is a firm choice of and longing for God. It is important for us moderns to understand that for the author, the human *will* is the key to sinlessness, sincerity, and salvation. The same concept is present in the writings of the author's fellow mystics: Julian of Norwich and Walter Hilton. What is called for is a kind of "mega-choice" in which the will *chooses* God above everyone and everything else, *longs* and *yearns* to be one-ed with that God, and willingly embraces any difficulty, discipline, stress, or pain in order to achieve that union. And the author sees this union as the ultimate peak of human spiritual attainment—"the perfection of a human soul is nothing but a one-ing formed between God and the soul in perfect charity."[62]

It should also be underlined that the author is clear in his understanding that in this great "reunification process" it is God who is the prime actor, and the human is mainly available and consenting. "He wills that you both gaze on Him and leave Him alone."[63] Indeed, it is not wholly inaccurate to say that it is the "bit of God" in us from our creation that responds to God's eternal Self and draws us as if by magnetic attraction toward perfect union—God *in us* bonding with God *in heaven*! Here spirit relates to Spirit, like to like, deific to the Divine.[64]

Like the other fourteenth-century English spiritual writers, our author tends not to see sin itself as the dread obstacle it is taken to be by many earlier medieval writers (for some of whom it seems the all-encompassing reality). He certainly sees sin as an ugly and obnoxious thing, but with repentance and forgiveness, the "unpretentious affirmation of love ...

removes the ground and the root of sin."[65] Indeed, our author suggests that "often it happens that some who have been foul and habitual sinners reach the perfection of this Work sooner than those who were not."[66] The sinner may find the Work difficult, but one's past history of sin (absolved in confession, of course) is not an impediment—and, curiously, may often be a benefit. Sin is certainly never belittled or ignored, but it need not be stressed or made a central issue; it is simply a matter for confession, since the church has always known what to do with sin: she forgives it and moves on! No need for fastings or flagellations or deprivation of sleep or hard beds.

One of the traditional mystical dimensions of spiritual life is what came to be called "deification" or "divinization" or *theosis*. It is a mystical tradition that had its roots mainly in the Eastern Christian traditions but was kept alive as part of monastic spirituality in the medieval West. Our author puts it plainly: "Only by His mercy—without your deserving it—*you are made a God by grace*, one-ed with Him in spirit without any separation both here and in the bliss of heaven without end."[67] A modern reader is usually a bit shaken to read such a simple idea, since we tend to be trained to recognize the vast *differences* between humans and God rather than to recognize our similarities. But the roots of this idea lie deep in Scripture and in the early Fathers: "He has granted to us his precious and very great promises, so that through these you may become partakers of the divine nature," reads 2 Peter.[68] Then, Saint Athanasius wrote: "For he was made man that we might be made God."[69] Saint Augustine put it very simply: "In fact, God wishes to make you God."[70] And Thomas Aquinas: "The only begotten Son of God, desiring to make us sharers in his divinity, took on our nature, so that he, made human, might make humans gods."[71]

Of course, the entire concept of *theosis* has its basis in the Genesis story of Adam being created "in the image of God"—thus having an innate compatibility with the Godhead. It is perhaps easier for a modern Christian to grasp this concept by recognizing the more familiar idea that we Christians, by our baptism, are made "members" of the body of Christ— and as Christ has ascended into heaven as a Person in the Holy Trinity, so we who are "within Christ" mystically participate in that divine Trinity.

However, no matter what degree of union with God one may be innately capable of, intellectual *knowledge* of God remains beyond reach—

for those who accept the principles of the apophatic *via negativa*. This understanding—that God is intellectually unknowable to human beings in this life—lies, of course, at the very heart of *The Cloud*. And for those of us raised in an essentially evangelical Christian environment, the idea of an unknowable God seems crazy at least and heretical at best. But that is mainly because our approach to God has tended to be either intellectual (through creeds, dogmas, literal Scriptures, and the like) or emotional (by being "saved," having "Jesus in your heart," religious ecstasy, and the like). Both of those approaches are strained when one recognizes that God is either being institutionalized and shrunken to fit human intellectual possibilities or anthropomorphized to such a degree that the Divine Being tends to end up being rather like a big perfect daddy. We seem generally unwilling to look beyond our own intellect or emotion to recognize that in dealing with divinity, we are going to be far beyond our intellectual depth, and will be called to turn to our third medium: our intuition—which works only with hints, metaphors, and poetry.

In his book *This Sunrise of Wonder*,[72] Michael Mayne says, "I know then, with a conviction I can no more deny than fly, that in the depths of myself, in stillness, I am aware of the 'other' that is not me and yet, paradoxically, is the very ground of my existence. And I believe that it is precisely this intuitive sense of the transcendent, the muffled presence of the holy, that makes me human." Frederick Buechner calls it "the occasional, obscure glimmering through of grace."[73]

An example of the problem we face in trying to approach God with our limited earthly tools appears if we were to try to define eternity. We can say the words that "eternity is beyond time," but our minds cannot grasp such a concept, because we are all entirely and unqualifiedly time-bound. So, most of us will tend to think of eternity as a very, very long (or even endless) time—whereas the reality is that eternity has nothing whatsoever to do with time. Eternity is the *absence* of time and, therefore, the absence of change, and the absence of even the concept of past-present-future. It is like either an endless "now" or an endless extension of the present moment. These are the only two ways the human intellect can think about eternity. No human being can comprehend it because there is no human experience or human permutation of thought that can lift us out of our own time-bound reality. For God, eternity is home—and has no beginning and no end and does not "go on." God is not "old" (regardless of the common image of an ancient bearded man on a throne), and God is not "young" or "middle-aged" either. Nor is God visible, since God is pure invisible spirit (rather like an idea that is alive). As theologian James Alison recently put it, "God is more like 'nothing' than 'something.'"[74]

We can never "understand" God, "grasp" God, or squeeze God's immensity into our minds, or turn any emotional sensation into an "experience of God." We can never know God in the same sense that we can understand, grasp, or know anyone or anything else, since God is metaphorically concealed behind "the cloud of unknowing," which can be pierced only with the "lance of longing love" (which love is unselfish and sacrificial and godly) after all past earthly experience has been repudiated. By this means we *may* be granted at least a momentary experience of union with this unknown, indescribable God.

But even if this supreme rarity of union occurs (through a specific stirring by God and special gifts of God's grace—see the next section of the "Work"), it will remain indescribable in words and accessible only to the intuition and only in poetry—as all great mystics have discovered. If one were to ask our author what this experience of union with God was like, he would reply: "It was like nothing!"—that is, it is unlike anything that anyone has ever known or experienced in earthly life.

It is extremely important to the author that his protégé come to understand that most of the words we use to describe our relation to God are merely metaphorical, so he exerts considerable efforts (which seem oddly overemphasized to us) dealing with locations, directions, bearing, and states—convincing his charge that "up" or "down," "within" or "without," and "cool" or "warm" did not refer to physical or geographical directions or states (as clearly *some* spiritual practitioners of his day were claiming), but were to be taken in the spiritual sense; that is, "lifting one's heart to God" had no *physical* implications concerning the location of one's beating, blood-pumping organ.

THE "WORK"

Before any consideration can be given to the actual contemplative processes promoted in *The Cloud*, it must be clearly stated that the procedures, methodology, and goal of the practices are, as it were, "post-graduate spirituality." That is, they assume a prior extensive, thorough, and deep knowledge and practice of fundamental Christianity, and so they may be fully relevant only to a small group—although the basic contemplative teachings and insights can enrich every Christian soul.

Ronald Rolheiser makes a distinction between discursive meditation (at the Singular level) where we are active and think verbally, on the one hand, and wordless contemplation on the other. He says that we are often like the young fish who asks his mother: "Where is this water I hear so much about?" The mother has some options: she can set up a projector or open a book and show her child pictures of the ocean, or she can say, "Close your eyes, feel it around you and let it flow over you and through your gills." Rolheiser suggests that that is the difference between discursive meditation and contemplation.[75] (And I might add that she could have taken the little fish to the surface, stuck his nose into the air, and said, "There, that is what water is *not!*"—a piscatorial *via negativa!*)

Some readers will note that in *The Cloud* there seems relatively little mention of Jesus Christ and the soteriology of the Incarnation, nothing much about the Trinity, hardly any reference to Holy Scripture, very slight emphasis on the details of a life of virtue, and scarcely a word about neighborly charity toward others. The point is, of course, that these are all *precedents* to the contemplative way being described in *The Cloud*. The author takes all these things for granted, since it would be inconceivable to him that one could even desire—to say nothing of actually undertaking—a direct, unmediated contemplation of God without a serious and extensive history of Christian learning, worship, and virtuous life in one's past. (This is a point I will make and remake multiple times in the text of this book, and it is especially evident in *The Letter of Privy Counsel* where the author seems to be trying to clarify what may have been confusing in *The Cloud*.)

One might say that *The Cloud* primarily involves post-incarnational Christianity and even a post-Trinitarian Christianity. That is, generally the

Christ referenced in *The Cloud* is the *risen* Christ, the Second Person of the threefold Divine Being within the cloud of unknowing.[76] As Karl Steinmetz put it: "If a person focuses on Christ as presented in Holy Scripture he or she will find the visible Christ as the entrance and door though which one can approach God. Such a turn to the visible Christ, though, cannot be regarded as the highest form of communication with God. Since God revealed himself as God in Jesus Christ, the humanity of Christ is only the door to God. In order to really attain God one must walk through the door, cross the threshold and then proceed to the Godhead, by which Christ is sitting, so to speak, behind the door as porter."[77]

When one has developed a settled life of study, virtue, and worship following Holy Scripture and the revelatory teachings of Jesus, then one is ready to move attention and orientation away from the things—even the *good* things—of earth and to direct oneself wholly to the *Deus Absconditus*, the hidden God of heaven itself.[78] And at that point, the emphasis is not on the distinctions between the Persons of the Holy Trinity, but upon the Divine Unity itself. Indeed, it is one's union with this unseen and unearthly Divine Unity that is the goal and purpose of *all* Christian belief and practice, since it was this very union with God that was the purpose for the creation of human beings in the first place—and the author's contemplative Work is meant to return human beings to the original unfallen state of perfect union with God.

The author makes the daring claim that for those who are so stirred by the Holy Spirit and overwhelmed with certain intent and fervent longing for God's very Self, a brief and momentary glimpse of heaven is possible in this ultimate and radical contemplative Work.

"The 'werk' that the Cloud describes is the recovery, through the grace of Christ, of that intuitive awareness of God and conformity to his will which Adam lost, and which is to be regained, especially through the attainment of a habit of contemplative openness to God."[79]

The basic pattern of the Work will certainly be confusing to the first-time reader. It involves an understanding of human and divine nature that will seem alien to most Christians who are used to a fairly anthropological version of God's nature and a somewhat sentimental concept of how a human relates to that God.

At its core, the Work involves a sorting process by which one delineates between what could be called the core reality of God and the core reality of the human being. This means the hard (and truly painful) work of purging from one's consciousness all dimensions, attributes, qualities, characteristics, descriptions, and properties of oneself and of one's idea of God. The facts that one is male or female, tall or short, smart or stupid, young or old, poetic or prosaic, interesting or boring, skilled or unskilled, tired or rested, present or past, and all such aspects or attributes must be disowned, rejected, and disavowed. They must be cancelled from one's mind and obliterated from one's consciousness, placed (as our author has it) under a "cloud of forgetting." For the purposes of the Work, such aspects are not only irrelevant, but also harmful, impeding the longed-for union with God. What one seeks is the consciousness of oneself as absolutely nothing more than "I AM"—not *what* I am, but only *that* I am. The point of this is the detachment of the "self" from any and all earthly connections of any kind—from anything that would contaminate the pure spirituality of one's core self—an awareness, as it were, of absolutely nothing about the self except the core of one's soul alone, and the unqualified, undifferentiated longing and craving for God out of willed love.

But then comes the second challenge, and that is to strip from our minds absolutely everything we have ever heard, read, known, believed, thought, or expected about God—any qualities or attributes or aspects of God that we have held in the past, such as goodness, omnipotence, fatherliness, or divine aspects of judgment, anger, or punishment—until the only thing we can hold as true about God is that "God IS"—One whose very being is simply to "be"—intentionally denying all else and putting it also under the "cloud of forgetting."

One can see that in both instances, the practitioner and God have been stripped down in the Worker's mind to the barren reality of "mere being"— and the point of such brutal ascetics is to discover the total *commonality* of one's pure spirituality with the pure spirituality of God. It is there—in the realm of the exclusively spiritual—that a one-ing between oneself and God is possible. As Hodgson has put it: "If the will reach only towards God, that alone is sufficient; there is no need for meditation on past sin or for devotional exercises to acquire virtue."[80]

A useful mechanic in achieving this liberation from divine and human attributes may be the mental repetition of a simple one-syllable word. The author suggests the words "God" or "Love." That word is then used repetitively in a way that ultimately liberates it from any literal meaning or definition and makes it only a kind of hollow touchstone, a home base to which one can return when faced with distractions.

The Work of *The Cloud* can be said to be human-essence-seeking-divine-essence. Like all Christian mystics, the author understands the potential for this exchange of life and vitality between the contemplative and God. When a contemplative has been able to extract the self from the morass of earthly entanglements and to clear away the underbrush of intellectualism and sentimentality by which God has been obscured, then there can be a virtual exchange between the created soul and its Creator. As Simon Tugwell, OP, put it: "The contemplative does not 'see God'; he enters into God's seeing. The abolition of any clear notion of God in the cloud of unknowing thus goes with the abolition of any clear awareness of the knowing subject. Our being must approach God in such nakedness that it is clothed not even in itself."[81]

The soul is left with nothing except a sense of being and a "naked" intention toward God—and, of course, toward a God whom one does not "know," a God who is beyond any human thought or concept or belief. So one's loving intention toward God is toward a "no-thing-ness," a non-known being, a divine mystery whom one can only approach with an unqualified act of will (which is the act of love). One cannot help but recall Paul's words: "Knowledge merely puffs one up, but love creates something real. So if someone assumes that he knows anything [about God], he has not yet discerned the right way to know. However, if one loves God, then God is known by such a one."[82]

One must come, then, to the point of saying (or thinking), "God, I don't really know a single thing about you or what you are like or anything except that I know there is a 'you' and I love you and long to be one with you." This is the "lance of longing love" with which one is to pierce the cloud of unknowing. "I am here, God, and I want nothing but you."

The upshot of this immeasurably difficult and deeply complicated Work may be literally nothing—in fact, if one practices the Work regularly, much of the time there may well be no noticeable result aside from a peaceful calm. But rarely, and for only momentary instances, one may be aware of sensing an indescribable union with the entire Presence of one we call "God." One has thus been given the grace to pierce the cloud of unknowing and to come into contact with heaven for a moment while still alive on earth.

As Jan van Ruysbroeck, whose life probably overlapped that of our author, and whose spirituality is representative of the mystical spirituality of that century, wrote in his essay "The Sparkling Stone":

> But if above all things we would taste God, and feel eternal life in ourselves, we must go forth into God with our feeling, above reason; and there we must abide, one-fold, empty of ourselves, and free from images, lifted up by love into the simple bareness of our intelligence. For when we go out in love beyond and above all things, and die to all observation in ignorance and in darkness, then we are wrought and transformed through the Eternal Word, Who is the Image of the Father. In this idleness of our spirit, we receive the Incomprehensible Light, which enwraps us and penetrates us, as the air is penetrated by the light of the sun. And this Light is nothing else than a fathomless staring and seeing. What we are, that we behold; and what we behold, that we are: for our thought, our life, and our being are uplifted in simplicity, and made one with the Truth which is God. And therefore in this simple staring we are one life and one spirit with God: and this I call a contemplative life.[83]

NOTES ON THE TRANSLATION

In his "Bookends" column in the *New York Times*, Daniel Mendelsohn recently wrote about the great Lawrence of Arabia, who when trying to make a prose translation of Homer's *Odyssey* produced six different drafts of only the first 441 lines (out of some 12,000), and finally wrote: "I see now why there is no adequate translation of Homer. He is baffling. He has me beaten to my knees."

Why, one might ask, would a person translating from Middle English to Modern English have any problems? Is it not the same language, after all? The answer is a very strong and emphatic "NO"—because translating from Middle English often involves multiple deceptions and snares that trip up an unsuspecting translator. The challenge arises because the simple Middle English word frequently does not mean the same thing in Modern English.

Some examples:

1. In the Preface, for instance, the text has *thanke God*, which seems simple, but the word *thank* in Middle English can be a variation of the word *think* with a sense of "remember with favor"—so I translate *thanke God* as "keep God always in your mind."

2. In the third chapter, the text has the word *wonderful*—but in Middle English the word is much stronger than our modern use. It has the sense of "magical," or "miraculous," or even "dreadful," or "horrible"—so I translate it as "frightening."

3. In the fourth chapter, the text has *comprehende*, but it is something of a false cognate. The original meaning of the word (which I use) was "to grasp," "to include," "to enclose," or "to contain." It is still occasionally used in that original sense, but usually it now means "to understand," and that leads to much confusion.

4. In the fifth chapter the text has *cortesye*, which literally means "courtliness" or "befitting the court of a prince." It does *not* mean "courtesy," or "politeness," or "good manners" in its modern sense.

5. In the sixth chapter the text has *scharp darte of longing love*, which has become a treasured catchphrase, but "dart" is a false cognate. In

Middle English, it means "an arrow," "a crossbow quarrel," "a spear," "a lance," "a javelin," or "a missile carrying a firebrand." It is *not* merely a meager projectile used in a pub game!

6. The text frequently includes the verb *worschep*—in Middle English it does *not* mean "to worship," but "to honor." (When a person was referred to as "Your Worship," it simply meant "Your Honor.")

7. The word *grace* appears hundreds of times, and it has a vast variety of meanings. The Middle English Dictionary lists some twenty possible translations: "God's gift," "favor," "forgiveness," "God's help," "token of favor," "miracle," "supernatural gift or power," "a virtue," "a benefit from God," "providence," "fortune," "one's lot," "fate," "good will," "kindness," "love," "beauty," "charm," "thanks," "prayer of gratitude," and the like. And it changes meaning constantly.

8. The words *can* and *may* actually exchange meanings in Middle English (and *can* is also sometimes a form of *canne*, meaning "to know").

9. The word *corious* always has the negative sense of "probing into what is not your business," or "odd," "peculiar," "weird," or "eccentric."

10. The word *kynde* means "nature" and never refers to flora and fauna, but to the inherent character or basic essence of a being.

11. The word *blinde* can mean "unseeing," "invisible," "insensitive," or "utter."

The translation challenge is summed up in the Italian adage *Traduttore traditore*—"A translator is a traitor"—because it is a literal impossibility for any translator perfectly to convey an author's exact meaning in another language. The innuendos, ambiguities, and cultural overtones of any piece of writing can never be perfectly captured in another culture or in another time or in another tongue. The best that can be hoped for is that a translator may share something of the values and practice of the writer, so that in translating *The Cloud of Unknowing*, for instance, a serious practicing contemplative hermit-monk may have a better chance of accuracy than a highly competent multi-degreed academic.

The reader needs to be aware of certain aspects of this translation that require explanation:

1. In general, I want to take my readers along on the translation project itself, so—especially where my work varies from that of others—I have frequently included the source of my translation and often noted

several alternate varying choices that would be accurate. There is a lot of vocabulary in my commentary.

2. All Scripture verses cited are from the Latin Vulgate Bible, and scriptural translations that are not actually part of the text of *The Cloud* are my own translations. (When there is a variation between the textual references in the Vulgate and the more familiar modern Bible versions, the modern reference is included in brackets, e.g., "Psalm 26 [27]" means "Psalm 26 in the Latin Vulgate, but Psalm 27 in the more familiar modern numbering."

3. All translations from cited works in Latin, Greek, French, or Spanish are my own translations from the original texts unless otherwise indicated.

4. All parenthetical citations of sources provide the name of the author and the page of the book listed in the bibliography: "(Kelsey, 8)" refers to "Kelsey, Morton; *The Other Side of Silence: A Guide to Christian Meditation*; Paulist Press; New York; 1976, p. 8." Sometimes an author's name appears in the text proper followed by the appropriate page number in her/his work, such as "Cowan (132)." When I cite an author who has more than one book in the bibliography I have added roman numerals in both the bibliography and the reference, e.g., "(II Clark, 49)."

5. When references are made to books not in the bibliography, the full citation is included: for instance, "(Irenaeus, *Against Heresies* 3.18.1)."

6. There are many abbreviations in the commentary: "ME" means "Middle English"; "MED" refers to *The Middle English Dictionary*; "ODEE" refers to *The Oxford Dictionary of English Etymology*; "NOAD" refers to *The New Oxford American Dictionary*; parentheses with a dagger and date refer to the death date of the person named, as in "Hugo De Balma († 1439)."

7. Because I think they accurately convey some of the style of the original, I have not hesitated to use some dated expressions—such as "Yea!" or "Ah …" or "Aye"—and to preserve sometimes stilted translations for the sake of loyalty to the author's work.

8. The author of *The Cloud* refers to his contemplative practice as *the Werk*. Most translators translate this as "the pattern," "the procedure," "the method," "the technique," or "the system." I have chosen to use the author's own word, but to capitalize it to make it distinctive, as in "at the time you propose to take up this Work…."

9. Wherever possible, I have tried to avoid male pronouns in gender-neutral statements and in references to God, but occasionally and rarely some have been unavoidable without engaging in literary gymnastics.

10. I have tried always to capitalize pronouns and possessive adjectives (e.g., "Him" and "His") referring to God—merely for literary clarity of the antecedent.

11. Occasionally I have retained Middle English words since they have no exact parallel in English—such as "one-ed" or "one-ing," or "seemly" or "full" (when it means "very" or "entirely") or "stirring."

12. I have often inserted parentheses, brackets, or em dashes in order to clarify the author's often long and complicated sentence structure.

THE
CLOUD OF
UNKNOWING

a. Like all English mystics, the author uses the ME verb *onyd* to suggest "united with," but it is subtly stronger than that and carries the sense of being "one with," so I modernize the spelling and retain the verb: "one-ed."

b. The ME has *on the prologe*, but the ME *on* can mean "on" or "upon" or "over" or "before" (MED).

c. The substance of this prayer is found in the medieval missals of Sarum, York, and Hereford as a Collect for a Mass of the Holy Spirit. In Sarum use, it is also part of the priest's private preparation for Mass while vesting—usually said by heart and silently. This may actually be an indication that the author was a priest, since the laity would simply not have known this prayer. "*Deus, cui omne cor patet et omnis voluntas loquitur, et quem nullum latet secretum, purifica per infusionem Sancti Spiritus cogitationes cordis nostri, ut te perfecte diligere et digne laudare mereamur. Per Dominum nostrum Jesum Christum, Qui tecum vivit et regnat, in unitate ejusdem Spiritus Sancti, per omnia sæcula sæculorum. Amen*" (Maskell, 6). The Collect also appears at the beginning of the Eucharist in *The Book of Common Prayer*, 1979 edition.

d. See Col. 3:14: "But above all these things have charity, which is the bond of perfection." The author is here appealing to the bond of love between two monastic Christians—almost certainly between two solitaries—himself (a solitary, probably Carthusian) and the addressee (probably a Carthusian novice).

e. A distinction is made here that is crucial in understanding this work—the distinction between the "active life" (which describes the lives of most devout and pious Christians—avoiding sin, doing good works, caring for one's neighbor, attending church, saying one's prayers) and the "contemplative life" (which transcends the active life and makes all of life oriented solely to spiritual union between the self and God). The contemplative way, however, seems extreme, foolish, and impractical to those without that commitment, so the book offers little to anyone except those who are committed to the contemplative way. Note that the author here makes his claims "by the *authority* of charity," whereas in the preceding paragraph, his appeal is to "the *bonds* of charity." Toynbee uses this phrase: "Love's authority, like conscience's, is absolute. Like conscience, too, love needs no authentication or validation by any authority outside itself" (Toynbee, A. J., *Experiences* [Oxford Univ. Press; Oxford; 1969], 155).

Here begins a book of contemplation that is called
"The Cloud of Unknowing" in which
a soul is one-ed[a] with God.

HERE BEGINS THE PRAYER BEFORE THE PROLOGUE[B]

God, unto whom all hearts are open, and unto whom every desire reveals itself, and unto whom no secret is hidden: I beseech you so to cleanse the intention of my heart with the unspeakable gift of your Grace, that I may perfectly love you and worthily praise you. Amen.[c]

HERE BEGINS THE PROLOGUE

In the Name of the Father and of the Son and of the Holy Spirit.

I charge you and deeply beg you, with as much power and strength as the bonds of charity[d] can allow, whoever you are that shall have this book in possession—whether it belongs to you, or you are keeping it for someone else, or carrying it as a messenger, or borrowing it—that in as much as is possible by choice and consideration, neither read it, nor write or speak of it, nor even let it be read by, or written to or spoken of to anyone unless, in your opinion, it be someone who by true desire and a sound intent, has made commitment to be a perfect follower of Christ—not only in active living, but in the highest achievement of the contemplative life that is possible for a pure soul to attain by grace while still living in this mortal body—and someone who, in your opinion, by means of a long and virtuous active life has been able to come to a contemplative life.[e] For otherwise, this book offers nothing to him.

a. Probably a reference to the scourge of scrupulosity in which a person never allows himself or herself to believe that any good work or prayer has been done adequately—a kind of spiritual obsessive-compulsive behavior.

b. The ME *corious* generally carries the sense of "weird" or "odd" as well as "curious." For the author the word almost always has negative implications.

c. In the previous sentence, the ME has *lettred or lewed men. Lettred,* of course, means "educated" and *lewed* broadly means "uneducated" or "unlettered," but in the fourteenth century it was also used to refer to the laity and non-clerics who were often unable to read or write—and especially those who knew no Latin. Note: Even King Edward II's queen, Isabella, could read but could not write (Weir, Alison, *Queen Isabella* [Ballantine; New York; 2005], 11.

d. At this point the author provides a six-page-long table of contents listing each of the seventy-five chapters with a heading for each. Since there were no chapter headings in the oldest manuscripts (Hodgson, 181) it is omitted here, but each heading has been attached directly in italics to its chapter.

e. The ME has *cours,* which means "direction" or "path." (Others have translated it as "progress," but that is true only in the sense of a king's "royal progress" when he visits his kingdom.) It is unclear whether the author asks his reader to look at the *way in which* he was called or the *direction* his calling has taken; I chose the latter interpretation.

f. The ME has *thank God,* but that is a false cognate. In ME, *thank* can actually be a variation of the word "think" (see my essay in *Mystics Quarterly,* 1989) with a sense of "remember with favor"—I use "keep God always in your mind."

g. There is a fourteenth-century distinction between *bodily* and *goostly* enemies as between physical, earthly, human versus spiritual, mystical, demonic. The author's distinction is between people and evil spirits. (See Eph. 6:10–13.)

h. See Jas. 1:12: "Blessed is man who endures temptation; for when he has been tested, he will receive the crown of life which God has promised to those who love him."

And more than that, I charge you and deeply beg you, by the authority of charity, that if any such shall read it, write or speak of it, or hear it read or spoken, that you charge them—as I do you—to take time to read it, speak or write of it, or hear it from beginning to end. For, it may be that there are some subjects there—in the beginning or in the middle—that are left hanging and are not fully explained where they stand, but if not there, the explanation comes shortly after or else at the end. Because of that, if a man were to see one subject and not another, possibly he might easily be led into error. And therefore in avoiding this mistake both in yourself and in all others, I beg you, for the sake of charity, that you do as I tell you.

Worldly prattlers, public flatterers, those who disparage themselves or others[a], slanderers, gossips, and tellers of tales, and all kinds of detractors—I saw to it that they never saw this book. For my intention was never to write such a thing for them. And therefore I prefer that they not meddle with it—neither they nor any of those merely curious[b] educated or unlettered men. Even though they may be truly good people who live active lives, this material offers nothing to them;[c] unless it be for those among them who, although they are fully active in the outward form of living, nevertheless by inward guidance from the mysterious Spirit of God (whose decisions are hidden) they may be seriously disposed by grace (not continuously, of course—as is appropriate for true contemplatives—but now and then) to share in the highest degree of this contemplative act—if such men were to see this book, they would by the grace of God be greatly comforted by it.

This book is divided into seventy-five chapters. The last chapter of all offers some sure signs by which a soul may truly prove whether it be called by God to be a participant in this holy undertaking or not.[d]

My devout friend in God, I earnestly beg and strongly implore you that you make a careful examination of the direction[e] and practice of your calling. And keep God always in your mind[f] so that by means of the aid of His grace, you can stand valiantly against all the subtle assaults of your human and spiritual enemies.[g] and win through to the crown of life[h] that lasts for evermore. Amen.

a. The four ME degrees might perhaps be more accurately translated as "Ordinary, Distinguished, Exceptional, and Complete," but the classifications of "Common, Special, Singular, and Perfect" have become a part of the tradition of *The Cloud*, so I have retained them—but I also capitalize them.

b. It has always been a matter of faith for the mystics that silent, contemplative prayer is the *only* mode of prayer that is actually practiced in heaven.

c. The ME has *comoun degree*—the first level of spiritual growth.

d. Following Paul in Rom. 5:12–21, it was believed that all mankind was mystically "in Adam" when Adam sinned—just as all were "in Christ" when they were redeemed from that sin. For example: "that what we lost in Adam ... we might recover in Christ Jesus" (Irenaeus, *Against Heresies* 3.18.1).

e. The *lyame of longing*—"a leash of longing" (MED)—is a unique metaphor, possibly its first use in English! Cowan (12) favors its translation as "chain."

f. The addressee was almost certainly a lay brother (*conversus* or *redditus*) and thus a "servant" of "Special servants," i.e., the cloistered monks.

g. The ME has *sith thou were oughtes*: "since you were of any being."

h. ME has *lystly* that some have translated as "deftly" (Hodgson, 183).

i. The *solitary forme and maner of leving* seems to indicate that the addressee is becoming a hermit—probably a Carthusian (where all monks live separately as solitary hermits).

j. This is a highly colloquial bit of guidance—a humorous Middle English prod: "Don't just sit there, but get your love on its feet and step up to the next level" (Augustine: "the foot of the soul is love" [Commentary on Psalm 9: *PL* 36:124]).

HERE BEGINS THE FIRST CHAPTER

Of the four degrees in Christian life, and of the progress of one's calling that this book was made for.

My devout friend in God, I want you to understand that I find, in my humble observations, four levels and forms of Christian life, which are these: Common, Special, Singular, and Perfect.[a] Three of these can be begun and ended in this life; and the fourth can by grace be begun here but it shall always last without end in the joys of heaven.[b] And just as you see how they are established here in order—each one after the other—first Common, then Special, after that Singular, and lastly Perfect—so I think that in the same order and in the same progression, our Lord has of His great mercy, called you and led you to him by the yearning of your heart.

For you are well aware of this: that when you were living at the Common level[c] of Christian life, living in the company of your worldly friends, it seems to me that the everlasting love of His Godhead—through which He made you and created you when you were nothing and afterward redeemed you with the price of His precious blood when you were lost in Adam[d]— could not allow you to be so far from Him in your form and level of life.

And therefore with great kindness He kindled your desire and bound it fast by a leash of longing,[e] and led you by it into a more Special state and form of living, to be a servant of His Special servants[f] where you might learn to live more specially and more spiritually in His service than you did—or could do—in your previous Common level of living.

And what more? Even then it seems that He would not leave you thus thoughtlessly because of the love of His heart that He has had for you ever since you were born.[g] So what did He do? Do you not see how gently[h] and how kindly He has drawn you up to the third level and manner of life, which is called Singular? In this solitary form and manner of life[i] you must learn to lift up the foot of your love and step forward[j] toward that state and level of living that is Perfect, and the last state of all.

a.   *Wreche* is the actual ME word. It generally means a miserable, unfortunate, or poor person—and in many cases carries the sense of "sinner." I have simply retained the ME word, thinking that it seems to be a somewhat overstated amiable poke-in-the-ribs of the spiritual son by his spiritual father.

b.   Sloth (or *acedia* as it is often called in monastic language) is one of the major curses and dangers of monastic life: it is an apathy and spiritual indifference or torpor that sucks the spiritual vitality out of a person.

c.   The ME has *in this while.*

d.   One is reminded of Rom. 12:16b: "Give yourself humble tasks. Be not wise in your own self."

e.   One of the universal counsels the author gives to his reader is not to try to climb the spiritual levels on his own, but *always* to depend on God's active grace and the good advice of a spiritual guide or director.

f.   While it is not unknown for spousal figures of speech to be used for relationships between males and God, it is more typical in female-God relationships.

g.   1 Tim. 6:15: "in his times he shall show who is the Blessed and only Mighty, the King of kings and Lord of lords."

h.   The "place of pasture" is quite apparently a monastic setting—almost certainly a Carthusian Charterhouse.

i.   It was widely believed—based on Mk. 10:29–30 ("There is no one who has left houses or brothers, or sisters, or father, or mother, or children, or lands, for my sake and the Gospel who shall not receive a hundred times as much now in this time … and in the world to come life eternal.")—that *all* monks and nuns were automatically guaranteed heaven in the afterlife.

j.   Another reminder that spiritual growth is the result of *God's* action in one's soul and all one needs to do is to consent to God's action and call.

k.   This mention of "flies" is another moment of droll amiability with almost a wink of the eye: in the New Testament one of the names given the devil is "Beelzebub"—Hebrew for "Lord of the Flies." The flies are "little demons." There is also reference to the plague of flies visited on Pharaoh by Moses.

l.   Very strong ME words: *put apon him with preier*—literally, "throw yourself upon Him with prayer."

m.   As if to say: "So, the ball's in your court! What are you going to do now?"

⤳ HERE BEGINS THE SECOND CHAPTER

A short exhortation to humility and to the spiritual Work of this book.

Look up now, poor feeble wretch,[a] and see what you are. What are you, and what have you done to deserve to be called in this way by our Lord? What heart—dull, wretched, and asleep in sloth[b]—is it that is not awakened by the weight of this Love and the Voice of this calling?

In this period of time,[c] poor wretch, beware of your Enemy; and do not think of yourself as holier or better because of the worthiness of your calling and the Singular form of life you are in.[d] On the contrary, you will be more wretched and afflicted unless you do what is godly in you—by grace and by counsel—to live according to your calling.[e]

And in view of that, you should be more humble and loving to your spiritual Spouse[f] so that He—that is, the Almighty God, King of kings and Lord of lords[g]—would make Himself so lowly to you, and out of all His flock of sheep would graciously choose you to be one of His Specials, and then set you in the place of pasture.[h] where you can be fed with the sweetness of His love in promise of your inheritance: the kingdom of heaven.[i]

Go on then, I pray you, earnestly. Look forward now and leave the past behind. And pay attention to what you are *lacking*, not what you have, for that is the best way to gain and hold on to humility. For all your life now you must persist in longing for God if you would advance in the level of Perfection. This longing must always be formed in your will by the hand of Almighty God and your own consent.[j] But one thing I tell you: God is a jealous lover and permits no other relationships, and He chooses not to work in your will unless He is with you alone by Himself. He asks no help, but only your self. He wills that you both gaze on Him and leave Him alone. And that you keep the windows and the door closed against flies and enemies attacking.[k] And if you are willing to do this, you must humbly set upon Him with prayer,[l] and soon He will help you. Go ahead, then: let us see how you carry yourself. He is fully ready, and waits only for you. So what shall you do, and how shall you proceed?[m]

a. The ME *werk* is used throughout the book to describe the process one follows in contemplative prayer. It is usually translated "exercise," "effort," or "practice." But the ME means an "activity" or a "deed"—especially one that is a commendable act of piety (MED)—so I retain and capitalize the word "Work."

b. There is a word play in ME between *God* and *goodes*.

c. I have translated the ME word *streche* as "extended." *Streche* was commonly used to describe the difficult Work of contemplation (I Walsh, 120).

d. Notice the laidback way the author deals with earthly things and matters. They are not "wrong" or "bad" but only, as it were, "in the way"—so just let them lie.

e. This is a difficult—albeit central and vital—element in understanding contemplative prayer. Since such prayer apparently produces no evident or valued results for the world, it is often seen as useless and impractical. But the author emphasizes the mystical impact of contemplative prayer on *all people*—based on an understanding of mystical solidarity in which good done by any member of the Body of Christ benefits the rest of the Body.

f. The ME has *wonderful*, but it is much stronger than its modern cognate. It has the sense of "magical" or "miraculous" or even "dreadful" or "horrible." I have used the modern "frightening."

g. We do not know how the author came up with the famous title "cloud of unknowing," but it is likely he was influenced by the Exodus story of Moses's ascent of Mount Sinai (Exod. 24:15–18: "And when Moses had gone up, a cloud covered the mountain … and entering into the midst of the cloud, Moses ascended the mountain"); and Paul's discussion of the Latin translation of Dionysius's *Deonise Hid Diuinite* (which our author later translated) refers to the "darkness" or "fog" (*caligo*) of unknowing (Hodgson, lxii). The earlier Old English sense of the word *clude* was "rock" or "hill" (related to "clod"), and "unknowing" would have carried the sense of "unacknowledged" (ODEE, 183).

h. The ME has *a nakid entent unto God*—a very powerful and poetic phrase. It has even been taken as the title for both an excellent out-of-print *Cloud* commentary by Douglas Cowan and a creditable current anonymous blog on *The Cloud*. *Nakid* carries the sense of "uncontaminated" or "uncompromised" or "clear."

ᕮ HERE BEGINS THE THIRD CHAPTER

How the Work[a] of this book shall be done, and of the worthiness of it before all other works.

Lift up your heart to God with a humble impulse of love—and I mean to His very Self and not to any of His goods.[b] And in this, see to it that you refuse to think on anything but Himself, so that nothing fills your mind or your will but only Himself. And do all that is in you to forget all the creatures that God ever made and all their works so that neither your thought nor your desire is directed or extended[c] to any of them—neither in general nor in particular. But just let them be and take no heed of them.[d]

This is the Work of the soul that most pleases God. All the saints and angels take joy in this Work of yours and hasten to assist it with all their powers. All the devils are enraged when you do this, and they try as hard as they can to chop your Work down. And although you do not understand how it can be, everyone living on earth is wonderfully helped by this Work of yours.[e] Yes, even the souls in Purgatory are eased of their pain by virtue of this Work and you yourself are cleansed and made virtuous by no work so much as by this one. And yet it is the easiest Work of all and quickly finished when, aided by grace, a soul feels this desire—otherwise it would be difficult and frightening[f] for you to do it.

Do not delay, then, but do your best in this Work until you sense the desire. For the first time you do it, you will find only a darkness, and, as it were, a cloud of unknowing,[g] which you do not understand, except that you feel in your will a naked longing for God.[h] No matter what you do, this darkness and this cloud is between you and your God, and it stops

a. The ME has *reson*—literally, "reason" or "mind" or even "talk."

b. The ME has *criing* —literally, "singing" or "chanting" or "weeping" or "praying."

c. The ME has *it behoveth*, which is extremely difficult to translate since its meanings reach from "it is necessary" to "it is proper" to "it is inevitable."

d. The ME word is *athomus*. It represents the smallest measure of time in the medieval world—literally, 15/94ths of a second! According to the philologist Charles Du Cange (1610–88), there are 22,560 such "atoms" in an hour (Hodgson, 186). Contemplation takes only a moment: "Infinity is present in that which is indivisibly finite" (Cowan, 22).

e. One is reminded of the words of Gandalf in J.R.R. Tolkien's *Fellowship of the Ring* (chapter 2): "All we have to decide is what to do with the time that is given to us."

f. It cannot be stressed sufficiently that the author recognizes the primary human agent of one's salvation and union with God to be one's *will*—that element of one's internal self that chooses and makes decisions. For the author, the will is morally more significant than any action or deed—and, as we shall see, it is the determination and resolve of the will alone (joined with God's grace) that will make union with God possible for the soul.

g. Our spiritual nature is close to God because God, too, is pure spirit—and God is close to us because we are made in his image. This is a statement about human nature: that as humans, we have an inborn affinity with God. The Quakers put it: "There is that of God in every man" (Fox, 14).

h. Because of the way humans are made, only God and God alone can ever fully satisfy the longings and yearnings of our soul. Whatever else we desire—no matter what it may be—it will never wholly fulfill our spiritual hunger.

you so that you can neither see Him clearly in your mind[a] by the light of understanding, nor sense Him in the sweetness of love in your affection. And therefore prepare yourself to remain in this darkness as long as you can, always begging[b] for Him you love, for if ever you can see Him or feel Him, it is fitting[c] that it always be in this cloud and in this darkness. And if you will struggle diligently as I bid you, I trust that in His mercy you shall come to that place.

HERE BEGINS THE FOURTH CHAPTER

Of the simplicity of this Work, and how it may not be achieved by the curiosity of intellect nor by imagination.

But so that you shall not err in this Work, or think that it is something other than what it is, I shall tell you a little more about it as I understand it.

This Work requires no long time before it can be truly done (as some men think) for it is the shortest work of all that a human may imagine. It is neither longer nor shorter than a split second[d] which, by the definition of true philosophers in the science of astronomy, is the smallest particle of time, and is so little that because of the smallness of it, it is indivisible and nigh on inconceivable. This is that moment of time of which it is written: "All the time that is given to you, it shall be demanded of you how you have spent it."[e] And it is reasonable that you give account of it, for it is neither too long nor too short but exactly long enough for each single impulse in the primary active power of your soul, which is your will.[f] For there are as many choices or selections made in your will in one hour—neither more nor less—as are split seconds in an hour. And if we were to be restored by grace to the first state of man's soul as it was before sin, then we would always, by the help of that grace, control that impulse or those impulses so that none would go astray but all of them would aspire to the most desirable and the highest that can be sought—which is God.

For He is actually close to our soul by virtue of His Godhead; and our soul is actually close to Him by the dignity of our creation in His image and His likeness.[g] And He by Himself—with nothing more and none but He—is fully capable (and much more) of satisfying the will and desire of our soul.[h] And our

a.   God created all rational beings—humans and angels—with the dual tools of reason/intellect and love, and there is much that our reason/intellect can tell us about God, but a complete encounter with Godself can only be accomplished through the agency of love—but this love is not the familiar emotional paroxysm or the sentimental wallowing that we often think of as "love." This salvific love is an action of the will, not of the emotions.

b.   The ME has *comprehende*, but it is something of a false cognate. The original meaning of the word was "to grasp," "to include," "to enclose," or "to contain" (MED).

c.   Coming to embrace God in love is heavenly (i.e., "endless bliss") while not doing so is infernal (i.e., "endless pain"). It is important for us to remember that *The Cloud* was written to some degree as a counteraction to the Scholastic rationalism of the thirteenth century with its almost exclusive emphasis on the intellect and dialectical reasoning as the best way to comprehend divinity.

d.   The ME word is *refourmyd* and still carried the sense of "being formed again" or "being remade"—much more strongly than modern use conveys.

e.   Psalm 33:9 [34:8]: "Taste and see that the Lord is sweet."

f.   ME has *fulle food*. In Christian literature, heaven is frequently described as a banquet (see Matt. 22:1–4 and Rev. 19:17), and I have translated *fulle food* as "full banquet."

g.   The author's extravagant and potent claim: that it is contemplative union with God that is the very purpose for which mankind was originally created and, hence, the means by which we can return to the original sinless state.

h.   The ME is *defaylyng* and means "feebleness" or "weakness." Without apology, the author sees contemplative prayer as the very center of Christian life.

i.   "As the devout Saint Bernard [of Clairvaux] says, 'Nothing is more precious than time, and nothing today is considered so worthless'—the same Saint Bernard also says that God will examine us carefully on how we have spent all the time granted us." (Hanbridge, Paul, tr., *The Capuchin Constitutions of 1536* [Collegio San Lorenzo da Brindisi; Rome; 2006], 5:10–12).

soul, by virtue of His restoring grace, is made fully capable of comprehending Him completely by means of love—He who is incomprehensible to all created powers of knowing, such as to the souls of angel and man. (I mean He is incomprehensible to their "knowing" but not to their "loving," and therefore I refer in this case to the "powers of knowing."[a])

But see: all rational creatures—angels and men—have in them, individually, a major active power which is called "a power of knowing" and another major active power which is called "a power of loving." Concerning these two powers: to the first (which is a "knowing power") God who is the maker of both is always incomprehensible; and to the second (which is a "loving power") in each one separately God is entirely comprehensible in detail, insomuch so that a single soul by virtue of love could by itself enclose[b] Him who is capable—without limit and much more beyond measure—of filling all the souls and angels that ever may be. And this is the endless marvelous miracle of love that shall never have an end. For He shall always do it and never shall He cease doing it. Understand this (whoever by grace may do so), for experiencing this is endless bliss, and its opposite is endless pain.[c]

And so whoever would be thus reshaped[d] by grace so as to continue in control of the impulses of one's will—since one cannot avoid natural impulses—would never in this life be without some taste of the eternal sweetness[e] or in the bliss of heaven without the full banquet.[f] And so have no wonder that I direct you to this Work, for this is the Work you will hear of later in which humanity would have continued had they never sinned, and for which Work humanity was made, and all things for humans to help them and assist them to it, and by which humans shall be restored once again.[g] And because of lack of interest[h] in this Work, a person falls deeper and deeper into sin and further and further from God. But by heeding and continually doing this Work alone, without anything else, a person evermore rises higher and higher above sin and nearer and nearer to God.

And so keep good heed of time and how you spend it, for nothing is more precious than time.[i] In one little moment of time—as tiny as it is— heaven may be won and lost. This is a sign that time is precious: for God,

a. The linear character of time matters to the author. One cannot lay claim to the moment yet to come nor retrieve the moment past. "For that whatever is made in time is made both after and before some other moment of time—after what is past and before what is future" (Augustine, *City of God* 11.6).

b. One is reminded of Jesus's words that express the same principle: "The sabbath was made for man, and not man for the sabbath" (Mk. 2:27).

c. This is an extremely difficult paragraph. First, the author puts these panic-stricken words on the lips of his twenty-four-year-old protégé. Second, it is an indication that the author has had this experience himself and is not speaking merely theoretically (Cowan, 25). Third, all these "time" references are very confusing. In essence, the author's basic point is that if one pays attention to the present moment—neither dwelling on the past nor thinking only of the future—then one cannot be faulted by God and will be able to account for one's time well spent.

d. The ME is *aseeth*. It is a difficult word with the sense of "settle" or "arrange." I have translated it as "deal adequately with" after Gallacher (33 n.).

e. Even if he now at last understands the importance of every moment of time, the protégé cannot go back and undo the past but can only take responsibility for the times that are yet to come.

f. The ME has *habundaunce of freelté and slowness of sperite*—literally, "abundance of frailty and slowness of spirit."

g. The ME has *conclude*, which in the fourteenth century meant "enclose," "close down," "infer," or "prove" (MED). (Walsh translates this line very poorly as "My reasoning is irrefutable.")

h. This plea is intended to be addressed by the protégé to the author.

i. The ME word is *comoun*, but the thought is that the protégé is not left alone with his fears, but love brings everything into community with Jesus, the saints, and the angels. So it has the sense of being "in common."

j. The ME has *in kepyng of tyme*. The author's idea: it was Mary's willingness to *wait* for the birth of the Child that made her "full of grace."

k. The ME has *never may lese tyme*. *May* translates as "can," and since the angels are in heaven, they are beyond time and cannot "lose" or "waste" time.

who is the giver of time, never gives two times together, but each one after the other.[a] And He does this because He chooses not to reverse the order or the ordinary course in the cause-and-effect of His creation. For time is made for humanity, and not humanity for time.[b] And therefore God, who is the ruler of nature, will not in the granting of time leap ahead of the natural progression in a person's soul which exactly corresponds to one-moment-at-a-time. So that a man shall have no accusation against God in the Judgment and at the giving of his account of how he spent time, saying: "You gave two moments at once, but I have only one impulse at a time."

But[c] now you say mournfully: "How shall I accomplish this? And since what you say is true, how shall I account for every past moment individually? I, who to this day—now four and twenty years of age—have never paid much attention to time. Even if I wanted to repair it, now—as you well know by very reason of your words written before—it could not be by following the course of nature nor through just any ordinary grace that I would be able to notice or even deal adequately with[d] any times other than those that are yet to come.[e] Yea, and moreover I know well by true proof that even of those times that are to come—because of my abounding weakness and spiritual sluggishness[f]—I shall in no way be able to heed one in a hundred; so I am truly depressed[g] by these thoughts. Help me now, for the love of Jesus!"[h]

Right well have you said: "for the love of Jesus," for there within the love of Jesus shall be your help. Love is so powerful that it makes everything available to all.[i] Therefore, love Jesus, and all that He has is yours. He, by His Divinity, is the maker and giver of time. He, by His Humanity, is the true custodian of time. And He, by both His Godhead and His Manhood together, is the most faithful judge and the one who will ask for an accounting of how we spent our time. Therefore, bind yourself to Him by love and by faith; and then by virtue of that bond you shall be a regular partner with Him and with all who by love are also bound to Him—that is to say, with Our Lady Saint Mary (who was full of all grace in her waiting[j]), with all the angels of heaven that never can waste time uselessly,[k] and with all the saints in heaven and earth that by the grace of Jesus pass time full righteously because of love.

a. This time business is confusing. The ME *lese tyme* ("lose time," MED) means "waste time," but also may suggest "losing credit for time well spent"—like losing "good time credit" in a prison sentence.

b. Meister Eckhart also frequently refers to a "spark [*fünkelin*] of the soul" that grasps God as God truly is (Mojsisch, Burkhard; *Meister Eckhart* [John Benjamins Publishing; Amsterdam; 2001], 15). The same is true in Richard of Saint Victor's *Benjamin Major* and Walter Hilton's *The Scale of Perfection* (Hodgson, *Cloud*, 187 n.). Bonaventure called it a "spark of conscience," and the poet Henry Vaughan called it "*Silex scintillans*" ("a sparkling hint") (Gallacher, 6, 108). The image also appears in Saint Jerome, Peter Lombard, and Thomas Aquinas (Davies, Oliver; *God Within*; New City Press, Hyde Park, NY; 2006], 48).

c. The ME has *maner of this worching*—literally, "the manner of this working."

d. It cannot be emphasized strongly enough that for the author this working of love lies entirely and completely *within the will*, without the working of the imagination or the emotions or the intellect. He describes an ecstatic intuition or insight and not merely a "good feeling."

e. The *blynde stering of love* is one of the foundational expressions the author uses throughout the book to describe the contemplative process. *Blynde* here means "invisible" or "secret" or "incomparable." I have tended to leave the author's original words in frequently recurrent phrases like this one.

f. The ME has *proude, coryous, and an ymaginatif witte*—all negatives!

g. In fact, there are references to some driven insane by reclusive contemplative life—see Dom Halys "ailing in body and in mind" (Hendriks, 76) and "[Father George] went crazy with terror and despair" (Taylor, 76).

h. The author intends that this be taken with the greatest gravity: by "fooling around" with contemplation, one can put oneself in extreme spiritual jeopardy. This can be seen among some modern bogus evangelists who claim personal familiarity with God and are capable of doing severe and grave damage to their own and others' souls. It is not merely a case of not straying from the path but of actually stumbling headlong into the abyss, for there are "spirits of evil in the high places" (Eph. 6:12).

Look! Here [in love] lies comfort: interpret it clearly and gain some benefit. But one thing I warn you of above all others: I cannot see how anyone can truly claim this fellowship with Jesus and His virtuous mother, His high angels, and also His saints unless he exerts every effort with the help of grace in keeping track of time[a]—so that he can be seen as one who is personally bringing benefit (however little that may be) to the community, just as each one of them does as well.

And therefore pay attention to this contemplative Work and to the marvelous way it acts within your soul. For if it is truly understood, it is nothing if not a sudden stirring without warning, as it were, suddenly springing up to God as sparks from a live coal.[b] And it is also marvelous to count the stirrings that can happen in one hour in a soul that is predisposed to this Work. And yet, in one stirring out of all these, the soul may suddenly and wholly forget about all created things. But immediately after each stirring (because of the depravity of the flesh) the soul drops down again to some thought or to something done or left undone. But, so what? Because immediately afterward it surges up again just as abruptly as it did before.

And here one can quickly understand the pattern of this process[c] and be convinced that it is far from any fantasy or any false imagination or fanciful opinion[d] (which had been brought about not by such a devout and humble blind stirring of love,[e] but by an arrogant, inquisitive, and an imaginative wit[f]). Such an arrogant, inquisitive wit ought always to be brought down and soundly trodden underfoot if this Work is truly to be undertaken in purity of spirit.

For whoever hears this Work either read or spoken, and thinks that it can or should be approached by intellectual effort, will therefore sit and seek in their wits how it may be done, and in this curiosity they belabor their imagination—probably beyond its natural capability—and they pretend a way of working that is neither bodily nor spiritual. Truly this person, whoever it is, is dangerously deluded—to such a degree that unless God of His great goodness shows His miraculous mercy and makes this person quickly abandon the Work and humble himself to the counsel of experienced contemplatives, he shall fall either into frenzies[g] or else into other great misfortunes of both spiritual sins and diabolical deceits through which he may easily be lost both soul and body for all eternity.[h]

a.   The contemplative way does not involve "thinking about God" or "imagining God" or "reflecting on God" or "explaining God" or "identifying God" or "comparing God to anything else." It is much more radical than that. In fact, the great mystic Meister Eckhart went so far as to say that one needs to forget "god"—that is, to forget any ideas or impressions or notions we may have had about what "god" was like—and to open ourselves to the unexpected, surprising, even shocking reality when or if God's Self is revealed to us in contemplation (MacKendrick, 88).

b.   It is interesting that in the two translations of *The Cloud* into Latin, one was by Richard Firth, a Carthusian of Methley, in 1491 and titled *Nubes Ignorandi* ("The Cloud of Not Knowing") and the other from the Pembroke College Cambridge MA 221 and titled *Divina Caligo Ignorancie* ("The Divine Fog [or Mist] of Ignorance").

c.   See Richard of St. Victor's [† 1173] *Benjamin Major* 5:2: "To enter the cloud of unknowing is to rise above mind, and by means of the cloud of forgetfulness, to hide from the mind the awareness of whatever lies at hand" (I Walsh, 128).

d.   "Creatures" is an awkward word because, in spite of its literal meaning, to the modern ear it suggests unpleasant animal beings (i.e., "critters")—but there is simply no other word that clearly means "all that is created including things, animals, and people," which is what is intended in the author's use of "creatures."

e.   The author now establishes his vertical cosmology: (1) At the bottom is the world and all its creatures—both good and bad; (2) above which is the cloud of forgetting; (3) above which is the contemplative seeking soul; (4) above which is the cloud of unknowing; (5) above which is the Perfect Presence of God (the Beatific Vision).

f.   The ME has *werkes and conditions*. The ODEE (202) gives "modes of being" as the fourteenth-century meaning of the ME *conditions*. Not only are the creatures themselves (both good and wicked) to be immersed in the cloud of forgetting, but also anything that might be related to them in any way. The author calls for a complete repudiation of absolutely *everything* that is "of the world."

So, for the love of God, take extreme caution in this Work, and do not struggle in your intellect or in your imagination in any way. For I tell you truly, it cannot be attained by laboring in them, and, therefore, leave them and do not work with them.[a]

And do not suppose that because I call it "a darkness" or "a cloud" that it is just any cloud produced by the vapors that drift in the air nor yet any darkness such as is in your house at night when the candle is out.[b] For truly such a darkness and such a cloud you can imagine with the phenomenon of wit to bring before your eyes on the brightest day of summer, and also, in the same way, in the darkest night of winter you can imagine a clear shining light. Let be such falsehood—I do not mean that kind of thing. When I say "darkness," I mean "the absence of knowing"—like everything that you do not know or else that you have forgotten is dark to you, because you do not see it with your spiritual eye. And for this reason it is not called a "cloud of the air" but "a cloud of unknowing" that is between you and your God.

⌁ HERE BEGINS THE FIFTH CHAPTER

That during this Work all the creatures that have ever been, are now, or ever shall be, and all the works of those same creatures, should be hidden under the cloud of forgetting.[c]

And if ever you shall come to this cloud, and wish to remain and work within it as I bid you, then just as this cloud of unknowing is above you (between you and your God) just so you ought to put a cloud of forgetting behind you (between you and all creatures[d] that have ever been made).[e] It may seem to you, perhaps, that you are very far from God in that the cloud of unknowing is between you and God, but surely (if it is well-considered) you are much further from Him when you have no cloud of forgetting between yourself and creatures that have ever been made. Whenever I say "all created things that have ever been made" I mean not only the creatures themselves, but also all the works and ways of life[f] of the same creatures. I make exception for no creature (whether they are bodily or spiritual creatures) nor yet any way of life or work of any creature (whether they are good or evil), but in short I say that all should be hidden under the cloud of forgetting in this instance.

a.   The author is considering that while the thought and remembrance of virtuous acts or honorable people (perhaps even saints) could be of benefit in living one's Christian life, they are useless in seeking God's own Presence in contemplation.

b.   The author now begins to enter what is very confusing and dark water for the modern Christian because he declares that *any* thought, *any* action of the mind, *any* intellectual consideration of *anything*, no matter what—even if it is a thought specifically intended to bring us closer to God—becomes the focus of the "eye of our soul" and thereby removes that focus from God's very Self. This is radical and barely comprehensible to the modern mind. We are used to the idea that "thinking about God" brings us closer to God—when in fact all it does is bring us closer to the *thought of God*, not to God's own Self.

c.   A good example of a false cognate. The ME word is *cortesye*, which literally means "courtly" or "befitting the court of a prince," not just "well-mannered" or "polite" in its modern sense. I have chosen to translate it as "respectful."

d.   Here we meet the vital central image of the entire *Cloud*: the unwillingness of the author to accept any dilution or compromise or attenuation of his primary principle: that there is nothing (i.e., no thing) that the mind can use to lead us to God's own true Self except silence and the obliteration of our thoughts and memories of anything else whatsoever. In an active sense, this is a repudiation of the thirteenth-century Scholastic conviction that the intellect alone can lead us to God and concurrently a repudiation of the more modern belief that the emotions provide that divine path.

e.   The ME has *can no man thinke* and the false cognate fools all previous translators, because *can* does not mean "can" but is from the ME verb *conne*, meaning "to know" or "to know how" (Bradley, 145).

f.   The ME has *leve*, which carries the sense of "cede" or "forfeit" more than merely "leave" (Bradley, 396).

g.   The ME has *thinke*, but in modern use, the only thing one can "think" is an idea—but one can "rationalize" anything.

h.   It seems odd that the author uses the word *thing* to describe God. I have taken the liberty of at least capitalizing the word.

For although it may be truly profitable to think of certain qualities and deeds of some certain special creatures, nevertheless in this contemplative Work it is of little or no benefit.[a] Wherefore, because of this memory or thought of any creatures that God ever made, or even any of their deeds, it is a kind of spiritual light, for the eye of the soul is opened on it and even fixed upon it (as the eye of an archer is upon the mark he shoots at). And one thing I tell you: that every thing that you think about is situated above you for that time, and lies between you and your God. And in that same degree, if anything is in your mind except God alone, you are that much further from God.[b]

Yea, and if it be respectful[c] and seemly to say so, in this Work there is little or no benefit in thinking of the kindness and excellence of God, nor of Our Lady, nor of the saints and angels in heaven, nor even of the joys of heaven itself—that is to say, having a special focus on them, as if you could by that attention feed and further your purpose. I trust that it would in no way be so in this instance and in this Work. For although it is good to think upon the kindness of God, and to love Him and praise Him for that, yet is it far better to think upon His own unadorned essence *itself*, and to love Him and praise Him for Himself *alone*.[d]

HERE BEGINS THE SIXTH CHAPTER

A brief conception of the Work of this book, dealt with by means of questions.

But now you ask me and say: "How should I think about His own Self and what He is?" And I cannot answer you except thus: "I have no idea."

For with your question you have brought me into that very same darkness and into that same cloud of unknowing where I wish you were yourself. For of all other creatures and their works—yea, and of the works of God as well—a person through grace can have complete knowledge and can easily ruminate about them, but about God Himself no person knows how to think.[e] And therefore I want to forfeit[f] everything that I can rationalize[g] and choose for my love that one Thing[h] that I cannot comprehend. Because He may well be loved, but never comprehended. By love He may be both

a. The ME is *getyn* meaning "to guard" or "to grasp" (ODEE, 396).

b. The ME has *it be a light*, meaning "it is something that sheds light."

c. The "casting down" and the "covering over" are done by the person involved, not by God.

d. A difficult translation. The ME word is *listely* and means "artfully" or "cunningly" (Bradley, 402) or "cleverly" or even "by trickery" (Mossé, 458) or "with eager longing" (Gallacher, 36).

e. The ME is *plesing,* and its first sense is "beautiful" or "attractive."

f. The ME has *smyte,* and virtually all translators have "smite" or "beat upon," and both may be appropriate for "pounding with one's fists," but not for "stabbing with a sharp instrument." I have chosen "pierce" as more specific.

g. The ME has *scharp darte of longing love*, which has become a treasured catchphrase, but "dart" may actually be a false cognate. In ME, it means "an arrow," "a crossbow quarrel [bolt]," "a spear," or "a lance" (ODEE, 244), also "a javelin" or "a missile carrying a firebrand" (MED). It is obviously related to the traditional arrow of Eros (Cupid). *Scharp* meant "shrill" or "piercing."

h. In this chapter, the author personifies the "thought" as though it were a person, exchanging questions and answers, and assigning human characteristics to the thought itself.

i. This is a difficult sentence which has confounded most translators—*And in Him sei thou kanst no skile*. Walsh (I 132) has "You have no part to play." McCann (15) has "In him," say, "thou hast no skill." Johnston (55) has "You are powerless to grasp him." Cowan (37) has: "You have no argument." They all miss the rare translation of *skile* as "distinction" or "definition."

j. The ME has *steryng*: "stirring" in the sense of "moving about."

k. "The soul is straining toward an immediate perception of God. Any discursive thought, however holy, will be an obstacle" (Hodgson, 187 n.).

embraced[a] and held—but by thought, neither. And therefore although it is good sometimes to think of the kindness and majesty of God in particular, and although it is source of light[b] and a part of contemplation, nevertheless in this Work it should be cast down and covered over[c] with a cloud of forgetting. And you shall stand above it resolutely (but longingly[d]) with a devout and fair[e] stirring of love, and strive to pierce that darkness above you. Strike[f] against that thick cloud of unknowing with a piercing lance[g] of longing love, and do not leave off no matter what happens.

⌁ HERE BEGINS THE SEVENTH CHAPTER

How a person shall bear himself in this Work against all thoughts, and especially against all those that rise from his own attention to learning and natural intelligence.

And if any thought were to rise and impose itself constantly over you—between you and that darkness—and if it were to demand of you, saying: "What do you seek, and what would you like to have?"[h] say that it is God that you would like to have: "I want Him, I seek Him, and nothing but Him." And if you are asked what that God is, say that it is the God that made you and redeemed you, and that has by grace called you to His love. And say that you know no other definition of Him.[i] And therefore say: "Get you down, once more!" And trample down that thought firmly with an arousing[j] of love, even though it may seem to you to be very holy, and may seem to you as if it would help you to seek Him.[k]

Perhaps that thought will bring to your mind varied, beautiful, and wonderful qualities of God's kindness, and it may say that He is very sweet and wholly loving, very gracious and very merciful. And if you will listen to that, the thought wants nothing better, for at the last it will chatter ever more and more until it brings you down to the memory of His Passion. And there it will let you see the wonderful kindness of God; and if you listen to it, it seeks nothing more. For soon thereafter, it will let you see your old wretched life; and perhaps in seeing and thinking of that, it will bring to your mind some place that you dwelled in before now. So that at the last, before you know it, your attention will be dispersed you know not where. The cause of this

a. This is one of the most difficult aspects of the author's thought: that in order to reach the full and perfect Presence of God, one must reject all concepts of divinity—no matter how good they seem. The author sees nothing "wrong" about having thoughts of God, the saints, and the virtuous active life, but they fall short and are impediments to the direct experience of the Godhead.

b. This is the author's first specific inclusive provision for women. Perhaps the author caught himself and realized that there were some notable female contemplatives in his recent history (e.g., Julian of Norwich).

c. "It is the process of opening ourselves to the realm of nonphysical reality in which God can touch us far more directly than in the physical world. It is that kind of prayer in which we seek relationship with God, and in this sense meditation is the preparation and foundation for prayer" (Kelsey, 8).

d. We need to remind ourselves throughout the book that the author does not mean to discredit or dishonor "sweet meditations" on moral and theological subjects, but to point out that they are appropriate only for the "lower" levels of spiritual development, and that here, at the very pinnacle, they must be put away with all thoughts and activities of the past, no matter how good.

e. The author reminds his protégé that he is not undertaking some frivolous or lighthearted task, but one of such significance that the practitioner needs to sense it as an actual vocation—a clear calling from God to take these extreme and potentially dangerous spiritual steps.

f. Curiously, in the Latin translations of *The Cloud*, the word the author promotes for "God" is *Deus* and for "Love" is *Amor*—both of which are, of course, *two*-syllable words!

g. The author will describe later how this single word is used as a spiritual watchword. In modern use it has come to be called a "mantra"—a Sanskrit word meaning "formula" or "sacred counsel"—and is used in the Hindu, Buddhist, Sikh, and Jain practice and promoted as well as by Christian contemplatives (especially John Main, William Meninger, and Thomas Keating). The word serves as a "cancellation" of all other thought and distraction by its mindless repetition, giving no thought to its literal meaning.

splintering is that at the first you listened to that thought deliberately, then you answered it, then you took it in, and let it have its way.[a]

And yet, nevertheless, the thing that it said was both good and holy—yea, and so holy that whatever man or woman[b] who expects to come to contemplation without many such sweet meditations on their own wretchedness, the Passion, the kindness and great goodness and the majesty of God coming before, surely that one shall err and fail of His purpose.[c] And yet, nevertheless, it is necessary that a man or a woman who has used these meditations for a long time must abandon them completely and put them aside and press them far down under the cloud of forgetting, if he shall ever pierce the cloud of unknowing between him and his God.[d]

Therefore, at the time you propose to take up this Work, and feel by grace that you are called by God,[e] then lift up your heart to God with a humble stirring of love. And know that what you mean is the love of God that made you, and redeemed you, and that by grace has called you to this Work—and admit no other thought about God—and not even all *these* thoughts unless it pleases you—for a clear longing directly to God is sufficient without any other cause than Himself.

And if it pleases you to have this longing wrapped and enfolded in one word (in order to have better grasp of it) take only a little word of one syllable (for in that way it is better than two—for always the shorter it is the better it will be in harmony with the work of the spirit). And such a word is the word "God" or the word "Love."[f] Choose which you prefer—or another word of one syllable that you like best, if you wish. And fasten this word in your heart so that it never goes from there no matter what happens.[g]

a. Another reminder that what lies in the future during this "Work" can involve serious spiritual dangers characterized as "in peace or in war."

b. Once again the author personifies the "thought" and writes of it as though it were a human being. (The author uses male pronouns—"he," "him," and "his"—to describe the thought.)

c. The author makes a gibe at academics by discounting "book-learning"— this is especially a dig at the Scholastics whose process was mainly analysis and classification. (Notably, the ME word for "book-learning" is *clergie*.)

d. The author now uses the ploy of posing loaded questions in order to clarify his earlier meaning about the spiritual challenges presented to a contemplative even by "virtuous thoughts." One suspects that the author becomes increasingly aware that his words will probably be read not only by a young male religious novice, but by a wider audience who will require greater clarity in these radical teachings.

e. The ME has *febeli*, and it is inevitably translated as "feebly"—but that is completely contrary to the meaning of this sentence, in which the author wishes to pay very special attention to his answer. This is a rare instance in which the word does *not* have negative connotations and should be translated as "delicately" or "deftly" (ODEE).

f. The ME has *beam*. In the fourteenth century that could refer either to a ray of light or the branch of a tree (ODEE, 82). Since God is not described in "light" terms here, I have chosen the idea of "reflection" to convey the idea that the source of goodness is God's own likeness.

This word shall be your shield and your spear, whether you ride in peace or in war.[a] With this word you shall strike down all manner of thoughts beneath the cloud of forgetting to such a degree that if any thought presses upon you to ask you what you would like to have,[b] answer it with no more words than with this one word. And if it should offer you out of its great book-learning[c] to explain that word for you and to tell you the specifications of that word, say that you will have it all whole and neither broken nor undone. And if you will hold fast to this purpose, you may be sure that that thought will not stay long. And why? Because you will not let it feed itself on such sweet meditations we spoke of above.

∽ HERE BEGINS THE EIGHTH CHAPTER

A reliable explanation of certain doubts that may arise in this Work, treated by question;[d] the quenching of one's own intellectual curiosity and natural intelligence; and distinguishing the various degrees and the parts of active and contemplative life.

But now you ask me: "What is this thought that thus presses on me in this Work, and is it a good or evil thing?" "And if it is an evil thing, then I wonder," you say, "why is it that it increases one's devotion so much? For sometimes I think that it is a passing comfort to listen to its stories. And sometimes, I think, it makes me weep full heartily for the Passion of Christ; sometimes for my wretchedness, and for many other reasons that I think are entirely holy and that do me much good. And therefore I think that it ought not in any wise be evil. And if it is good, and with its sweet stories does me much good besides, then I have a great wonder why you bid me put it down and put it away so far beneath the cloud of forgetting?"

Now assuredly it seems to me that this is a well-moved question, and therefore I plan to answer it as delicately[e] as I can. First, when you asked me what this thought is that presses so hard upon you in this Work, offering to help you in this undertaking, I answer that it is a sharp and clear insight of your natural intelligence, impressed on your reason within your soul. And where you ask me about it, whether it is good or evil, I answer that it is utterly essential that it be good in its nature, because it is a shining reflection[f]

a. It has long been understood that human reason is the aspect of humanity that is shared with God—that human reason is the promised "image of God" in humanity—so it must in its own nature be good, but it is also vulnerable to misapplication and abuse.

b. The ME has *moche clergie and letterly conning*—"a lot of learning and literary skill"! Note: *Letterly conning* could also be translated as "scriptural science" (Mayhew, 134, 50).

c. A clear intended affront to the ordinary clergy of the day—in contrast to the monastics. The fact is that many fourteenth-century parish clergy were very poorly educated—many unable even to understand the Latin they were reading from their Mass books.

d. The ME has *prees*, normally translated as "press," but in rare cases it can be translated as "hasten" (Bradley, 484).

e. It is obvious that the author respects sincere, humble, and devout scholars as much as he dislikes false and prideful academics—just as in the next sentence he sees one's natural wisdom and intellect (which is good in itself) perverted by pride and covetousness.

f. The author now lays out his fundamental spiritual cosmology. It is based loosely on the classical ladder of perfection (*scala perfectonis*) in which the committed Christian soul passes through progressive states of spiritual realization: (1) the Purgative Way, (2) the Illuminative Way, and (3) the Unitive Way. The Purgative Way is for the spiritual beginner who is working to rid the soul of worldly and carnal temptations and to increase charity. The Illuminative Way follows once the avoidance of mortal sin has become habitual and one begins to sense the deeper divine and mystical truths about Godself and the true nature of God begins to be revealed. And the Unitive Way is the final perfection of the soul when it is freed from sin and desires nothing but God's own Presence and is in perfect union with God. Our author's version of this is the fourfold low-active, high-active, low-contemplative, and high-contemplative. These correspond to the "Common, Special, Singular, and Perfect" states in chapter 1. (Common = virtuous, but precedes serious spiritual development; Special = Purgative; Singular = Illuminative; Perfect = Unitive).

g. The ME has *goodly*, which can mean "fitting" or "suitable" or "fair" or "proper" or "excellent" (MED).

of the image of God.[a] But the application of it can be both good and evil: good, when it is opened by grace in order to see your wretchedness, the Passion, the kindness, and the wonderful works of God in His creatures physically and spiritually—and then it is no wonder that it increases your devotion as much as you say. But then there is the evil use: when it is swollen with pride and with the aberration of much learning and literary skill[b] (as in clerics[c]), and makes them rush[d] to be recognized not as humble scholars and masters of divinity or of devotion,[e] but proud scholars of the devil and masters of vanity and of falsehood. And in other men or women whoever they are—religious or secular—the use and working of this natural intellect is evil when it is swollen with proud and cunning urgings of worldly things and carnal thoughts in coveting worldly honors and having riches and vain pleasure and the flattery of others.

And where that you asked me why you should put this thought down beneath the cloud of forgetting since it seems that it is good in its nature, and when it is well-used it does you so much good and increases your devotion so much—to this I answer and say that you shall well understand that there are two manners of life in Holy Church.[f] The one is active life, and the other is contemplative life. Active is the lower and contemplative is the higher. Active life has two degrees: a higher and a lower—and also contemplative life has two degrees: a lower and a higher. Also these two lifestyles are so coupled together that although they are different in some degree, yet neither of them can be complete without some part of the other—because the part that is the higher part of active life, that same part is the lower part of contemplative life. So that a person cannot be fully active unless he is in part contemplative, nor yet fully contemplative (as it can be here on earth) unless he or she is in part active. The state of the active life is such that it is both begun and ended in this life. But not so the contemplative life, for it is begun in this life, and shall last without end, because that part that Mary chose "shall never be taken away." Active life is "troubled and worried about many things," but the contemplative sits in peace with only one thing.

The lower part of the active life consists in good and honest corporal works of mercy and of charity. The higher part of the active life and the lower part of the contemplative life lie in suitable[g] spiritual meditations and the earnest

a. This sentence presses beyond the possibilities of a translator to make it "easy." The author speaks ecstatically as only a true contemplative could speak—because the actual Beatific Vision of God is beyond grammar and literary possibility. Here, in fact, the reader must recognize that the author speaks of actual experience—and the only language he can possibly use is paradox and poetry. So *hongeth* <u>could</u> be omitted (or made into "suspended"), and *steryng* <u>could</u> be made into "impulse," and the paradox of *blinde beholding* <u>could</u> be turned into "dark gazing," and *nakid beyng* <u>could</u> be made into "simple being" (all from I Walsh, 137), and then we would no longer be dealing with the truth—nor with the experience of the author! Of course the contemplation "hangs"—swinging, dangling, undulating in cosmic winds; of course there is "darkness"—frightening, directionless, impenetrable; of course there is a "cloud of unknowing"—fog and mist incomprehensible, overwhelming; of course there is a "loving stirring"—a movement, a twinge of adoration, a spasm of devotion; of course there is a "blind investigation"—a seeing without eyes, a vision without sight, an inexplicable seventh sense; and, of course, there is the "naked being of God"—the stripped, unadorned, unembellished, unimagined, unnamable Divinity. And this is the essence—what contemplation itself is all about!

b. In this sentence, a person's concerns are with the external world ("outside himself") and the lower parts of himself that are carnal, not spiritual ("beneath himself"). Here we see the evidences of the influence of neo-Platonism that presumes some degree of enmity between the material and spiritual realms.

c. In the "middle state" (higher active and lower contemplative) a person is concerned about one's spirituality ("within one's self") and with one's better parts ("with one's self")—but is still absorbed with "self" and so not free to move to the "higher part" of contemplative life.

d. Without the grace of God, no one can by oneself naturally attain to the highest part of contemplation (i.e., the cloud of unknowing).

e. A person cannot undertake the contemplative life if one's mind is filled with the virtuous acts of the past—one needs to "disconnect" from the past level when moving up to the next level. Something like the modern "been there done that."

f. The ME has *unleveful* that can mean "unlawful" or "impermissible" (Bradley, 649).

consideration of one's own wretchedness with sorrow and contrition, of the Passion of Christ and of His servants with pity and compassion, and of the wonderful gifts, the kindness and works of God in all His creatures—both physical and spiritual—with thanksgiving and praising. But the higher part of contemplation (insofar as it may be reached on earth) hangs wholly in this darkness and in this cloud of unknowing, with a loving stirring and a blind investigation into the naked being of God Himself alone.[a]

In the lower part of the active life a person is outside one's self and beneath one's self.[b] In the higher part of active life and the lower part of contemplative life, a person is within one's self and evenly balanced with one's self.[c] But in the higher part of contemplative life, a person is above one's self and under one's God: one is above one's self because one means to get to a place by grace where a person cannot come by nature.[d] That is to say, to be knit to God in spirit, and in the union of love and harmony of will.

And just as it is impossible to human understanding for a person to come to the higher part of active life unless one closes down for a time the actions of the lower part—so it is that a person shall not be able to come to the higher part of contemplative life unless one closes down for a time the actions of the lower part.[e]

And it would be just as intolerable[f] and just as much a hindrance to a person who sat in meditation if one were at that time to be distracted by thoughts of one's outward corporal works (which one had done or else shall do—even though they may have been very holy works in themselves), surely it would be just as unlikely a thing and would be just as much a hindrance to a person who ought to be working within this darkness and in this cloud of unknowing with an ardent stirring of love to God for Himself, if one were to allow any thought or any consideration of God's wonderful gifts, kindness, and works of any of His creatures, bodily or spiritual, to rise

a. A confusing paragraph reiterating at length the ideas of the previous paragraph.

b. Here is the core concept of the entire book: that access to the Presence of God can never come by use of the intellect, but finally only by love. But it is important that we differentiate the author's meaning of "love" from our present-day sentimental idea. The love that leads us to Godself is utterly sacrificial, utterly the intentional act of the will, not an act of the romantic heart.

c. The reader needs to be prepared for hyperboles that are common attention-getters for the author. In this subtitle the author makes his point: that *any* ratiocination or intellectual activity—even the thinking process of a saint—would serve to hinder one's soul's ascendance to the cloud of unknowing. The intellect is of inestimable value through all human life until one begins this last great Work of the contemplative way—the wordless, indescribable encounter with the cloud of unknowing—and the Divine Being hidden within it. Even the holiest saint would have to stop thinking about God and turn to loving him if union with God was the goal.

d. The ME has *werk blynd*. Walsh translates it as "dark contemplation," but the author constantly refers to the inability to "see" before the cloud of unknowing, so I am convinced he would call it a "blind Work."

e. One of the author's frequent adages—a mnemonic aid. Cowan (51) refers to it in his commentary: "Suppress them, or they will suppress you!"

f. Even when one means to be concentrated on the contemplative Work, very often one's attention drifts to something or someone other than God, and that distracts from "the Work."

upon him to push in between him and his God—even if those thoughts might be very holy, pleasant, and comforting.[a]

And it is for this reason that I bid you put down any such clever, cunning thought, and cover it with a thick cloud of forgetting—no matter how holy it is or how much it may promise to help you in your undertaking. Because love may reach to God in this life, but not knowledge.[b] And all the while that the soul dwells in this mortal body, always the cleverness of our understanding in considering all spiritual things—but most especially God—is muddled with a sort of illusion because of which our Work might well be contaminated and it would be a wonder if it did not lead us into great error.

⌒ HERE BEGINS THE NINTH CHAPTER

During this contemplative Work the intelligence of the holiest creature God ever made would hinder the Work more than it would help it.[c]

And therefore the intense activity of your understanding (that will always thrust itself upon you when you commit yourself to this blind Work[d]) ought always to be brought down. For unless you bring it down, it will bring you down[e]—to such a degree that when you believe it best to remain in this darkness, and you believe that nothing is in your mind except God alone, if you look truly, you may well find that your mind is not occupied with this darkness at all, but rather with a clear vision of something less than God.[f] And if that is so, then certainly during that time that thing is actually above you and between you and your God. And therefore, commit yourself to bring down such clear visions, no matter how holy or pleasant they may be.

For one thing I will tell you: this blind activity of love toward God for His own sake—such a secret love which thrusts against the cloud of unknowing—this is more beneficial for the health of your soul, more worthy in itself, and more pleasing to God and to all the saints and angels in heaven (yea, and more helpful to all your friends both bodily and spiritually, whether they be living or dead), and it is better for you to have this and to feel it spiritually in your affection than it is to have the eye of your soul

a. An extremely extravagant claim: that it is better to be spiritually thrusting blindly against the cloud of unknowing than to see or hear the heavenly communion of saints and angels! It is hard for us to make the distinction: that seeking *anything* other than God—no matter how holy or sanctified it may be—is an impediment to the "blind love" of the Beatific Vision.

b. The Latin version of *The Cloud* translates this confusing sentence as follows: "But be secure in this, that no mortal will be able without the cloud and the darkness to have a clear image of the divine. Paul attests this who says: 'We see now through a glass in a dark manner,' although in this case by those who will be able to obtain this feeling by grace" (*Nubes Ignorandi* in McCann, 21 n.).

c. The author points out that since an unintentional wandering of mind can impede one's contemplative Work, how much more will *voluntarily* or *intentionally* turning one's mind to "anything less than God" obstruct one's movement toward the cloud.

d. Similarly, if even thinking of holy saints hampers the Work, certainly thinking of ordinary friends or anything worldly from one's past would be an even greater obstacle.

e. The author knows he is in deep water here and is certainly aware that many of the neo-Platonists of his day were strict dualists who claimed that *everything* earthly or worldly was actually evil and only what was spiritual was good. He is very definite about denying that stance, presenting his denial with the strongly emphatic "No!" and "God forbid…"

f. The author makes his point by showing that one would not "settle" for awareness of a mere angel or saint when one seeks awareness of God's Self.

opened in contemplation either in gazing directly upon all the angels and saints in heaven, or in hearing all the jubilation and the music that is among them in bliss.[a]

And you need not wonder at this: for if you could once see it with the same clarity that you come to touch it and feel it in this life by grace, you would think as I say. But be assured that humans will never have that clear sight here in this life—only the feeling that a person might have through grace when God bestows it. And therefore lift up your love to that cloud.[b] Or, to speak more truly, let God draw your love up to that cloud; and try to make a commitment to yourself, through the help of His grace, that you will forget all other things.

For since a plain recollection of anything less than God, coming *against* your will and your understanding, puts you further from God than you would be if it were not there—and hinders you, and makes you to that degree less able to feel in your experience the fruit of His love—how much more, then, do you think that a recollection *deliberately* and *willingly* entertained will hinder you in your purpose?[c] And since the recollection of any particular saint or any pure spiritual thing will hinder you so much, how much more do you think the recollection of any ordinary person living in this wretched life, or any manner of bodily or worldly thing, would hinder you and obstruct you in this Work?[d]

I am not saying that just a simple sudden thought of any good and pure spiritual thing under God, thrusting against your will and your understanding, or else intentionally drawn to you deliberately to increase your devotion (even though it is hindering this manner of Work), is therefore evil. No! God forbid that you take it so.[e] But I say that although it is good and holy, yet *in this particular Work* it hinders more than it helps—that is to say, while one is doing the Work. Because certainly one who seeks God perfectly will not settle finally for the mere awareness of any angel or saint that is in heaven.[f]

a. A reader must understand the medieval moral system in which the gravity of a sin is classified by the sinner's intention, the circumstance in which it happens, the effect it has on others, the degree to which one is addicted to the sin, the other options for choice, and the like. By and large, sins were classified as either mortal or venial. Mortal sins (called *deedly* in ME) were believed to be serious enough to breach one's relationship with God and to bring about damnation after death—unless they are absolved in confession. Venial sins were minor infractions involving no intent to do serious evil and can be forgiven merely by repentance.

b. The medieval church, following Saint Augustine, believed that the sin committed by Adam in the Garden of Eden was inherited by every human being since then (i.e., "original sin"), and that while the individual *guilt* of that sin is removed by Holy Baptism, the human *inclination* to sin (or "concupiscence") remains.

c. The section in italics represents seven lines that had been crossed out in the original manuscript we are following (Harleian, 674). Hodgson (20) suggests that the cancellation may have been made by an early critic who was opposed to monasticism—possibly a Lollard.

d. See note "c" above. This is the ME word *entent*, which the author uses frequently—as in *a nakid entent unto God* in chapter 3. Intention is a significant dynamic in the author's explanation of "the Work."

e. The monastic state (in which the author's protégé apparently has chosen to remain) was thought to be a guarantee for salvation—based on Matt. 19:29: "Everyone who has left houses, even brothers, or sisters, or father, or mother, or wife, or children or lands for my name's sake ... shall inherit everlasting life."

f. The words in italics were crossed out in the original manuscript we are following (Harleian, 674) and omitted in some later manuscripts (Hodgson, 7).

g. Notice that the author equates "the spiritual heart" with "the will," not with the emotions as a modern might do. The author sees the will as the primary determinant of human morality and salvation.

h. The author uses this paragraph to expound a catalog of the traditional Seven Deadly Sins. It is both interesting and remarkable to note that unlike more modern cataloging, he places the sin of Anger first and the sin of Lust last.

⟲ HERE BEGINS THE TENTH CHAPTER

How one shall know when one's thought is not sin; and if it be sin, when it is mortal and when it is venial.[a]

However it is not the same regarding thoughts of any man or woman living in this life or of any bodily or worldly thing—whatsoever that may be. Because plain sudden recollection of any of them thrusting against your will and your understanding, although it is no sin attributed to you—for, beyond your control, it is the torment of original sin of which you were cleansed in baptism[b]—nevertheless, if this sudden stirring or recollection is not struck down rapidly, then quickly, because of its frailty, your fleshly heart may be bound to it with some kind of pleasure (if it be something that pleases you or has pleased you before) or else with some kind of complaint (if it be a thing that you think distresses you or has distressed you before). This binding—although it can be mortal in worldly men and women who have been living in mortal sin—nevertheless, it is only venial sin in you and in all others that have with a true will forsaken the world, *and are obligated in any degree to devout life in Holy Church (whether it be private or public) and therefore wish to be ruled not according to their own will and their own thought, but by the will and counsel of their superiors, whoever they may be, religious or secular.*[c] The reason for this is the grounding and rooting of your intention[d] in God, made in the beginning of your life under vows in the state that you remain in[e] *by the witness and counsel of some discrete father.*[f] But if it were to happen that this pleasure or complaint is bound to your *fleshly* heart and is allowed to remain there for a long time without being renounced, then it will in the end be bound to your *spiritual* heart (that is to say, the will[g]) with full consent—then it is mortal sin.

And[h] this occurs when you, or any of those of whom I am speaking, intentionally bring to mind the thought of any man or woman living in this life, or of any bodily or other worldly thing, insomuch that—if it is a thing that grieves or has grieved you before—there rises in you an angry passion and an appetite for vengeance, which is called Anger; or else a wicked disdain and a kind of loathing for that person with spiteful and contemptuous thoughts, which is called Envy; or else a weariness and antipathy to any good work, physical or spiritual, which is called Sloth.

a.   The ME word here is *catel*. Some have translated it as "cattle"—but it is actually the word that comes to us as "chattel" or "moveable personal property" (MED).

b.   The ME word is *glosing*, which is generally defined as "flattery" or "deception" or "perversion" (Bradley, 298). Walsh (I 144) translates it— perhaps wisely—as "seduction."

c.   It is curious that the author considers "fleshly indulgence, perversion, or flattery" *of oneself* as a sin of lust, rather than of gluttony, greed, or pride.

d.   The ME word is *charge*, and carries the sense of "put in right order" or "lay blame on" or "attach importance to" (Gallacher, 43).

e.   The ME word is *distroie* and carries the sense of "demolish," "pull down," "put an end to" (ODEE, 260). Richard Methley (the XV c. Latin translator) uses *destitutionem* ("abandon" or "desert").

f.   The ME word is *rechlesnes* and means "absence of consideration" or "not paying proper attention to" or "overlooking" (Bradley, 498). I have chosen "neglecting" as the most literarily comprehensive word.

g.   1 John 1:8: "If we say that we have no sin we lead ourselves astray, and truth is not in us."

h.   The ME word *trew* is added here in some of the later manuscripts.

i.   It is fundamental spiritual advice that paying no attention to small and seemingly insignificant moral compromises in relatively unimportant issues almost inevitably results in greater and greater compromises, blossoming eventually into full-blown mortal sin. There is an old spiritual saying: "Stealing a penny today means stealing a dollar tomorrow."

And if it is a thing that pleases you or has pleased you before, there wells up in you an inordinate delight to think about that thing, whatever it may be, to such a degree that you rest in that thought and finally bind your heart and your will to it, and feast your fleshly heart on it, so that you think for the time that you covet no other wealth but to live always in such a peace and rest with that thing that you think about. If this thought that you draw to yourself or else receive when it is put to you, and in which you rest yourself with delight, is of natural worth or knowledge, of grace or degree, of favor or beauty, then it is Pride. And if it is any kind of worldly goods, riches or property[a] or what a person may own or be master over, then it is Greed. If it is dainty meats and drinks, or any kind of delights that one can taste, it is Gluttony. And if it is love or desire or any kind of fleshly indulgence, perversion,[b] or flattery of any living man or woman, or even of yourself, then it is Lust.[c]

⌇ HERE BEGINS THE ELEVENTH CHAPTER

That a person should recognize[d] each thought and each stirring for what it is, and always avoid carelessness in venial sin.

I do not say this because I believe that you or any of the others I spoke of are guilty and encumbered with any such sins, but because I want you to recognize each thought and each stirring for what it is, and because I want you to struggle earnestly to subdue[e] the first stirring and thought of these things in which you might thus sin. For one thing I tell you: that the one who does not recognize or pays little attention to the first thought—yea, though it is no sin to him—that person, whoever it may be, shall not be able to avoid neglecting[f] venial sin. No one can absolutely avoid venial sin in this mortal life,[g] but neglecting venial sin ought always to be avoided by all [true][h] students of perfection. Otherwise I would not be amazed if before long they were to sin mortally.[i]

a. Richard of Methley (who translated *The Cloud* into Latin) says he practiced "the Work" for fourteen years and knows that it is only "in intention" that it can be practiced "all the time" (cited in I Walsh, 145, n.).

b. The ME has *go not thens*—"do not go from there" (i.e., "from the Work").

c. The reader is reminded of 1 Cor. 13:3: "If I give all I possess to feed the poor, and if I deliver my body to be burned, and have not love, I gain nothing."

d. The author lists all the traditional corporal castigations for monastic penance: fasting, forgoing sleep, rising at midnight, sleeping on hard boards or the floor, wearing a shirt made of rough goat's hair, and flogging one's body with a whip of cords knotted with thorns.

e. This list of supposedly beneficial spiritual practices—even extreme ones—is totally repudiated by the author as useless in ending sin. This may seem obvious to a modern reader, but it would have been unspeakably radical to a fourteenth-century Christian monk who was taught that these specific practices were considered the best guarantee against sin.

f. The reader needs to be reminded that the author is speaking of all "good things" only in relation to their ability to facilitate the "blind stirring of love" of his contemplative ideal.

g. The reference, of course, is to the biblical account of Martha and Mary (Lk. 10:38–42) in which Martha, who was busy with much serving, is judged for being "troubled by many things," and Mary, who sat at the Lord's feet and listened to him, is praised for having "chosen the best part, which shall not be taken away from her." Virtually every medieval mystic (including our author) used the Mary and Martha story as evidence for the superiority of the contemplative life over the active life.

h. The ME word is *comprehended* in its ancient sense of "contained" or "included" (Latin: *com* = completely + *prehendere* = to grasp).

i. The author is wholeheartedly committed to the contemplative experience of the "blind stirring of love" and makes the claim that all virtues—if truly understood—can be seen to be present within that "stirring."

j. The ME word is *crokid*—literally "corrupted" or "deceitful" (MED).

◌ HERE BEGINS THE TWELFTH CHAPTER

That by virtue of this Work, not only is sin destroyed,
but virtues are also gained.

And therefore if you wish to stand and not fall, never weaken in your intentions but strike evermore against this cloud of unknowing that is between you and your God with a piercing lance of longing love.[a] And refuse to think on anything less than God. And do not desert[b] this Work no matter what may happen. For this alone by itself is the only work that actually demolishes the ground and the root of sin. No matter how much you fast,[c] no matter how long you keep vigil, no matter how early you rise, no matter how hard your bed, no matter how coarse your hairshirt,[d] yea, and if it were lawful to do (as it is not), even if you put out your eyes, cut out the tongue from your mouth, totally plugged up your ears and your nose, though you were to cut away your private parts and to give all the pain to your body[e] that you could imagine—all this would not help you at all. The stirring and increase of sin will still be in you.

Yea, and what more! No matter how much you weep for sorrow over your sins or over the Passion of Christ, or no matter how much you think about the joys of heaven, what can it do for you? Certainly it would gain for you much good, much help, much benefit, and much grace, but in comparison to the blind stirring of love, it does (or can do) but little without that stirring.[f] This by itself without the other things is the "best part" of Mary.[g] Without contemplation, they benefit little or not at all. This stirring destroys not only the ground and root of sin—as much as it can here on earth—but it also gains virtues. For if it is truly understood, then all virtues shall be subtly and perfectly conceived, and deemed to be included[h] in the stirring,[i] without any confusion of the intention. And no matter how many virtues a man has without this stirring, they are all tainted by some corrupt[j] intention because of which they are imperfect.

a. This definition is undoubtedly borrowed from Richard of St. Victor's *Benjamin Minor* (chapter 7) where he has "Virtue is nothing else than the ordered and moderated affection of the soul." But the author adds "plainly directed to God for Himself" (Hodgson, 190).

b. The ME word is *medelid*, which means "muddled" or "mixed up." (Sheila Upjohn told me in conversation that "muddled" remains a familiar and common East Anglian/Midlands word.)

c. Saint Augustine and Saint Bernard called humility the chief virtue (Cowan, 63). See Phil. 2:3: "Let nothing be done through contention, nor by vain glory, but in humility let each esteem others as better than themselves."

d. Saint Bernard in his *Of the Degrees of Humility* wrote: "Humility is a virtue in which a man is most true to himself in his own eyes" (Hodgson, 190).

e. The author is not one for compromise or softening of tone: he declares emphatically and in very strong language the universally sinful state of all humans "no matter how holy they are" (sic!). And this is the first good reason for a person to be humble. See Rom. 3:23: "For all have sinned, and lack the glory of God."

f. The ME word is *clerkes*, which can mean either "clerics" or "scholars" (Mayhew, 46). Again, the author derides the ostensibly well-educated—compared to the great glory of God even those who claim to be learned are fools.

g. In a rare harangue on God's love and glory, the author holds forth on the terrifying and unbearable reality of God—so great that it would destroy those who "see" it if God had not moderated and mitigated some of his divine glory. See Exod. 33:20: "And again [God] said: 'You cannot see my face: for a man may not see me and live.'"

h. Like contemplative prayer itself, true humility has no end—it will continue in heaven after bodily death.

For virtue is nothing but a well-ordered and moderate affection, clearly directed to God for Godself.ᵃ Because He in Himself is the pure source of all virtues, insomuch that if anyone is guided to any single virtue by any other cause mingledᵇ with Him—yea, even though it be the chief virtue— yet that virtue is then imperfect. As thus, by example, may be seen in one or two virtues in place of all the others. And well may these two virtues be humility and charity, for whoever could gain these two clearly would need no more, because he would have them all.ᶜ

⟡ HERE BEGINS THE THIRTEENTH CHAPTER

What humility is in itself, and when it is perfect and when it is imperfect.

Now, let us consider first the virtue of humility—how it is imperfect when it is caused by any other thing mingled with God even though it may be the chief virtue—and how it is perfect when caused by God Himself. And first we must know what humility is in itself if this matter is to be clearly envisioned and conceived. And then we can more rightly consider in truth of spirit what the source of it is.

Humility in itself is nothing more than a true knowledge and awareness of oneself as one truly is.ᵈ For surely anyone who could really see and know one's self as one actually is would truly be humble. Two things there are that are the cause of one's humility which are these: one is the lewdness, the wretchedness, and the weakness of persons into which they have fallen by sin, and which in every way they are bound to feel in some degree while they live in this life—no matter how holy they are.ᵉ Another is the superabundant love and the praiseworthiness of God Himself, at the sight of which all nature quakes, all scholarsᶠ are fools, and all saints and angels are blinded—insomuch that were it not that, through the wisdom of His Godhead, He tempered their vision in keeping with their natural and grace-filled ability, I cannot say what would happen to them.ᵍ

The second cause of humility is perfect, because it will last forever.ʰ And the previous cause is imperfect not only because it shall fail at the end of this life, but also because very often it can happen that a soul in this mortal body—through the abundance of grace which magnifies his desire (as often

a. One of the marks of a genuine mystical incident is that it is inevitably very brief. Cowan (66) quotes the philosopher William James: "Mystical states cannot be sustained for long. Except in rare instances, half an hour, or at most an hour or two, seems to be the limit beyond which they fade into the light of common day" (James, William *The Varieties of Religious Experience* [Modern Library/Random House; New York;1902], 381).

b. This is the experience of the "lower part" of the contemplative way—the intuitive awareness of God's love and goodness. It is still short of knowing God "as He really is" which is the "higher part" of the contemplative way and the encounter with the cloud of unknowing.

c. As he makes clear in the next chapter, "imperfect humility" is not a bad thing. The author's point is that *all* humility is good, but one aspect is more perfect than the other.

d. Much of what the author speaks of in this book is beyond the ordinary reach of typical Christian understanding—it is a more rarified ascetic than most Christians encounter. Consequently, the author may relegate to second or third place some dimension of Christian spirituality that most of us would consider the very apex or peak of Christian practice. That is to say, most Christians are taught and are satisfied with a level and degree of spiritual practice far lower than what the author proposes. We may recall the degrees or levels the author set out in the first chapter: "Common, Special, Singular, and Perfect." Most Christian spiritual understanding and practice is "Common"; some devoted Christians reach the "Special" level. Very few are interested in or are able to reach the "Singular" degree. And only a handful of people, specially called by God, will be among the "Perfect" in this life. "[I]f imperfect humility does not lead us to perfect humility, then it has not performed its mystical function" (Cowan, 67).

e. Jn. 1:18: "No one has seen God at any time: the only begotten Son, who is in the heart of the Father, has described him."

f. Matthew 11:27: "[Jesus said,] 'All things have been handed down to me by my Father. And no one knows the Son except the Father, and neither does anyone know the Father except the Son, and anyone to whom the Son chooses to reveal him.'"

and as long as God is willing to cause it)—shall suddenly and completely lose and forget all consciousness and sense of its own being, not even considering whether it has been holy or sinful. But whether this happens frequently or seldom to a soul that is well-disposed to it, I believe that it lasts only a very short while.[a] And during this time the soul is in perfect humility, for it knows and senses no foundation except God's immense love and goodness.[b] But whenever it knows and feels any *other* source associated with it (even though this remains the chief source) yet that makes it imperfect humility. Nevertheless, it is good and should always be sought, and God forbid that you understand it in any other manner than I say.[c]

✑ HERE BEGINS THE FOURTEENTH CHAPTER

That unless imperfect humility comes first, it is impossible
for a sinner to come to perfect humility in this life.

For even though I call it "imperfect humility," yet I would rather have this true understanding and sense of myself as I really am—because I believe that it would gain for me the perfect source and virtue of perfect humility by itself, sooner than it would if all the saints and angels in heaven, and all the men and women of Holy Church living in earth, religious or seculars, in all degrees, were set at once all together to do nothing else but to pray to God for me to obtain such perfect humility. Yea, for it is impossible for a sinner to gain the *perfect* virtue of humility—or to retain once it is acquired—without this *imperfect* humility.[d]

And therefore struggle and sweat in every way you know of and can do in order to gain a true knowledge and sense of yourself as you really are. And then I am sure that soon afterward you will receive a true knowledge and sense of God as He really is—not as He is in Himself (for that no man can do except Godself[e]) nor even as you shall eventually know Him in heaven (both body and soul together), but as He really is to the extent that He allows Himself to be known and sensed by a humble soul living in this mortal body.[f]

And do not think that because I have presented two sources of humility— one perfect and the other imperfect—that I wish you to give up the efforts to gain imperfect humility and set yourself entirely to gain the perfect. No!

a. The ME has *a prevé love put in clennes of spirite upon this derk cloude of unknowyng*—"a hidden love pressed in purity of spirit against this dark cloud of unknowing." Here is the central core of the author's spiritual goal for his protégé: to be able to press one's secret will of love against the dark cloud of ignorance—and then, with the "piercing lance of longing love," to penetrate that cloud and be one-ed with God … even momentarily!

b. Song of Songs 8:6: "Set me as a seal over your heart, as a seal over your arm, for love is strong as death …"

c. The ME has *make thee more meek*, but usually *make* is erroneously translated as "make" (meaning "cause"), but in the fourteenth century *make* more often had the sense of "to form" or "to shape" or "to build" (ODEE, 547). We should also note the emotional connection between the author and his protégé: "do it for you and for me."

d. An apparent contradiction that one can be prideful about ignorance—but the author's subtlety shows: if one doesn't know real humility, he can confuse it with a lesser or false humility and be proud of what, in his ignorance, he thinks he has but, in fact, lacks.

e. A serious spiritual claim: that humility alone will help to keep one from sinning! This may be so since humility is the opposite number to pride, which is the chief and source of all other sins. C. S. Lewis wrote: "The vice I am talking of is Pride or Self-Conceit: and the virtue opposite to it, in Christian morals, is called Humility. According to Christian teachers, the essential vice, the utmost evil, is Pride. Unchastity, anger, greed, drunkenness, and all that, are mere flea bites in comparison.… Pride leads to every other vice: it is the complete anti-God state of mind" (Lewis, 103).

f. Another very personal comment, revealing the close relationship between the author and his protégé.

g. "The rust of sin" is a common image in fourteenth-century England and appears in the author's *Letter of Privy Counsel*, in the work of Walter Hilton, and in *The Ancren Riwle* (Hodgson, 191).

h. Walsh quotes Hugo De Balma († 1439): "For just as a file is applied to iron, so that by its special function the rust on the iron is removed, so after the infusion of grace, this humility rids itself of the rust left by sin" (I Walsh, 152 n.).

i. Note that two witnesses are called for: one's conscience (inner) and one's spiritual director (outer). See Jn. 8:17: "And in your law it is written that the testimony of two men is true."

Surely, I believe you would never bring it about in that way. But I have written as I did because I hope to explain to you and help you to see the value of this contemplative exercise above all other exercises—physical or spiritual—that a person can know or do by grace: how that a hidden love,[a] pressed in purity of spirit against this dark cloud of unknowing between you and your God, truly and completely contains within it the perfect virtue of humility without any special or clear vision of anything less than God; for I want you to know what perfect humility is and to set it as a token over the love of your heart[b] and do it for you and for me—for I would by this knowledge shape[c] you to be more humble.

For often, it seems to me, it happens that a lack of knowledge is the source of much pride.[d] For instance: if you do not know what perfect humility is, you might think—when you have a little knowledge and sense of what I call "imperfect humility"—that you had nearly achieved perfect humility. So you would deceive yourself and think that you were fully humble when, in fact, you were all wrapped up in foul, stinking pride. And therefore strive to toil for perfect humility, because its feature is such that whosoever has it (and as long as he has it) shall not sin, and only very little afterward.[e]

✑ HERE BEGINS THE FIFTEENTH CHAPTER

A short testimonial against the error of those who say that there is no more perfect path to humility than the recollection of one's own wretchedness.

Trust faithfully that there truly is such a perfect humility as what I speak of—and that it can be attained in this life through grace. And I declare this to confound the error of those who say that there is no more perfect source of humility than what is brought up by the recollection of our wretchedness and our previous sins.

I grant well that to them that have been in habitual sin—as I am now myself and have been[f]—it is the most necessary and beneficial source to be humbled by that recollection of our wretchedness and our previous sins, until the time comes that the great rust of our sin[g] is in large part rubbed away,[h] witnessed by our conscience and our spiritual director.[i]

a. The canonical requirements for formal auricular confession to a priest and reception of absolution are: (a) true *contrition* and penitence for the sins committed; (b) full *confession* of all known sins committed since previous confession; and (c) the fulfillment of *reparation* or satisfaction (e.g., returning something stolen, or apologizing for an offense against another, or somehow "undoing" the results of sin insofar as possible).

b. The author is being very prudent and cautious here: the mystics have always been accused of attempting to bypass the Church in seeking the experience of God's direct and immediate Self without intermediary. The author is assuring his readers that his extremely mystical project very much includes and respects the part played by the Church.

c. The author catalogs those whose humility would not involve recollection of wretchedness or inclination to sin—Jesus, Saint Mary, the saints and angels—and claims thereby that there is, in fact, a path to humility that may not need to include such recollection of sins.

d. Matt. 5:48: "Therefore, be perfect just as your Father in heaven is perfect." The author is clear that every perfection is a gift of grace, not something arising naturally (by nature).

e. This chapter is a turning point in the first part of the book. Previous chapters discussed humility, and that discussion is completed in this chapter as the author begins here to discuss the important distinction between the active and contemplative ways.

f. It must be clear that past sin does not disqualify one from undertaking the deep Work of contemplative prayer—with the four provisos: (1) amendment, confession, restitution, absolution; (2) a calling/stirring to the contemplative way; (3) assent of a good conscience; (4) consent of one's spiritual director. It is interesting to note that this late-medieval mystic considers sin a horrendous and ugly thing—but also has the rare insight to think of it as easily correctable and not damning in itself.

g. It is difficult to explain to a modern mind, but to a medieval churchman, all of the biblical Marys (except the Blessed Virgin herself) and several other anonymous women were all thought to be one and the same person: including Mary Magdalen (Lk. 8:1–3 and elsewhere), Mary of Bethany (Jn. 11), the sinful woman who washed Jesus's feet with her tears (Lk. 7:38), the woman who anointed Jesus's feet with perfumed ointment (Jn. 12:3), and the woman taken in adultery (Jn. 8:3–11).

But to others who are, as it were, innocents who never committed mortal sin with any definite persistence and intention (but only through weakness and ignorance), and who determine themselves to be contemplatives—and to both of us, if our spiritual director and our conscience witness our legitimate amendment in contrition, confession, and reparation[a] according to the rules and regulations of the entire Holy Church,[b] and if we also feel ourselves stirred and called by grace to be contemplative—then (if these prerequisites are present) there is another source for humility. This one is as far above that first imperfect source as is the life of Our Lady above the life of the most sinful penitent in Holy Church, or as the life of Christ is above the life of any other person in this life or else as the life of an angel in heaven who never felt (nor ever shall feel) weakness is above the life of the weakest person here in this world.

For if there were no perfect path to humility except to see and feel one's wretchedness, then I would like to know from those who say so: what would be the source of humility for those who never saw or felt a wretchedness or inclination to sin and never shall—such as our Lord Jesus Christ, Our Lady Saint Mary, and all the saints and angels in heaven?[c] It is to this and every other kind of perfection that our Lord Jesus Christ Himself calls us in the Gospel where He bids that we be perfect by grace as He Himself is by nature.[d]

⟡ HERE[e] BEGINS THE SIXTEENTH CHAPTER

That by virtue of this Work a sinner who is truly converted and called to contemplation can attain perfection more swiftly than by any other work, and can most rapidly obtain forgiveness of sins from God.

Let no one consider it presumptuous that one who is the worst sinner of this life dare take upon himself—after having properly amended himself, and after he has felt stirred to that life that is called contemplative (by the consent of his director and his conscience)—to offer a humble stirring of love to his God, secretly pressing against the cloud of unknowing which lies between him and his God.[f] Our Lord said to Mary[g] (who stands for

a. Refers to the woman who anointed Christ's feet with ointment in Lk. 7:47–48: "her sins, which are many, are forgiven, for she loved much, but one to whom less is forgiven loves less. And he said to her, 'Your sins are forgiven.'"

b. See how important this centrality of love is to the author: a rhetorical question, followed by an emphatic affirmation, followed by a sudden exclamatory, followed by a grammatical extremity!

c. Lk. 7:38: "And standing behind at his feet, she began to wash his feet with her tears, and wiped them with the hairs of her head."

d. The ME words here are extremely strong: *hidous and wonderful sorow*.

e. The author uses Mary here as an exemplar for the Christian contemplative for whom one's willful love is the virtual center of one's entire spiritual life. For him love overwhelms even penitential recollection of one's sins.

f. The ME word is *devision*—a word that carries not only the sense of a "separation" but also a "de-vision"—a "blocking off of vision" (Mayhew, 62).

g. A deep insight: that by a lack of loving, one languishes in sickness!

h. The ME words are *foule stynkyng fen and dunghill of hir sinnes*. One is reminded of Julian of Norwich's description of the body as "a bloated heap of stinking mire" (I Julian, 305). The author writes almost hyperbolically in order to make his point: there is no benefit in dwelling obsessively on one's sins.

i. Note that like all mystics, the author locates some kind of Divine Presence or grace within the human soul. It is helpful to think of grace as God's own life shared with human beings. See Rom. 10:8: "The word is near: on your lips and in your heart."

j. Constant preoccupation with one's past sins can reignite the temptations that led one to those sins—and so be worse off for the obsession with those sins.

all sinners who are called to contemplative life) "Your sins are forgiven you"[a]—not because of her great sorrow, nor for recollection of her sins, nor yet for her humility that she had in paying attention to her wretchedness only. But why then? Surely, because she loved—Look! Here we can see what a hidden love offered may gain from our Lord—more than all other actions one can think of.[b]

And yet I agree strongly that Mary had very great sorrow, and wept greatly over her sins,[c] and she was very humble in recalling her wretchedness. And so should we do as well—we, who have been wretches and habitual sinners throughout our lives, should feel dreadful and astonishing[d] sorrow for our sins, and be extremely humbled in thinking of our wretchedness.

But how? Surely just as Mary did. Although she could not rid herself of the deep heartfelt sorrow for her sins—because all her life she had them with her wherever she went, like a burden wrapped up and laid away in complete secrecy in the depths of her heart, in a manner never to be forgotten. Nevertheless it can be said and affirmed by Scripture that she had a more heartfelt sorrow, a more mournful desire, and a deeper sighing, and she languished more—yea! nearly unto death—for the *inadequacy* of her love (even though she had a great deal of love), than she had for any recollection of her sins.[e] And there need be no amazement at that, for it is the condition of a true lover that the more one loves, the more one longs to love.

And yet she knew well (and felt it deeply in herself) in a sober certainty that she was a wretch—more foul than all others—and that her sins had built a barrier[f] between her and her God whom she loved so much; and also that those sins were to a great degree the cause of her languishing sickness through lack of love.[g] But what of that? Did she therefore come down from the height of desire into the depths of her sinful life, to search in the foul, stinking quagmire and dunghill[h] of her sins, dragging them up one by one, with all the incidents surrounding them, and sorrowing and weeping thus upon each one of them by itself? No, surely she did not do so! And why? Because God let her know by His grace within her soul[i] that she could never accomplish anything that way. For thus she might more likely have raised in herself an inclination to sin more often rather than to have won by those efforts any clear forgiveness for all her sins.[j]

a. Lk. 10:39: "Mary, who also sat at Jesus's feet and heard his word." There
    was a strong tradition that Jesus was physically beautiful. Nicholas of Cusa:
    "O Lord, all beauty that can be conceived is less than the beauty of your
    face" (Cusa, 26); Augustine: "Christ is beautiful in heaven; beautiful on
    earth" (*Enarrationes in Psalmos* 44.3); Clement of Alexandria: "Our Savior
    is beautiful and is loved by those who desire true beauty" (*Stromata* 2.5);
    Basil the Great: "In the blessed sight of the image [the Son] you will see
    the inexpressible beauty of the archetype [the Father] (*De Spiritu Sancto*
    9.23).

b. Luke 10:38–42: "But it happened that, as they journeyed, [Jesus] entered
    into a certain village: and a certain woman named Martha received him
    into her house. She had a sister Mary as well, who sat at Jesus's feet, and
    listened to his words. But Martha was busy with much serving and she
    came up, and said: 'Lord, have you no care that my sister has left me to
    serve alone? Tell her to help me.' And he answered and said unto her:
    'Martha, Martha, you are full of care and troubled about many things.
    But only one thing is necessary. Mary has chosen the best part, which
    shall not be taken away from her.'"

c. The author—like so many medieval mystics—sees Mary as the prototype
    of the contemplative, and he even applies to her his own belief/teaching
    about the cloud of unknowing, giving a practical illustration of what
    "pressing against the cloud of unknowing" looks like: paying attention
    to the Divinity with love: unaware of one's physical surroundings; sitting
    entirely still; enwrapped in a "sweet secret and longing love."

And therefore she hung up her love and her longing desire in this cloud of unknowing, and learned to love a thing which she might not see clearly in this life by the light of understanding in her reason, nor yet truly feel in a sweetness of love in her affection—insomuch that she had often paid very little particular attention to whether she had ever been a sinner or not. Yea! And very frequently I expect that she was so deeply disposed to the love of His Divinity that she had very little particular awareness of the beauty of His precious and blessed body in which He sat full lovely, speaking and preaching before her[a]—nor even of anything else, corporal or spiritual. It appears by the Gospel that this is the truth.

HERE BEGINS THE SEVENTEENTH CHAPTER

That a true contemplative does not wish to meddle with the active life nor anything that is done or spoken against him, nor yet to answer his critics to explain himself.

In the Gospel of Saint Luke, it is written that when our Lord was in the house of Martha her sister, all the time that Martha busied herself about the preparing of His food, Mary her sister sat at His feet.[b] And, listening to His word, she did not notice the busyness of her sister (although all that busyness was completely good and holy, for it is the first part of the active life), nor yet to the preciousness of His blessed body, nor to the sweet voice and the words of His Humanity (although that was even better and holier, because it was the second part of active life and the first of contemplative life), but only to the most supreme wisdom of His Divinity wrapped in the dark words of His Humanity—to that she paid attention with all the love of her heart. For she would not wish to move from there for anything that she saw or heard spoken or done around her—but sat entirely still in her body with many a sweet secret and longing love pressed against that high cloud of unknowing between her and her God.[c]

For one thing I tell you: that there was never yet (nor ever shall be) so pure a person in this life thus transported on high in contemplation and love of the Divinity, that there was not always a high and wonderful cloud of unknowing between that person and his God. It was in this cloud that

a. This is an unapologetic claim of absolute and exclusive rights to the contemplative way by way of his image of the cloud of unknowing. And he makes free to project onto Mary his own experience of "many a secret thrust of love" under the cloud of unknowing and slots her experience in at the top tier of his spiritual cosmology: the highest part of contemplation—even though there is no such detailed evidence in the biblical account.

b. The author is certainly not the last person to tailor biblical exegesis to one's personal interests and needs. Of course there is no mention at all in Luke's account of Mary's response to Martha (or lack thereof), and so the author embroiders that scriptural silence to speak even of Mary's facial expression!

c. Now the author steps back from storytelling to his role as teacher and advisor—making certain that his protégé understands the Mary/Martha story as an allegory. This allegorical treatment of that biblical account was virtually universal among medieval spiritual writers and was often used to justify the monastic life over the secular life.

d. "Active" now becomes a noun: those living an active life are called "actives" as those who lead a contemplative life are called "contemplatives."

e. The author's observation is quite literally and historically true—and remains entirely true to this very day. As a contemplative monk, I am often asked, "What do you all do?" I answer, "We pray." And the response is inevitable: "Well, I know that, but what do you *do*?" The author's warning that critics will say that a contemplative is "doing nothing" is specifically and exactly accurate. Indeed, in the same week in which I write this note, I have been accused by a critic of "gnostic spiritualities." The reason for this is that the strict apophatic contemplative tradition has to a great degree been overlooked in the modern Church. In an era when output, efficiency, and the production of material things and the manufacture of worldly pleasure has become central to the culture, there can be little comprehension (coupled with little experience) of the contemplative way, which is so counter-culture, so unproductive of material goods, so ascetical, and so cloaked in mystery. The contemplative's justification is extremely simple: God created human beings to be united with the Godhead in heaven—and while most Christians consider that union to be something that occurs (if at all) only after death, the contemplative recognizes that given his or her "call" to that special vocation, and with the careful guidance and oversight of a competent spiritual director, such a union is at least conceivable, if transitory, during earthly life.

Mary was occupied with many a secret thrust of love.[a] And why? Because it was the best and holiest part of contemplation that is possible in this life. And it was her wish never to move from this part insomuch that when her sister Martha complained to our Lord about her and bade Him tell her sister to rise and help her, and not leave her to work and labor by herself, Mary sat entirely still and answered not one word, nor showed as much as a peevish expression toward her sister for any complaint that she could make.[b] And no wonder: because she had another work to do that Martha did not know of, and so she had no time to listen to Martha or to respond to her complaint.

[c]See, my friend, that all these works, these words, and these looks that were shown between our Lord and these two sisters are set down as an example for all actives and contemplatives in Holy Church that have lived since then and shall live until Judgment Day. For by Mary is understood all contemplatives—for they should conform their living to hers—and actives[d], by Martha in the same way, and for the same reasons.

⟿ HERE BEGINS THE EIGHTEENTH CHAPTER

How that until this day all actives complain against contemplatives—as Martha complained of Mary—and what the cause of these complaints is.

And just as Martha complained about Mary back then, just so up to the present day actives complain about contemplatives.[e] For if there is a man or woman in any company in the world—no matter what company it may be, religious or secular, I make no exceptions—that men or women (whichever it may be) feel stirred through grace and by advice to forsake all outward business and to give themselves entirely to live a contemplative life, following their intelligence and their conscience, and with the agreement of their spiritual director—immediately their own brothers and their sisters, and all their good friends, with many others who do not know of their stirrings nor the way of life they had set themselves to, with a great complaining spirit shall rise upon them, and say harshly to them that they are doing nothing! And immediately they gather many true and false tales of the failing of men and women that have given themselves to such a life in the past, with never a good word of those that persevered.

a. The author's point is well taken even today: a rough estimate is that at least 80% of those who undertake any kind of monastic vocation will depart the monastic life before final vows—and some, albeit a much smaller percentage, *after* life vows. (Indeed, there has developed an entire genre of trendy popular literary accounts replete with praise for those who have "leapt over the wall.")

b. Cowan (82) suggests that these ending sentences were intended to have a humorous tone—since the entire last chapter was spent in a "distracting" (or at least tangential) biblical story—exactly what the author here disclaims.

c. Martha of Bethany was venerated as a saint in both the Roman Catholic and Eastern Orthodox Churches on July 29. More recently her commemoration has been added to the liturgies of the Church of England, the Episcopal Church, and the Lutheran Church. In the Eastern tradition she is also thought to have been one of the women who brought myrrh to the tomb of Jesus. Note: The medieval commemoration of Martha as a saint in England appeared *only in the York missal and Breviary* (i.e., only in the north: another evidence of the author's geographical origins).

d. In moral considerations, ignorance can be an alleviating circumstance that eliminates the culpability for an act done without knowing or intending any evil. One must *intend* to do wrong for an act to be judged a sin.

e. It seems to be the author's belief (or perhaps his bias) that the details of the contemplative life that he provides in his book were clearly known and specifically practiced in first-century Palestine. Historically, that is virtually impossible—but like many of the great medieval and Renaissance painters who clothed biblical figures in contemporary dress, so our author consistently projects his own contemporary thought and practice into the past.

f. No matter how charitable his admonitions to forgive the critics of the contemplative way, the author cannot resist the temptation for a little covert jab at the critics for their crudity: "They really are quite nasty people but as good Christians, we should forgive them."

I grant you that many of those who to all appearances forsake the world do fall and have fallen in the past.[a] And where they should have become God's servants and His contemplatives, because they did not let themselves be guided by true spiritual direction they have become the devil's servants and his contemplatives and have turned out to be hypocrites or heretics or have fallen into trances and many other misbehaviors in scandal to all Holy Church. (Of these I shall say no more at this time for fear of distracting from our subject.[b] But nevertheless later on—when God grants and if need be—we can say something about their circumstances and the cause of their failings. But therefore no more of them at this time—but let us get on with our subject.)

HERE BEGINS THE NINETEENTH CHAPTER

A short clarification by the author of this book, explaining that all contemplatives should pardon all actives for their critical words and deeds.

Some may think that I give little honor to Martha—that outstanding saint[c]—because I compare her words of complaint about her sister to this-worldly people's words, or theirs unto hers. And truly I intend no dishonor to her or to them. God forbid that I should in this book say anything that could be taken in condemnation of *any* of the servants of God in *any* degree, and in particular, of His outstanding saint. For I think that she should be well and fully excused for her complaint, considering the time and manner in which she said it, because her ignorance was the cause of what she said.[d]

And no wonder that she did not know at that time how Mary was occupied—for I believe that before that she had heard very little about such perfection.[e] And also, what she said was both courteous and in few words. And therefore she should always be excused.

And so I think that those men and women living the active life in this world should also be wholly excused of their critical words mentioned above—even though they may speak their words crudely[f]—in view of their ignorance. Because just as Martha knew very little of what her sister Mary was doing when she complained of her to our Lord, just so in the same

a. That is, contemplative novices—like the author's protégé for whom the book is written.

b. Increasingly from here on the author begins to speak of "active" and "contemplative" as nouns rather than merely modifying adjectives—of persons who are "actives" or "contemplatives."

c. The author understands that the contemplative way may simply be so far from the actual personal experience of the actives that they cannot comprehend any life that might be of higher merit than their own familiar lives.

d. The reference, of course, is to the words of Jesus in Matt. 7:12 (and in Lk. 6:31): "Everything whatsoever you would that men should do to you, do you also to them. This is the law and the prophets."

e. A tiny gentle poke at his own contemplative brethren: that is, if they were as committed to and as involved in contemplation as they ought to be (and as they claim to be), their detachment from things of this world would mean that they would be impervious to such external criticism.

f. The phrase "unto whom no secrets are hidden" is from the Collect (prayer) for the Mass of the Holy Spirit in the Sarum Missal (which was the common liturgical use throughout England in the fourteenth century). It was also part of the private prayers said by the priest while putting on the vestments for Mass (Hatchett, 318).

g. Again we see the author transferring his fourteenth-century contemplative practice back to Bethany in the first century: one is given the vision of a Mary so entranced and rapt in Jesus's divinity that she is unable to speak, to relate to her sister, or to defend herself. The author draws all this from the simple words: "Mary, who also sat at Jesus's feet and heard his word" (Lk. 10:39).

h. A subtle dig at Martha who asked Jesus to "judge" against Mary, and Jesus refused to accept the role she asked of him.

way these folk nowadays know very little—or even nothing—of what these young disciples of God[a] mean when they turn themselves away from the business of this world and commit themselves to be God's special servants in holiness and righteousness of spirit. And if those actives[b] were to understand, truly I dare say that they would neither do nor speak as they do. And therefore, I think that they should always be excused because they know of no better kind of life than the one they live themselves.[c] And also when I think on my innumerable faults which I have committed myself in the past in words and deeds because of my lack of knowledge, I think that if *I* would be excused by God for my ignorant faults, that I should then charitably and compassionately entirely excuse *other* people's ignorant words and deeds. And surely otherwise I would not be doing to others as I would that others did to me.[d]

✎ HERE BEGINS THE TWENTIETH CHAPTER

How Almighty God will graciously answer on behalf of
all those who do not wish to leave their business of loving Him
in order to make excuses for themselves.

And therefore I think that they who set themselves to be contemplatives should not only excuse active people for their critical words, but also I think that they should be so involved in spirit that they ought to take little or no heed of what people did or said about them.[e] Thus did Mary, our supreme example, when Martha her sister complained to our Lord. And if we will truly do this, our Lord will do for us now what He did for Mary.

And what was that? Surely it was thus: our loving Lord Jesus Christ, unto whom no secrets are hidden,[f] although He was asked by Martha to be judge and to bid Mary rise and help her serve Him, nevertheless, He recognized that Mary was fervently occupied in the spirit with the love of His Divinity, and therefore, courteously—and as it was fitting for Him reasonably—He Himself answered on behalf of her who would not leave the love of Him in order to excuse herself.[g] And how did He answer? Surely not as judge (as He was called to be by Martha[h]) but as an advocate, formally defended

a. Jesus also uses a repetition of a name in another reproach: "Simon, Simon, behold, Satan has asked for you that he may sift you as wheat" (Lk. 22:31).

b. An extremely confusing phrase. The ME has *Twies for spede. Spede* can mean "profit," "success," "issue," "fortune," "abundance," or (less commonly) "speed." Other versions of this phrase: McCann: "Twice for her good"; Walsh: "In his urgency he called her name twice"; Johnston: "He called her name twice to be certain she heard him"; Underhill: "Twice for speed he named her name"; Wolters: "He named her name twice for her good"; Cowan: "Jesus called Martha twice ... in urgency"; Butcher: "He said it twice, to be sure she heard him." (There is also the very ancient British adage "Once for love. Twice for luck," which may have been in the author's mind.)

c. Again the author assures his reader that the active life—inferior though it may be compared to the contemplative life—is in itself "good and beneficial for her soul."

d. It is interesting that the original Greek of this Gospel story uses the word *agathein* meaning "good," "profitable," or "beneficial." The NRSV translates it as "better." Only the Latin Vulgate Bible (which our author would have used) has the word *optimam* that means "best."

e. McCann reminds us that the virtues of faith and hope disappear at death but the virtue of love is present now and is "continued uninterruptedly in heaven." He refers to 1 Cor. 13:8: "Love never ends" (McCann 35 n.).

f. Following Augustine, the author believes that the "true explanation" of the Gospel words is frequently allegorical—and there is a flavor here of a paragon revealing the truth to his lowly protégé.

g. This statement seems excessive, but it represents the formal teaching of the Church: *vpon peyen of dampnacioun.* (Simmons and Nolloth, 71).

h. The author makes the grammatical point that between two, one can only be "better," but among three, one can be "best."

her who loved Him, and said, "Martha, Martha!"[a] twice for her benefit.[b] He named her name, for He wanted her to hear Him and take heed to His words. "You are very busy," He said, "and bothered about many things." For those who are actives must always be bothered and troubled about many diverse things, that fall first to those who have them for their own use and then as works of mercy for their fellow Christians, as charity demands. This He said to Martha because He wanted to let her know that her activity was good and beneficial for the health of her soul,[c] but lest she should think that it was the best of all work a person could do, therefore He added to it and said, "Only one thing is necessary."

And what is that one thing? Surely that God alone be loved and praised above all other business that one can do—physical or spiritual—and at the same time to pay attention to the necessities of this life, in order to deliver Martha from uncertainty that she could serve God both in bodily and spiritual business together perfectly—imperfectly she could, but not perfectly. He went on and said that Mary had chosen the best[d] part that would never be taken from her. Because that perfect stirring of love that begins here is the same as that which shall last without end in the bliss of heaven—for both are entirely one.[e]

⤳ HERE BEGINS THE TWENTY-FIRST CHAPTER

The true[f] explanation of the words of the Gospel:
"Mary has chosen the best part."

What does this mean: "Mary has chosen the best"? Wherever the "best" is indicated or named, it assumes before it these two things: a "good" and a "better" so that it can be the "best" and the third in order. But what are these three good things of which Mary chose the best? They are not three lifestyles, for Holy Church recognizes only two: active life and contemplative life—which two lives are covertly understood in the story of this Gospel by these two sisters—Mary and Martha—by Martha the active, by Mary the contemplative. Without one or the other of these two lives no one can be saved,[g] and where there are no more than two, no one can be said to choose "the best."[h]

a. Chapter 8 above.

b. The author's intricate spiritual classification system:

	DEGREE OF LIFE	TYPICAL ACTIVITIES	QUALITY
4	Second level of the contemplative life	Doing the Corporal Works of Mercy and Charity.	Best
3	First level of the contemplative life	Meditation on one's sinfulness, on the life and Passion of Christ, and on the joys of heaven.	Better
2	Second level of the active life		
1	First level of the active life	Doing the Corporal Works of Mercy and Charity.	Good

Note: rarely and only by a special grace can a second-level active move to contemplative level one; and rarely only in great need can a contemplative level one move to active level two.

c. An important and primary distinction is made here: that the *good* activities of levels one, two, and three are all earthly activities and will end with death, but the activity of the fourth part will go on unendingly for eternity.

d. Here the author catalogs the classical Seven Corporal Works of Mercy, which have their basis in the list of six virtues in the parable of the sheep and goats in Matt. 25:34–46. The seventh is found in the Book of Tob. 1:17–19 and was added in the third century.

> To feed the hungry.
> To give drink to the thirsty.
> To clothe the naked.
> To shelter the homeless.
> To visit the sick.
> To visit the imprisoned.
> To bury the dead.

But although there are only two lives, nevertheless, within these two lives are three parts—each one better than the other. These three—each one by itself—have been specifically described in their places previously in this book.[a] For, as was said before, the first part consists of good and honest corporal works of mercy and charity—and this is the first degree of active life, as was said before. The second part of these two lives lies in spiritual meditations on one's own wretchedness, on the Passion of Christ, and on the joys of heaven. The first part is good, but this second part is better, because this is both the second degree of active life and the first of contemplative life. In this part the contemplative life and the active life are coupled together in spiritual relationship and made sisters—following the example of Martha and Mary. Thus far can an active come toward contemplation— and no farther—unless it be very seldom and by a special grace. Thus far can a contemplative come toward active life—and no farther—unless very seldom and in great need.

The third part of these two lives hangs in the dark cloud of unknowing with many a hidden love offered to God Himself. The first part is good, the second is better, but the third is altogether best.[b] This is the best "part" of Mary. And that is why it is plainly to be understood that our Lord did not say: "Mary has chosen the best *life*" because there are only two lives, and from only two no one can choose "the best." But of these two lives, "Mary has chosen," He said, "the best *part* which shall never be taken from her." The first and second parts, although they are both good and holy, yet they end with this life. For in the other life there shall be no need—as there is now—to do the works of mercy, nor to weep for our wretchedness, nor for the Passion of Christ.[c] For then—as is not true now—none shall know hunger or thirst, nor die of the cold, nor be sick, nor homeless, nor in prison, nor even need burial, for then no one shall be able to die.[d] But the third part that Mary chose, let the person choose who by grace is called to choose, or—to speak more truly—let those who are chosen by God eagerly turn themselves toward it. For that call shall never be taken away—and although it begins here, it shall endure without end.

So, therefore, let the voice of our Lord cry out to these actives, as if He were to say now for us to them, as He did for Mary to Martha: "Martha, Martha!"—"Actives, actives! Do as well as you can in the first part and in the second—now in the one and now in the other—and if you so wish and

a. The word "my" is not in the original ME, but it was added by Wolters in his translation—much in the true sense the author intended (Wolters, 89).

b. The ME is *Ye wote not what hem eyleth*—literally, "You know not what ails them." Walsh (I 165) has: "You do not know what they are about."

c. "To live with the true consciousness of life centered in Another is thus to lose one's self-important seriousness, and thus to live a 'play' in union with a Cosmic player" (Merton, Thomas; *Thoughts on the East* [Continuum; New York; 2000], 60, cited by Hodgson, 30/28 and Gallacher, 116).

d. The non-canonical *Gospel of Philip* (late third century): "Christ loved [Mary] more than all the disciples and used to kiss her often on her mouth. The rest of the disciples were offended by it and expressed disapproval. They said to Him, 'Why do you love her more than all of us?'" (cited in Cowan, 91). It is at least *conceivable* that our author may have known this document.

e. The ME has *alle the contynaunce that was bitwix Hym and hir*. *Contynaunce* is usually translated as "look" or "gesture" or "outward appearance" or "encouragement" or "favor" (Mayhew, 50). It is a courtly word often used in medieval stories to describe intimate relationships (Cowan, 92).

f. It should be understood once more that there was a medieval confusion among the various biblical Marys. Obviously, in this case, this Mary is Mary Magdalen who came to Jesus's tomb and was met by angels who told her of the Resurrection, which news she passed on to the disciples. However, the author has conflated the three accounts because the weeping and refusal to leave come from John's account but the angels are from Matthew's and Luke's (Matt. 28:1–7, Lk. 24:1–11, Jn. 20:1–18) (Clark, 123).

g. The ME has *take whoso take may*. *Take* can mean "accept" or "grasp" (Mayhew, 223) or "understand" (Gallacher, 54).

h. Julian of Norwich: "God brought cheerfully to mind David and others in the Old Law... and in the New Law He brought to mind first Mary Magdalen ... and how they are recognized on earth along with their sins and it is no shame, but all of their sins have been changed to honor" (I Julian, 181).

feel yourself inclined, boldly in both at once. But don't meddle with my[a] contemplatives. You do not know what troubles afflict[b] them. Let them sit in their rest and in their play[c] with the third and best part of Mary."

⋑ HERE BEGINS THE TWENTY-SECOND CHAPTER

Of the amazing love that Christ had for Mary, who represents all sinners truly converted and called to the grace of contemplation.

Sweet was the love between our Lord and Mary.[d] She had much love for Him but much greater was His love for her. For whoever would fully consider all the favor[e] that passed between Him and her (not as a gossip might tell, but as the account of the Gospel will witness—which in no way can be false) he would find that she was so heartily determined to love Him, that no thing less than He would comfort her nor keep her heart from Him. This is she, that same Mary, that when she sought Him at the tomb with tear-streaked face would not be comforted by angels.[f] For when they spoke to her so sweetly and so lovingly, and said, "Weep not, Mary, because our Lord whom you seek is risen, and you shall have Him and see Him live and full fair among His disciples in Galilee, as He said," she would not leave because of them, for her thought was that whoever truly sought the King of Angels ought not to leave the search on only angels' advice.

And what more? Surely whoever will look truly into the story of the Gospel shall find many amazing moments of perfect love written about her for our guidance, and as are also in accord with the Work of this book—as though they had been set down and written for this purpose. And indeed they were—accept it whosoever can comprehend it.[g] And if a person wishes to see in the Gospel writing the wonderful and special love that our Lord had for her (representing all habitual sinners truly converted and called to the grace of contemplation[h]), he shall find that our Lord would not allow any man or woman—yea, not her own sister—to speak a word against her without answering for her Himself. Yea, and what more! He blamed

a. Called "Simon the Leper" in Mk. 14:3 and "Simon the Pharisee" in Lk. 7:36–40. The identification is made in de Voragine (Clark, 124).

b. It is in Lk. 7:36–50 where Jesus reprimands his host for criticizing the "woman that was in the city, a sinner" who was ministering to Jesus, saying, "I entered into your house, you gave me no water for my feet; but she with tears has washed my feet and with her hair has wiped them. You gave me no kiss, but she, since she came in, has not ceased to kiss my feet. My head you did not anoint with oil, but she with ointment has anointed my feet." Note: Again, the unnamed biblical woman is wrongly identified by our author as Mary of Bethany.

c. Matt. 5:11–12: "Blessed are you when people insult you, and persecute you, and shall say all kinds of evil against you falsely, because of me. Be glad and rejoice, for your reward is very great in heaven. For so they persecuted the prophets who have been before you." And, of course, the reference to the criticism of Mary in note "f" above.

d. Augustine Baker in his analysis of *The Cloud* writes about this sentence "*if it stand well with those fault-finders*—that is to say, if they be such as have care of their consciences and would not willingly do anything that might displease God" (McCann, 372).

e. Ps. 6:11 [6:10]: "Let all my enemies be put to shame and greatly troubled; let them suddenly be converted and be ashamed." Note: The original Hebrew has "turned back," but the Latin Vulgate Bible has the verb *convertantur* that can mean "to be converted." It seems likely that the author has used the Latin version of this psalm to predict what will happen to critics of the contemplatives—i.e., they will be converted and be ashamed.

f. The author expresses an optimistic view, and he is surely describing his own experience as a contemplative whose needs were met by the charity of others. And as a contemplative monk may I certify the accuracy of this proposition—whenever we have been in need over the course of three decades, there has been a windfall of utterly unforeseen charity to fill that need.

g. The ME word is *leveful* and usually means "lawful," but in the thirteenth and fourteenth centuries it still had its original sense of "set down" or "placed" (ODEE, 518).

h. The ME verb is *sette* and is usually translated "set" but also carries the sense of "place" or "appoint" or "establish" (Mayhew, 204).

Simon the Leper[a] in his own house for his thoughts against her.[b] This was great love; this was transcending love.

⤳ HERE BEGINS THE TWENTY-THIRD CHAPTER

How God will answer and provide for those spiritually who, because of their obsession with God's love, have no desire to answer or provide for themselves.

And truly, if we will willingly conform our love and our life—insomuch as is in us by grace and by counsel—to the love and the life of Mary, no doubt but that God will answer in the same manner for us now spiritually every day, secretly, in the hearts of all those that speak otherwise or think against us. I say nothing except that endlessly some people will speak or think something against us while we live in the hardship of this life, as they did against Mary.[c] But I say that if we pay no more heed to their words, nor to their thoughts, nor anymore leave off our spiritual hidden Work because of their words and their thoughts than she did—I say that our Lord will answer them spiritually, as long as it shall be well with them who so speak and think[d]—that they should within a few days be ashamed of their words and their thoughts.[e]

And just as He will answer thus for us spiritually, so will He inspire other folk spiritually to give us the things we need that are part of this life—like food and clothing and everything else—if He sees that we will not abandon this Work of His love to bother ourselves about those things.[f] And this I say to refute their error who say that it is not set down[g] that people are to establish[h] themselves to serve God in the contemplative life, unless they are

a.   The author seems to be contrary to much of common practice at the time, for instance in this passage about medieval hermits and anchorites: "The bishop was careful not to license anyone unless he was satisfied that sustenation was secure and permanent" (Clay, 103) (compare II Clark, 124).

b.   This is an ancient proverb (Hodgson, 192 n.) that seems to imply (Johnston, 190 n. and Wolters, 91) that God will provide, but the receiver must do his or her part—something like "God helps those who help themselves" (Cowan, 95). At the foot of the page in one of the early manuscripts is the Latin verse: "*Ipse Labrator! Non dica, 'Dat Deum aurum'; Dat Deus omne bonum / Sed non per cornu taurum*"—"Work yourself! Do not say 'God gives the gold,' God gives all good but not by the horn of a bull" (McCann, 39 n.).

c.   The ME has *For alle comes to one in verrey contemplatyves*. It is likely that this means "It all comes to the same thing for true contemplatives."

d.   This is a harsh judgment, but it reflects "the intense spiritual climate of the fourteenth century" (Cowan, 96).

e.   This is the point of the last lines: "If you are a true contemplative, pay attention to God, not to how bad things are for you."

f.   One is reminded of Julian of Norwich's prayer: "God of Thy goodness, give me Thyself, for thou art enough to me ... and if I ask anything that is less, ever shall I be in want, for only in Thee have I all" (I Julian, 79).

g.   In chapter 12 the author announced two virtues that he would use as examples of all the virtues that would come to a contemplative: humility and charity. So far he has spoken of humility and now he turns to charity.

h.   The ME has *lityl blynde love put*—literally, "little blind love thrust."

i.   The Great Commandment: "You shall love the Lord your God from your whole heart, from your whole soul, from all your strength, and from all your mind; and your neighbor as yourself" (Lk. 10:27).

assured beforehand of their bodily necessities.ᵃ For they say that God sends the cow, but does not lead it by the horn.ᵇ And truly they speak wrongly of God as they well know. For trust steadfastly—whoever you are that truly turns yourself from the world to God—that one of the two things God shall send you, without troubling yourself, and that is, either abundance of necessities or strength in body and spiritual patience to bear the lack. What does it matter which of these a person has? For it is all the same to true contemplatives.ᶜ

And whoever is in doubt about this, either the devil is in his heart and deprives him of his faith, or else he is not yet truly converted to God as he should be—no matter how clever or holy the reasons he shows against it, whosoever he may be.ᵈ

And therefore you who set yourself to be a contemplative as Mary was, choose rather to be humbled under the awesome stature and worthiness of God (which is perfect) than under your own desolation (which is imperfect)—that is to say, see to it that you pay your special attention more to the worthiness of God than to your own desolation.ᵉ For to those who are perfectly humbled, nothing—neither physical nor spiritual—shall be lacking, because they have God in whom is all bounty; and whoever has Him—yea, as this book says—needs nothing else in this life.ᶠ

✐ HERE BEGINS THE TWENTY-FOURTH CHAPTER

*What charity is in itself, and how it is subtly and perfectly contained in the Work explained in this book.*ᵍ

And as it is said of humility—that it is mysteriously and perfectly contained in this little blind thrust of loveʰ as it assails this dark cloud of unknowing, with all other things put aside and forgotten—so, too, it is the same understanding of all other virtues and especially of charity.

For charity does not signify anything else to our understanding than the loving of God for Himself above all created things, and the loving of others for God's sake with love equal to the love of oneself.ⁱ And it appears fairly clear that in this Work God is loved for Himself and above all creatures, for—as it was said before—the essence of this Work is nothing but a naked

a. Once again, here is the harsh limitation the author places on the second degree of contemplation: that literally nothing—no matter how good or high or holy—may be placed next to God in the contemplative's spiritual cosmos. There is nothing inherently bad or evil about those rejected things, but they are merely inappropriate material for the highest contemplative way of life.

b. The ME word is *homliest* meaning "most familiar," most "home-like" (ODEE, 445–46).

c. "But I say unto you, Love your enemies, do good to those who hate you, and pray for those who mistreat you, that you may be children of your Father who is in heaven.... For if you were to love only those who love you, what reward shall you have? Do not even the tax collectors do the same? ...Be you therefore perfect, as also your heavenly Father is perfect" (Matt. 5:44–48).

d. The ME is *whan he condesendith*, and it means "when he comes down [from the heights of contemplation]." I have chosen "stoops" because it seems to have less of the sense of patronizing pomposity. The author suggests that it is possible to have occasional, necessary, minimal relations with others without sacrificing the whole of one's contemplative life— one can "ease off" a bit from the "pinnacle."

e. The author recognizes that there may well be practical instances when a devout contemplative needs to make temporary connection with others in the name of charity.

f. However, even in such instances of relaxation of the eremitical contemplative way, one is not to give over entirely and return to full social participation with others. In the Carthusian tradition, the hermit-monks came together ("into common") with the other monks for Matins, Mass, and Vespers daily and for a silent community meal on Sundays and feast days; and once a week the hermits took a communal walk (or *spacia)* in the countryside—the only time they are allowed to speak. The hermit-monk is also allowed two annual visits from family members. It may well be such departure from the private hermitage that is referred to in this paragraph.

g. The ME word here is *wille*, and it can mean "will" or "mind" or "desire" or "intention" (ODEE).

intent directed to God for Himself. A "naked intent" I call it because in this Work a perfect apprentice asks neither for a release from pain nor an increase of reward, nor (to put it briefly) anything except Godself—insomuch that he neither cares nor notices whether he is in pain or pleasure as long as the will of Him he loves is fulfilled. And thus it seems that in this Work God is perfectly loved for Himself—and that above all created things. For in this Work a perfect worker cannot allow the thought of even the holiest creature God ever made to have any share with Him in that love.[a]

And in this, the second and lower branch of charity to your fellow Christian, appears also by that argument to be truly and perfectly fulfilled. Because in this Work a perfect worker has no special regard for any person *individually*—whether the person be kinsman or stranger, friend or foe. For he considers every person alike his kinsman and no one a stranger. He sees all persons as his friends and no one his foe—so much so that he thinks those who cause him pain and do him damage in this life are his greatest and particular friends, and he thinks he is directed to wish them as much good as he would to the closest[b] friend he has.[c]

HERE BEGINS THE TWENTY-FIFTH CHAPTER

That during this Work a perfect soul pays no special attention to any one person in this life.

I do not say that in this Work one shall have a special regard for any person in this life—whether that be a friend or foe, kinsman or stranger, for that cannot be if this Work is to be perfectly done (as it is when everything less than God is completely forgotten—as is appropriate for this Work). But I declare that one shall be made so virtuous and so charitable by the quality of this Work that afterward, when he stoops[d] to join with or to pray for his fellow-Christians which is profitable and needful to do sometime, as charity demands[e] (not departing entirely from *all* this Work—for that cannot be without great sin—but from the *pinnacle* of this Work[f]), his intentions[g] shall then be just as particularly directed to his foe as to his friend, to a stranger as to his kinsman. Yea! And sometime *more* to his foe than to his friend!

a.   The ME word is *leveful*, and most translate it as "lawful" but its better meaning is "allowable" or "permissible" (Mayhew, 134).

b.   This reference is to John, "the disciple whom Jesus loved" (Jn. 21:7).

c.   This reference is, of course, to Mary Magdalen.

d.   The ME word here is *cause* and carries the sense of the "motive" or "source" (MED).

e.   The ME has *affecte*, suggesting "attracted to" or "impassioned by" (MED).

f.   The ME is extremely confusing: *not in the same maner, bot as it were in the same maner.* The author speaks metaphorically (as is clear in the next two sentences when he says the perfect disciple ought to "stretch out his spirit . . . as our Lord stretched His body on the Cross"). It seems the author is speaking of two things: the sacrificial life modeled by Christ; and the observation that the perfect disciple makes an unselfish (i.e., Christlike) vicarious sacrifice to bring others to perfection as well.

g.   Following traditional language for the Crucifixion (i.e., Christ "stretched" on the cross), I translate the ME word *streyne* as "stretch." Its literal meaning is "to draw tight" (Mayhew, 218). All others translate some form of "strain" (e.g., "expend himself" or "lift up his spirit" or "strain up his spirit").

h.   See the first sentence of chapter 24: "this little blind thrust of love."

Nevertheless in this Work one has no leisure to pay attention to who is his friend or his foe, his kinsman or a stranger. I do not claim that he shall not feel sometimes his affection more dearly to one, two, or three than to all the others—yea! and quite often too—for that is permissible[a] for many reasons, as charity demands. For such a close affection Christ felt for John[b] and for Mary[c] and for Peter above many others. But I say that during this Work all shall be equally dear to him, for then he shall feel no impetus[d] except for God—so that all shall be loved plainly and simply for God's sake—as one loves oneself.

For as all mankind were lost in Adam, and as all who give evidence of their wish for salvation by good works are saved and shall be by virtue of the Passion of Christ alone, therefore a soul that is perfectly disposed to[e] this Work and is thus one-ed to God in spirit (as the evidence of this Work testifies) will do what it can to make all others as perfect in this Work as it is itself—not in exactly the same manner as Christ, but in generally the same way.[f] For just as when a limb of our body feels sore, all the other limbs are in hurt and distress because of it, or if a limb thrives, all the rest are made happy along with it—just so is it spiritually with all the limbs of Holy Church. For Christ is our head, and we are the limbs, as long as we are in charity. And whosoever wishes to be a perfect disciple of our Lord ought to stretch out his spirit in this spiritual Work for the salvation of all his natural brothers and sisters, as our Lord stretched His body on the Cross.[g] And how? Not for his friends and his kinsmen and his dearest lovers, but far and wide, for all mankind—without any special regard for one over another. For all who wish to abandon sin and beg for mercy shall be saved through the power of His Passion.

And as it has been said of humility and charity, so it is to be understood of all other virtues as well—for all of them are subtly contained in this little thrust of love mentioned before.[h]

a. A wonderful human touch: the author has been pressing his protégé to work long and hard, and only here does he allow a little breathing space.

b. In all the Work, the author credits two elements that are able to alleviate some of the burden: (1) a gift of special, particular, specific grace—not your ordinary commonplace grace, but a unique extra gift; and (2) a long experience in the practice of the contemplative way. The latter alleviation is not so much a mitigation of the burden, but the assurance based on experience that what seems intolerable *can* be borne when one is called upon to do it.

c. The author gives assurance that the invisible "hand of Almighty God" is at work to aid the soul that is entering "the Work"—and that God has also been working unnoticed for "a long time beforehand."

d. See chapter 5 throughout.

e. The difficulty of the contemplative way is not in the motion of the soul toward the cloud of unknowing and the hidden God; the real, exhausting, and painful spiritual Work is the disposal in one's mind of all worldly things and matters from the past, and the discarding of most of what has been held to have value in the world—including much that is good in itself (like friendship, works of mercy, etc.) because even the good is an impediment to reaching the pinnacle of contemplation. This is certainly the most difficult aspect of the "Work" to modern eyes—indeed, it seems downright misguided to one unfamiliar with the higher degrees of Christian prayer and sadly conditioned to believe that emotional attachment is the highest good.

f. The ME has *do on thi werk*. Walsh has "Press on then earnestly" (I 174).

g. The ME has *Do on than fast*.

h. The ME has *devocion*, but it is a false cognate. In the fourteenth century it meant "dedication as by a vow" (ODEE, 263).

i. It is a familiar understanding among monastics that it is easier to endure poverty when one has taken a vow of Holy Poverty; it is easier to live chastely when one has taken a vow of Holy Chastity. The vow itself seems to carry with it a certain facility. Also evidence that at this point in his life, the protégé is about to take monastic vows.

➤ HERE BEGINS THE TWENTY-SIXTH CHAPTER

That without abundant special grace—or the prolonged exercise of ordinary grace—the Work of this book is very difficult; and within this Work, the distinction between what is the work of the soul aided by grace and what is the work of God alone.

And therefore work earnestly for a time and thrust against this high cloud of unknowing, and then rest afterward.[a] Nevertheless, a hard job shall one have whoever shall apply oneself in this Work; yea, surely! and an ample great labor at that—unless he has a more special grace, or else he has a prolonged time of applying himself in it.[b]

But I ask you, in what shall that labor be? Surely not in that devout stirring of love that is continually at work in one's will to enable one to do this Work (not by oneself, but by the hand of Almighty God—which is always ready to perform this Work in every soul that is disposed to the Work and that has done all that it can, and has done so for a long time beforehand).[c] But in what, then, shall this labor be? Surely, this labor is all in treading down the thoughts about all the created things God has ever made—and in holding them under the cloud of forgetting (as mentioned before).[d] In this is all the labor—for this is a person's work with the help of grace.[e] And the previous—that is to say, the stirring of love—that is the work of God alone. And therefore, get on with[f] your Work, and assuredly, I promise you, He shall not fail in His.

Go on then quickly![g] Let us see how you carry yourself. Do you not see how He stands and waits for you? For shame! Work eagerly for only a while, and you shall soon be eased of the burden and difficulty of the struggle. For although it is hard and troublesome in the beginning when you have no dedication,[h] nevertheless, after you have dedication to a vow,[i] it shall be made wholly restful and very light for you that before was very hard—and then you shall have either little labor or none at all. For then God will do the Work sometimes all by Himself, but not always, and not for long periods

a. The author catches himself slightly overstating and has to backtrack a bit
    and qualify his claim that God will work all alone—"but not always, and
    not for long periods of time."

b. The ME has *mery to late Hym alone.* This does not mean "to desert God,"
    but to stay out of his way and let him do what he chooses when he
    chooses.

c. "The highest experience of the mystic is the direct and sole work of God;
    it is an illumination which comes as a flash of lightning" (Richard of St.
    Victor, *Benjamin Minor*, chapter 82), and "God ... makes Himself known
    however rarely and rapidly, like a flash of light, by a certain, intelligible,
    and ineffable presence in the minds of the wise men, when their spirits
    are soaring above matter" (Augustine, *City of God* 14.102).

d. 2 Cor. 12:4: "[He] was caught up into paradise, and heard words that
    are not lawful for man to speak." There may be even a hint of a nuptial
    image here in that God shows *sum of His priveté* (II Clark, 134).

e. "Thou art not there yet, but by some small sudden lightnings that glide
    out of small caves from that City, shalt thou be able to see it afar off ere
    you come to it, for know thou well, that though thy soul be in this restful
    darkness without the trouble of worldly vanities, it is not yet clothed all
    in light, nor turned all into the fire of love" (Hilton, 175).

f. The ME has *the lesse peril of the two. Peril* translates as "danger" or "risk"—
    an indication that we are in the midst of a great spiritual power with
    the risks of both great reward and great danger. The author honors
    contemplation as a way of high threat—this is no Sunday School outing!

g. This chapter is really only a preface to sections dealing with who, when,
    how, and with what care. Chapter 27 deals with who should undertake
    the Work; chapters 29–30 speak of when it should be done; chapter 34–
    40 tell how the contemplative life is to be lived; chapters 41–49 deal with
    the care a novice must take in beginning the Work (Cowan, 111).

h. The ME word is *ordinaunce.* In ordinary text it refers to "common
    prescribed usage" (ODEE, 632), but in the late fourteenth century it
    came to mean specifically what is otherwise called "a sacrament"—either
    of which meaning would be appropriate here, since the reference is to
    the sacrament of Holy Confession or Penance.

of time, but whenever He wishes and as He wishes.[a] And then you will think it pleasant simply to leave Him to Himself.[b]

Then perhaps sometimes He will send out a beam of spiritual light,[c] piercing this cloud of unknowing that is between you and Him, and show you the whole of His mystery, of which a person neither can nor is allowed to speak.[d] Then you shall feel your passions all enflamed with the fire of His love[e]—far more than I can tell you (or am willing, or able) at this time. For of that work which is God's alone, I dare not take upon myself to speak with my blabbering, fleshly tongue—and, in short, even if I dared to speak, I would not. But of that work that is a human's (when one feels stirred and aided by grace) it pleases me to tell you well—for that is the less risky[f] of the two.

⟋ HERE BEGINS THE TWENTY-SEVENTH CHAPTER
Who should undertake the gracious Work of this book.

First and foremost, I will tell you who should undertake this Work, and when, and by what means, and what discretion you should have in it.[g] If you were to ask me who should undertake this, I would answer you: all that have forsaken the world with a true will, and have given themselves not to active life, but to that life that is called "contemplative life." Every one of those should labor in this grace and in this Work, whoever they are—whether they are habitual sinners or not.

⟋ HERE BEGINS THE TWENTY-EIGHTH CHAPTER
That a person should not presume to engage in this Work
before the time that he is canonically absolved in his conscience
of all his specific acts of sin.

But if you were to ask me when they should start in this Work, then I would answer you and say that not before they have cleansed their conscience of all their specific acts of sin done previously—following the common prescribed usage[h] of Holy Church.

a. This odd and later theologically repudiated idea: that there was a kind of sinful residue—flakes of original sin?—in the soul even after absolution.

b. The ME has *besy*. It usually translates as "busy" or "attentive" (Hodgson, 216), but it has a rarer meaning of "assiduous" or "thorough" (Gallacher, 58).

c. The ME has *lawefuly*. It means "lawfully" but in this case it refers to ecclesiastical canon law, so it is translated "canonically."

d. The ME has *lat him think*. The context requires a more reflective and self-deceiving word. Walsh has "consider" (I 176). Another option would be "suppose" or "pretend." The idea is that one should be eager for the Work—just as though prevented and held back from it for a long time (during which time God may have been working unnoticed in the soul).

e. The ME has *cumbrous*. It implies "cumbersome" or "heavy" or "thick."

f. The ME word is *prees*—usually used in the action of a printing press, so it is a particularly forceful and energetic word (ODEE, 707).

g. The ME word is *welthe* and, curiously, by the fourteenth century, it had come to mean "well-being" rather than "riches" (Bradley, 676). It remains in modern use in the word "commonwealth" as a "state founded by agreement of the people for the common good" (ODEE, 996).

h. The ME word is *wo* coming from the Old English *wä* and meaning "misery" or "misfortune" (ODEE, 1011).

i. The ME word is *sufre*, and in the fourteenth century it still carried the ancient sense of "undergo," "tolerate," or "endure" (ODEE, 883).

j. The ME words are *that is greet skyle* ("that is great reason"), and my translation is from Gallacher, (59).

k. The ME word is *horrible* and meant "rough," "shuddering," or "loathsome." (It is related to the word for hair "standing on end.")

l. One will notice that the author contradicts himself a little: in the two previous paragraphs he points out that everyone will struggle and suffer in "the Work," but in this paragraph he suggests that the worst sinners come through better/sooner/easier than others.

m. The ME word is *hope*, but it comes from the verb *hopien* that can mean both "hope" and "expect" (Bradley, 349).

For in this Work a soul dries up within it all the root and ground of sin that will always be left in it after confession,[a] no matter how thorough[b] it is. And therefore whoever will labor in this Work, let him first cleanse his conscience and afterward, when he has done what he can canonically,[c] let him set out boldly but humbly to the Work. And let him imagine[d] that he has been kept from it for a long time, for this is the work that a soul ought to be doing throughout its entire lifetime even though it never sinned mortally.

And while a soul is dwelling in this mortal flesh, it shall always see and feel this thick[e] cloud of unknowing between him and God. And not only that, but in the pain of original sin the soul shall always prompt us to see and feel that some of all the creatures that God ever made, or some of their works, will always press into one's mind between one and God. And this is the just judgment of God: that humanity, when it had sovereignty and lordship over all other creatures, made itself subservient to the stirrings of those it ruled, deserting the commandment of God his Maker, so that afterward when he wanted to fulfill the commandment of God, he became aware that all the created things that ought to be beneath him had now arrogantly pushed[f] in above him—between him and his God.

↷ HERE BEGINS THE TWENTY-NINTH CHAPTER

That a person should patiently labor in this Work, and
suffer the pain of it.

And therefore, whoever longs to come to the purity that he lost through sin and to gain that happiness[g] where all misery[h] is absent, it is necessary for him obediently to struggle in the Work and endure[i] its pain, no matter what he is—whether he is a habitual sinner or not.

Everyone has struggle in this Work—both sinners and innocents that never greatly sinned—except that those who have been sinners have far greater struggle than those who have not—and that is entirely reasonable.[j]

Nevertheless, often it happens that some who have been foul[k] and habitual sinners reach the perfection of this Work sooner than those that were not. And this is the merciful miracle of our Lord who so precisely gives His grace to the wonder of all the world.[l] Now truly I expect[m] that on Judgment Day

a. Cowan (117) alone of all the many translators recognized that the *Domesday schal be fayre* means not that "Judgment day will have good weather," but that it will be a "fair," a festival. One of the greatest events in the life of a medieval English town or village was to be given the royal permission to hold a fair. This was a huge commercial undertaking with merchants and craftsmen coming from miles around, and possibly the only time a distant farm family might come to town. At a fair there was a great sense of festivity—and on Judgment Day it will be *God's* "wares" that will be displayed.

b. The ME has *sette at lytil or nought*—"of little or no worth" (Cowan, 116).

c. *Helle calves* is a wonderful image of the demons, and generally everyone translates it as "devils" or "demons"—but Wolters (97) provides a valuable insight: that the ME *helle calves* could mean "caves of hell."

d. The ME word is *levefully*—"lawfully" or "legally" or "legitimately."

e. The ME word is *power*. In the fourteenth century it carried the sense of "rule," "ability," or "authority" (ODEE, 702).

f. The ME has *cure of theire soules*. The phrase "the cure of souls" is still used in the Church of England to describe a pastoral relationship between a vicar and the congregation.

g. This is a straightforward command: "Leave others alone!" Julian of Norwich: "the beholding of another one's sins makes ... a thick mist before the eye of the soul ... we cannot for the time see the fairness of God" (I Julian, 345)

h. The reference is to sacramental confession. It is general and universal understanding that no serious spiritual undertaking or moral effort ought to be undertaken without first resolving past sins, being absolved, and clearing away their remaining spiritual detritus.

shall be a festival[a] when God shall be seen clearly along with all His gifts. Then some that are now despised and considered of little or no worth[b] as common sinners—and possibly some who are now foul sinners—shall sit with dignity among the saints in His sight—while some of those who seem now so very holy and are honored by folk as angels, and perhaps some of those that have never committed a mortal sin, shall sit sorrowfully among the caves of hell.[c]

By this you can see that no one should be judged by another here in this life either for the good or evil that they do. However, the *deeds* may legitimately[d] be judged whether they are good or evil, but not the people.

HERE BEGINS THE THIRTIETH CHAPTER

Who should blame and criticize other people's faults.

But, I ask you, by whom shall people's deeds be judged? Surely, by those who have authority[e] and care of their souls,[f] whether that is given publicly by the statute and ordination of Holy Church or else privately and spiritually in perfect charity at the special inspiration of the Holy Spirit. Each person beware lest he presume to take it upon himself to blame and criticize others' faults unless he feels truly that he is inspired by the Holy Spirit as part of his work—for otherwise he can very easily err in his judgments. And therefore beware! Judge yourself as you wish, between you and your God or your spiritual father—but leave other folk alone.[g]

HERE BEGINS THE THIRTY-FIRST CHAPTER

How one should keep oneself, when beginning this Work,
from all thoughts and stirrings of sin.

From the time that you feel that you have done whatever you can do to amend yourself properly by the judgment of Holy Church,[h] then you shall set yourself vigorously to undertake this Work. And then if it happens that your previous particular sinful deeds are always pushing up in your mind between you and your God, or any new thought or stirring of any other sin,

a. The author does not spare any energy in describing the process of getting rid of any leftover past or present sins—he describes the danger of the thoughts of sin "pushing up in your mind"—and prescribes that one mount above those thoughts of sin and "trample them down under your feet." As a good spiritual director he knows that any compromise with even the *thoughts* of sin can be fatal to serious spiritual growth, and that the mere thought of sin itself can be seen as virtual sin.

b. The spiritual novice is found in the neutral no-man's-land between the "cloud of forgetting" below and the "cloud of unknowing" above. But there is a constant magnetic kind of attraction to the past sins—or even to the past virtues—which threatens to turn one's attention away from the search for God's very Self. He now provides some "techniques" or "schemes" to counter that attraction.

c. "On second thought, I *will* give you some advice…"

d. The author's first remedy is simply to ignore the thoughts and temptations as they arise— to "pretend" that they have no impact on you. It has been said that the fastest way to escape the devil's wiles is either to ignore his temptations or to laugh at them. Even serious struggling efforts to avoid the thoughts of sin will never work because they put the sin center stage in one's consciousness. Paying no attention is a far more effective method.

e. One of those wonderful moments when the ME *and* means "if"—what ODEE calls "a special development of meaning" (36). By the sixteenth century, the "if" sense was shown usually by spelling the word simply *an* (Mayhew, 9).

f. Most translate the ME *it deservith alweys to be esid* as "it deserves to be relieved"—but that carries the suggestion that one has "earned" the relief—and the fourteenth-century use of the word "deserve" means "to be worthy to have" (ODEE, 259), —a lessened sense of demanding reward.

g. The ME word is *think* and is sometimes a false cognate—it *can* mean "conceive," "consider," or "believe" (ODEE, 917).

h. Ps. 21:15a [22:14a]: "I am poured out like water, and all of my bones are scattered"; and Lam. 2:19: "Arise, cry out in the night … pour out your heart like water before the presence of the Lord."

i. See note "f" above.

you must staunchly step above those thoughts with a fervent stirring of love and trample them down under your feet.[a] And attempt to cover them with a thick cloud of forgetting—as though they had never been done in this life of yours, nor of any one else's either.[b] And if they arise often, put them down often and, to be brief, as often as they arise so often put them down. And if you think that the struggle is great, you can seek tactics and tricks and private refinements of spiritual techniques to put them away, which schemes are better learned from God by experience than from anyone in this life.

⤳ HERE BEGINS THE THIRTY-SECOND CHAPTER

Of two spiritual schemes that may be helpful to a spiritual beginner in the Work of this book.

Still I think I shall tell you something about these refinements.[c] Try them out, and do better if you are able.

Do what you can to pretend that you do not know that temptations press so hard upon you between you and your God. And try to look over their shoulders (as it were) as though you were seeking something else—which, of course, is God, enclosed in a cloud of unknowing.[d] And if you do this, I promise that within a short time you shall be relieved of your struggle. I promise that if[e] this technique is well and truly grasped, it is nothing else but a longing desire for God—to feel Him and see Him as much as possible here on earth. And such a desire is charity—and it is worthy of always bringing relief.[f]

There is another technique: try it if you wish. When you feel that you can in no way put down those thoughts, then cower down under them as a captive and a coward overcome in battle, and believe[g] that it is only foolish for you to strive any longer with those thoughts—and so yield yourself to God in the hands of your enemies. And then feel as though you were ruined forever. But be careful of this technique, I beg you, for I think that in the trial of this technique you could melt entirely into water.[h] And surely I think, if[i] this technique is subtly understood, it is nothing else but a true knowledge and sense of yourself as you truly are—a wretch and a foul thing,

a. This encouragement to see one's self as only *a wrecche and a filthe fer wers then nought* is uncharacteristically harsh of this author. One feels that in this paragraph he is a bit carried away by his own literary similes and style.

b. The author indulges his vivid imagination with this extravagant depiction of the fatherliness of God toward a sinner who has thrown himself on God's mercy.

c. The ME has *wode biting beres*—literally, "mad [or raging] biting bears." The reader is reminded that bear-baiting had been practiced in England since the thirteenth century, and the rage of the cornered, chained, and attacked bear would have been familiar. We are also reminded of the horrendous account where Elisha curses the children who jeered at him "and two she-bears came out of the woods and mauled the forty-two children" (2 Kgs. 2:24). And the wild boar was the favorite "beast of the chase" and was hunted widely for sport as well as for meat (*Britannica*).

d. The ME has *to fele the profe of these*—literally, "to experience the test of these."

e. An amazing humility: the teacher asks to be taught by the student!

f. The ME has *purgatory*, but it does not refer to the classic Purgatory, since that comes only after death. The author obviously means that the enduring of this pain is part of the cleansing (purging) process.

g. The ME has *goven*—literally, "given," but "supplied" is more refined (MED).

h. The ME has *graciously getyn in custume*—literally, "gotten into habit by grace."

i. Peter Lombard, following Augustine, explains (in his *Sententiae*) the theological understanding that while the guilt (*reatus*) of original sin is removed by baptism, the penalty and suffering (*pœna*) and concupiscence (*concupiscentia*) remains (cited in Clark, 94).

j. Ordinary concupiscence (i.e., the inclination to lust) is an example of the remnants of original sin. The human is plagued lifelong by the inclination and predisposition to sin.

k. One is ceaselessly presented with temptations to sin and can never let down one's spiritual guard against these inducements, so one can never simply relax spiritually and consider oneself unbothered by temptation and sin.

far worse than nothing. And this awareness and experience is, of course, true humility. And this humility makes you worthy[a] to have God Himself mightily descending[b] to avenge you against your enemies in order to take you up and cherishingly dry your spiritual eyes, as the father does a child that is at the point of perishing in the jaws of wild boars or savage[c] bears.

⬱ HERE BEGINS THE THIRTY-THIRD CHAPTER

That in this Work a soul is cleansed of both particular sins and of the torment of them, and yet how there is no perfect rest in this life.

I shall not tell you more about these techniques at this time, for you have the grace to test these two out on your own.[d] And I do believe that then you shall know better how to teach me than I you. For even if that were so, I truly think that I am very far from there. And therefore I pray you to help me—and do so both for your sake and for mine.[e]

Do it then—and work hard for a time, I beg you. And if you cannot learn these techniques soon, then accept the pain of these thoughts humbly. For truly this is your purging.[f] And then when the pain has passed, and your methods have been supplied[g] by God, and learned in ordinary usage,[h] by grace, then I have no doubt that you will be cleansed not only of sin, but also of the penalty for sin. I mean of the penalty for your particular sins of the past, and not the penalty for original sin—for that will always be with you until your dying day no matter how hard you work.[i] Nevertheless, it shall do little harm to you, as compared to the pain from your own particular sins—and yet you shall not be without great labor. For out of this original sin all day long will spring new and fresh stirrings of sin[j] that you must always strike down and work hard to cut away with the sharp double-edged sword of prudence. And by this you can see and learn that there is no true refuge, nor yet any true rest in this life.[k]

a. The author has to deal with some imponderable paradoxes here—and one is inclined to wonder if his confusion arises from questions about some harsh church teaching. He describes the sacrament of confession as the panacea for one's actual past sins (highly orthodox), but warns against the ongoing inclination to sin (highly orthodox), and then declares that if one has confessed, that inclination to new sins will "cause you little harm" (very theologically liberal).

b. The author is adamant that his protégé understand that there is absolutely nothing one can do to "earn" or "deserve" the gift of contemplation—it is a free gift of God, dispensed—almost recklessly (from our point of view).

c. The ME has *vouchesaaf,* which usually means "confer" or "bestow," but has a rarer meaning of "show a gracious willingness" (ODEE, 986).

d. "Then God brought cheerfully to my mind … how [sinners] are recognized in the Church on earth along with their sins, and it is to them no shame, but all of the sins have been changed to honor" (I Julian, 181).

e. This is an oddly circular issue: "The fact that one is able to have this grace indicates that the same grace is already prevenient and active in his soul" (Clark, 145).

f. The author is watchful that his protégé does not get the impression that the contemplative grace cannot be withdrawn—clearly, it can: precisely by the commission of actual sin.

g. The ME has *conseyve*—literally meaning "conceive," but since the rest of the sentence suggests something like "handling" the idea, I chose the option of "take this into your mind" (ODEE, 200).

Regardless of that, you must not fall back, nor yet be overly fearful of failing. For if you can gain grace to destroy the pain of your past particular deeds—in the way I have described (or better if you know how)—be certain that the threat of original sin, or else the new stirrings of sin yet to come, can both together cause you very little harm.[a]

∽ HERE BEGINS THE THIRTY-FOURTH CHAPTER

That God gives this grace of contemplation directly
without any mediator, and that it cannot be found
by using intermediaries.

And if you were to ask me by what means you ought to approach this Work, I beg Almighty God of His great grace and His great courtesy to teach you Himself. For truly I do you a favor to let you know that I am not able to tell you. And that is no wonder! Because that is the work of God alone, specifically accomplished in whatever soul pleases Him, without that soul deserving it in any way.[b] For without this work of God no saint nor any angel can even imagine wanting it. And I believe that our Lord as specifically and as often—yea! more specifically and more often—will be willing[c] to perform this Work in those who have been habitual sinners, rather than to some others who, in comparison with them, have never saddened Him greatly.[d] And He will do this in order to be seen as all merciful and almighty—and because He wants to be seen to work however He wishes, wherever He wishes, and whenever He wishes.

And yet He does not give this grace nor perform this Work in any soul that is unable to bear it. And yet there is no soul without this grace who is able to possess this grace[e]—none!—regardless of whether it is a sinful or an innocent soul. For the gift is not given because of innocence nor withheld because of sin. (Take good notice that I say "withheld" and not "withdrawn."[f] Beware of error here, I beg you—for the closer one comes to touching the truth, the more wary one must be of error.) I mean only good. If you cannot take this into your mind,[g] lay it beside you till God comes and teaches you. Do so then, and do not bother yourself.

a. The ME has *condicion*—literally, "mode of being" (ODEE, 202), which I mean to convey by the word "nature."

b. If this paragraph is confusing to the reader, it is no surprise. The author is dealing here with paradoxical imponderables, and every reader should take to heart his advice (above): "If you cannot take this into your mind, lay it beside you till God comes and teaches you." In brief, the author is saying, "If you find yourself longing for a contemplative life, then your will is probably being stirred by the grace of God to seek that life because without that stirring there would be no desire."

c. The ME word is *spille* and it is a false cognate. Virtually all others have translated it as "spill," but in ME it means "ruin" or "destroy" or "spoil" (Mayhew, 213).

d. The ME has *be thou bot the hous*—"be yourself only the house" (Clark, 147).

e. There are critics of *The Cloud* who have accused the author of Quietism. (This was a deviant Christian tradition—declared as heretical by Pope Innocent XI in 1687—that proposed that all one had to do to be with God was to be entirely passive and to undertake no actions or initiate any functional movement toward God or others.) As Hodgson puts it: "The difference between the exercise of contemplative prayer and Quietism is comparable to that between 'the tense stillness of the athlete and the limp passivity of the sluggard'" (Hodgson, 194).

f. The most important dimension of the contemplative way is what the author so accurately and beautifully calls "a naked intent to God"—the "longing love" which finally pierces the cloud. We may be reminded of Saint Francis's dictum that his followers offer themselves "naked to the naked Christ" (Brooke, Rosalind B.; *The Image of Saint Francis* [Cambridge Univ. Press; Cambridge; 2006], 322).

g. It is interesting that most mystics credit the devil with very little (or no) power. For example, Julian of Norwich: "I saw our Lord scorn the Fiend's malice and totally discount his powerlessness—and He wills that we do so, too" (I 109). The sole power the devil has is persuasion and temptation.

h. In most Middle English usage, the use of a *mene* ("intermediary" or "middleman") usually refers to the invocation of or actions by a saint (often in place of an unmediated direct relationship with God). The word *mene* can also be translated as "method," and it is suggested that the author is engaging in wordplay here with both meanings (Clark, 150).

Be on guard against pride, for it blasphemes God in His gifts and emboldens sinners. Were you truly humble, you would feel about this Work as I say: that God gives it freely without any warrant. The nature[a] of this Work is such that its very presence bestows on the soul the capability to possess it and to be aware of it; and no soul has that capability without it. The capability for this Work is inseparable from the Work itself, without distinction—so that whoever senses this Work is thereby capable of it—and no one else—so much so that without this Work a soul is, as it were, dead, and cannot either crave or desire the contemplative experience. For the degree to which you will it and desire it, to that degree you already possess it—no more and no less—and yet, it is neither a will nor a desire, but a thing that you will never comprehend that stirs you to will and to desire you-know-not-what.[b] Do not worry even though you understand no more, I beg you, but move forward ever more and more, so that you are always advancing.

And, to speak more briefly, let that thing do with you and lead you wherever it will. Let it be the worker, and you only the one acted upon; only look upon it, and leave it alone. Do not meddle with it as though you meant to help it, for fear that you spoil[c] everything. Think of yourself as only the wood and let it be the carpenter; let yourself be only the house,[d] and let it be the householder dwelling in it.[e] During this time, be blind, and rip away the desire to understand, for that will hinder you more than help you. It is enough for now for you to be lovingly aware of being stirred by something you-know-not-what, so that in your stirring you may have no special thought of anything less than God, and that your intent be nakedly directed to God.[f]

And if it is like this, then trust unwaveringly that it is God alone who moves your will and your desire, entirely by Himself, without any other intermediary on His part or on yours. And do not be afraid about the devil, for he cannot come so near. He can never come to move a person's will except rarely and only by indirect means, no matter how subtle a devil he may be.[g] For not even a good angel can adequately and without help move your will—indeed, to speak briefly, nothing can do that except God.

So that you can here understand by these words—but much more clearly by the experience—that in this Work people should use no intermediaries, nor yet come to the Work with intermediaries.[h] All good intermediaries

a. "By meditation here is not meant discursive prayer ... but consideration, whereby a man thinks how he ought to behave interiorly and exteriorly without sin, or else it means the exercise of immediate acts" (Hodgson, 194).

b. The ME has *Thinkyng*, but it implies more than mere rational exercise.

c. McCann strongly associates this teaching with the book *Scala Claustralium* by Guido II, prior of the Grande Chartreuse (Carthusian) monastery in the twelfth century, which was translated into English in the fourteenth century as "a ladder of four rungs by which ladder men may well climb to heaven." The four rungs are Lection, Meditation, Orison, and Contemplation (McCann, 50–51). This also underlines my opinion that the author was a Carthusian.

d. Probably the Carthusian Guido II's *Ladder of the Cloistered* (McCann, 50 n.).

e. The ME has *profiters*, meaning "those who have benefited or made progress." Following Walsh (I 188), I have used the single word "proficient."

f. The ME has *goodly*. Clark (II 152) suggests "hardly" as a rare translation.

g. The following is one of the most confusing sentences in the book and has been translated in multiple ways (e.g., "See how this is demonstrated in this same book" [I Walsh, 188]). The ME has "*See by the preof in this same cours.*" The ME word *see* has a very rare meaning of "that" (Bradley, 538); the word *preof* can be translated as "evidence" (ODEE, 715) and the word *cours* can mean "path," "line," "progression," "procedure," "direction," or "order" (ODEE, 222). "The exact meaning of this [line] is uncertain" (McCann, 195).

h. This is the first reference in the book to Holy Scripture as having any significant part in one's spiritual growth. Unlike the Continental mystics, it is *extremely* rare for the author to use the Bible as a "proof text" for his teachings.

i. The ME word is *custom* and means not only "habit," but a subtle hint at "tribute" or "mercantile trade" and faintly suggests "paying homage to sin."

j. The ME word here is *circumstaunces*, and it can be translated as "all that goes with it" or, more rarely, as "ceremonies" (ODEE, 177).

k. The ME has *blynde rote*—literally, "blind root." It refers to a person's *inclination* to sin that is the consequence and taint of original sin (II Clark, 153).

depend on the Work, and it depends on no intermediary—nor can any intermediary lead one to it.

⮑ HERE BEGINS THE THIRTY-FIFTH CHAPTER

Of preparations with which a contemplative apprentice ought to be occupied: reading, thinking, and praying.

Nevertheless, there are occupations in which a contemplative apprentice ought to be engaged, which are these: Lection, Meditation,[a] and Orison (or else for your understanding they might be called: Reading, Reflection,[b] and Prayer).[c] Of these three you shall find written in another book of another man's work much better than I can tell you[d]—and therefore it is not necessary here to tell you of their qualities. But this I can tell you: these three are so coupled together that for those who are the beginners and the proficient[e] (but certainly not those who are perfect, as some may be here) reflection cannot graciously be gained without reading and hearing preceding it. For reading and hearing are really one and the same: clerics reading books and unlettered people "read" the clerics when they hear them preach the word of God. And prayer can hardly[f] be gained by the beginners and the proficient without thinking preceding it. And[g] that by evidence of this same order.

God's word,[h] whether written or spoken, is like a mirror. Spiritually, the eye of the soul is one's reason and the conscience is one's spiritual face. And just as you are aware that if a foul spot is on your bodily face, the eye of that same face cannot see that spot nor know where it is without a mirror or someone else's pointing it out—just so is it spiritually. Without reading or hearing God's word, it is impossible for one's own intellect (whose soul is blinded by the habit[i] of sin) to see the foul spot on one's own conscience.

And so it follows that when a man sees in a physical or spiritual mirror or knows by someone else's instruction, where the foul spot is on his face—whether physical or spiritual—then at once and not before, he runs to the well to wash himself. If this spot is a particular sin, then the well to which one goes is Holy Church and the washing water is Confession with all its ceremonies.[j] But if it is both of an indistinct origin[k] and a stirring of sin,

a. "Where there has been an *impulse* to sin, but no *consent* and no *actual* sin, sacramental confession is not necessary" (II Clark, 153).

b. The ME has *goodly*. In the fourteenth century, it meant "excellently" or "properly" (ODEE, 405).

c. Baker calls these meditations "aspirations" and explains that they come without any warning and without any intention on the part of the recipient—and that their sudden and unintended natures indicate that they originate with the Holy Spirit within the soul (Baker, 510, cited in Hodgson, 195).

d. The ME has *conseites*, which translates usually as "notions" (Bradley, 130), and I have chosen the equivalent "insights," since "notions" may have mercantile implications.

e. The ME has *blynde felynges*—literally, "blind feelings," a strange phrase presenting the paradox of an adjective concerning sight with a noun concerning sense. I have chosen "vague" for "blind."

f. The author again allows his protégé to select his own single-syllable word to serve as what we today would call a "mantra"—i.e., a word bereft of clear meaning that is used to keep the mind clear of distractions.

g. With the coarse word "lump," one is reminded of Julian of Norwich: "I saw a body lying on the earth that appeared thick and ugly and fearsome, without shape and form, as it were a bloated heap of stinking mire" (I Julian, 305); and see Rom. 7:24: "O, wretched man that I am, who will release me from this body of death?"

h. An awkward passage: it means that one would be driven so mad by discovering himself to be merely a disgusting, congealed lump of sin that no one would be more insane or have greater need to be restrained than he—and yet that spiritual madness would not be visible to the outside world where everyone would think that person calm.

then the well is the merciful God, and the water is prayer, and all that goes with it.[a]

And thus you can see that no reflection can properly[b] be gained by the beginners and the proficient unless reading (or hearing) precedes it—nor does prayer come without reflection preceding it.

⌐ HERE BEGINS THE THIRTY-SIXTH CHAPTER

Of the meditations of those who persistently toil in the Work of this book.

But it is not so with those who persistently engage in the Work of this book. For their meditations[c] are like sudden insights[d] and vague sensations[e] of their own wretchedness or of the goodness of God, without any special methods of reading or hearing preceding them, and without any special awareness of anything under God. These sudden notions and these vague sensations are learned more quickly from God than from others.

It is of no matter to me if these days you had no other meditations on your own sinfulness nor on the goodness of God (I mean if you feel you are stirred that way by grace and by your director's counsel) except such as you can find in the single word *sin* and in the word *God* or in such other word as you wish[f]—neither deciphering nor expanding on these words with the aberration of your mind, nor in searching the attributes of these words, as if by that searching you would increase your devotion. I believe it should never be so in this case and in this Work. So keep all these words completely intact—if by "sin" you mean a whole *lump*, that is, nothing other than yourself.[g] I think that in this blind awareness of sin thus congealed into a lump (i.e., nothing but yourself) there should be no need to tie up anyone more insane than you would be at this time.[h] And yet, possibly, anyone looking at you would think you completely solemnly disposed physically, without any changing of expression, but simply sitting or moving, or lying down or leaning or standing or kneeling, as though you were in a very sober calm.

a. A contemplative would find thoughtful reflections rising spontaneously without intention or effort—and the same with their prayers.

b. The author is very careful throughout the book to emphasize that undertaking the contemplative way in no way vitiates one's responsibilities to the organized church, its rules, and its structures. We need constantly to remember that this book addresses a person already deeply involved and profoundly committed to the life of the institutional church, so such direction can simply be understood and assumed as already present and is referred to by our author only occasionally and in passing. It is likely that this passage refers to the Church's Divine Office of daily prayer—which would make good sense since the author and his protégé were very probably Carthusian monks.

c. Probably a reference to devout monastic predecessors.

d. "Mystical prayer has nothing in common with petition. It is not articulate, it has no forms" (II Underhill, 207)

e. "All the powers of the soul are rooted in the one essence of the soul" (Aquinas, *Summa Theologica* 1.2.37.1). "This essence of 'being' is what other mystics call the apex or ground of the spirit. By contemplating itself as it is in its essence, the soul rises to the contemplation of God" (Hodgson, 196).

f. The Latin translation of the passage (Clark, *Nubes Ignorandi*) has "*sicut illud est in Anglicis dictum* fyre; *vel illud* oute; *sive illud* helpe" ("as it is said in English *fyre*; or that *oute*, or that *helpe*"). "Out" is probably intended to mean something like "Let me out." The MED offers "Help" as one possible translation. It is interesting that the Latin translator added the third word *helpe* to make the meaning more obvious.

g. The ME has *sterith rather*. The translation of *rather* is the comparative (i.e., "more") of the adverb *rathe*, which means "early" or "quickly" (MED).

h. The author caught himself using the "height of the spirit" for the first time and needing to assure his reader that it meant the same as "depth of the spirit."

i. See Matt. 6:7: "When you are praying, do not speak much, as the pagans do, for they think that in their many words they will be heard."

j. The Latin version has *Brevis oratio penetrat cælum* (McCann, 54 n.) and probably finds its origin in Eccles. 35:17: "The prayer of one who humbles himself shall pierce the clouds: and until it comes near he will not be comforted: and he will not depart until the Most High faces him." The adage is found widely—e.g., in Gilbert of Holland, in Saint Bernard, in *Fasciculus Morum*, and in *Piers Plowman*, and later in John of the Cross (I Clark, 158).

ꙮ HERE BEGINS THE THIRTY-SEVENTH CHAPTER
Of the special prayers of those who habitually labor
in the Work of this book.

And just as the meditations of those who habitually labor in this grace and in this Work rise suddenly without any causes,[a] just so do their prayers—I mean their *singular* prayers not those prayers that are ordained by Holy Church,[b] for they that are true laborers in this Work honor no prayer so much as those, and therefore they do them in the form and under the procedures that were ordained by the holy fathers before us.[c] But their own prayers always rise immediately to God, without any mediators or specific premeditation coming before it or accompanying it.

And if they are in words—as they are only infrequently[d]—then they are only in few words—yea, and always the fewer the better. Aye, and if it is only a little word of one syllable, I would consider it better than two, and more in accord with the work of the Spirit since it is thus that a spiritual laborer in this Work should always be in the highest and most supreme place of the spirit.[e] That this is true, see by example of the course of nature: a man or a woman, fearful of any sudden risk of fire, or of one's death, or whatever else may be, suddenly in the intensity of one's spirit is driven to rush and to the need to cry out or to pray for help. Yea, how? Surely not in many words nor even in a word of two syllables. And why is that? Because he thinks it would be waiting too long to declare the need and the affliction of his spirit. And therefore he bursts out shockingly with great feeling, and cries out only a little word of one syllable, like the word "Fire!" or the word "Out!"[f]

And just as this little word "Fire!" moves more quickly[g] and more rapidly pierces the ears of the hearers, so does a little word of one syllable when it is not only spoken or thought but secretly intended in the depths of spirit—which is actually the height of the spirit (for in spirituality, all are the same: height and depth, length and breadth).[h] And more quickly it pierces the ears of Almighty God[i] far more than does any long psalm unmindfully mumbled in the teeth. And therefore it is written that short prayer pierces heaven.[j]

a. The words themselves are not "magic"—but they must be spoken in the utmost ardor and fervor and gravity of the one praying.

b. An outstanding example of the sheer literary skill of the author—the extended catalog of adjectives with their poetical implications is a masterpiece of English rhetoric at its best.

c. Eph. 3:17–19: "[I pray] that Christ may dwell by faith in your hearts, being rooted and grounded in love, that you may be able to comprehend with all the saints what is the breadth, and length, and height, and depth; and to know the love of Christ that surpasses knowledge so that you may filled with all the abundance of God"; 1 Cor. 13:12: "We see now through a glass mysteriously: but then face to face. Now I know in part: but then I shall know just as I am known."

d. "The everlastingness of God" is reminiscent of Julian of Norwich: "His goodness fills all His creatures and all His blessed works and surpasses them without end, for He is the endlessness" (I Julian, 79).

e. There is a hint here of the Parable of the Importunate Neighbor (Lk. 11:5–8) in which a friend finally agrees to help his neighbor because of his insistent demands. Here (in the author's joke) it is the "frightful clamor" of one word that will sway God.

f. "Yea! though it be on a midwinter's night" is probably a reference to the winter solstice, which is called "Midwinter" and usually occurs on December 21 to 22.

g. Another example of the personalization of this long letter to the author's protégé. There are such exclamations throughout the book, and I have tried to leave them in their original Middle English form whenever possible.

h. Ps. 119:73: "Your hands have made me and fashioned me."

i. This is a confusing statement: basically it argues that if a natural human being can be made compassionate even to one's enemies by grace, then surely God, who is compassionate by nature, would be merciful to a pleading sinner.

j. Mercy is part of God's own nature: God is "naturally" merciful. But humans do not have mercy naturally, but only by the inspiration and gift of God's grace. Hence mercy and compassion are a part of God's own nature ("closer to Him"), while mercy and compassion are only appliques or adjuncts that are added on to human nature by grace. (See McCann, 55 n.)

HERE BEGINS THE THIRTY-EIGHTH CHAPTER
How and why that short prayer pierces heaven.

And why does it pierce heaven, this little short prayer of one little syllable? Certainly because it is prayed with a full spirit, in the height and in the depth, in the length and in the breadth of the spirit of the one who prays it.[a] It is in the height—for it is with all the power of the spirit; it is in the depth—for in this little syllable is contained all the wisdom of the spirit; it is in the length—for if it were to feel over a stretch of time as it feels at the moment, it would cry then just as it cries now; it is in the breadth—for it desires for all others what it desires for itself.[b] In this moment it is that a soul has grasped (following the teaching of Saint Paul, with all saints[c]—not fully, but in a way and in part) what is the length and the breadth, the height and the depth of the Everlasting and All-loving Almighty and All-wise God. The everlastingness[d] of God is his length; his love is his breadth; his power is his height; and his wisdom is his depth. No wonder, then, that a soul that is so nearly conformed by grace to the image and likeness of God, his maker, would be quickly heard by God. Yea, even though it were a very sinful soul—which would seem to be an enemy of God—if through grace it could come to cry such a little syllable in the height and depth, the length and the breadth of its spirit, yet for the frightful clamor of this cry it would always be heard and helped by God.[e]

See this as an example: one who is your mortal enemy, and you hear him so afraid that he cries out in the height of his spirit this little word "Fire!" or this word "Out!"—yet, having no thought of him as your enemy but for pure pity stirred in your heart and raised up by the anguish of this cry, you rise up—yea! though it be on a midwinter's night[f]—and help him to quench the fire or to quiet him and ease him in his distress. Ah, Lord![g] Since a person can be made so compassionate by grace as to have such mercy and such pity on his enemy (not withstanding his enmity), what pity and what mercy shall God Himself have for the spiritual cry of a soul, made and fashioned[h] in the height and the depth, the length and the breadth of His spirit (which has all by nature that a human has only by grace[i]... and much more)? Surely God will have much more mercy by comparison, since it is so that what is possessed by nature is closer to its holder than that which is obtained by grace.[j]

a. Another intimate rhetorical question. It would be quite easy for the author—in the position of a tutor—to make simple statements without setting up these rhetorical flourishes. But they give us a sense of the intimacy and friendliness between tutor and protégé—it feels like the author is having some enjoyable literary fun with his young apprentice.

b. The ME word is *entent*, which in the fourteenth century meant "intention of the mind to its object" (ODEE, 480). Other translators have used "intention" (Cowan) or "reaching out" (Walsh) or "openness" (Johnston). I have chosen to retain "intent" throughout the book since its spare simplicity seems to accord with the author's teachings.

c. This definition is in the *Scala Claustralium* of the Carthusian Guido II (circa AD 1150): "Prayer is a devout desiring of the heart toward God for avoiding evils and in acquiring goods." Another evidence that the author is a Carthusian monk.

d. And now the author is about to set up his two words to serve as contemplative mantras for his contemplative protégé.

e. The author explains his justification for the promotion of the two words he recommends for mantras. "Sin" is the simple word/concept/summary that carries within it all the negative aspects/implications/properties that characterize the varied human experiences of evil. It is a kind of catchall word for badness.

f. Similarly, the simple word "God" implies everything a person experiences as good. It is a catchall word for goodness. (It ought also to be pointed out that the author identifies God not only as "good," but as "goodness" itself.)

g. There is a long tradition among contemplatives that one's mantra is to be assigned by one's spiritual director—lest the word one chooses be "contaminated" with too many personal and emotional elements. But the author here leaves room for his protégé to choose a different word for his mantra if he is led to that particular word by God.

h. There is a hint here of a thus far unspoken agenda with the author's words "if you are going to pray with words, *and not otherwise*." This is the first suggestion that true contemplative prayer can be (and, indeed, might advisably be) wholly and entirely wordless (i.e., apophatic).

i. Here the author gives another hint that the person he addresses lives an enclosed and reclusive life, since he values unlimited frequency of prayer— something impossible for anyone other than an eremitic monastic, a Carthusian.

➶ HERE BEGINS THE THIRTY-NINTH CHAPTER

How a perfect contemplative should pray and what prayer is in itself; and if a person were to pray in words, which words accord most with the property of prayer.

Therefore one ought to pray in the height and the depth, the length and the breadth of our spirit—and that not in many words, but in a little word of one syllable.

And what shall that word be?[a] Surely such a word would be best if it agreed with the nature of prayer. And what word is that? Let us first see what prayer is properly in itself, and thereafter we may clearly know what word will best accord with the nature of prayer.

Prayer in itself properly is nothing else but a devout intent[b] directed to God, for the gaining of good things and the removal of evil things.[c]

And[d] then, since it is understood that all evils are included in sin—either as the cause of sin or as sin itself—therefore, when we would intently pray for the removal of evils, let us neither say nor think nor mean anything else, nor any other words, than this little word *sin*.[e] And if we would intently pray for the gaining of good things, let us cry neither with word or with thought or with desire or anything else, nor any more words except this word *God*. Because God is all good—both the cause of good and goodness itself.[f]

Do not be amazed that I set these two words before all others. For if I knew any shorter words, as completely containing in them all good and all evils (as these two words do), or if I had been led by God to take any other words instead, I would have taken them and left these; and so I suggest that you do as well. (But do not analyze the words themselves, because in that way you would never come to your purpose nor to this Work, for it is never gained by analysis, but only by grace.) And therefore take no other words to pray in—even though I set these two here—except such words as you may be led by God to take.[g] But if God moves you to take these, I advise that you not reject them—I mean: if you are going to pray in word, and not otherwise—because they are very short words.[h]

But although the shortness of prayer is greatly commended here, nevertheless, the frequency of prayer ought never to be limited in that way.[i]

a. The ME has *lengthe of the spirite.* The meaning (based on chapter 38's broad application of the word *lengthe*) has to do with its "reach" or "extent," so I chose the word "extension."

b. The author now begins to give deeply serious and fundamental advice about the contemplative way. Here is a primary one: that investigation and excavation of every detail of each and every sin (as is recommended by many other spiritual directors) is actually a *diversion* from the Work one has set oneself to do. A contemplative must simply understand that since the life goal of contemplative prayer is total union with the Godhead, *any* sin is disruptive to that sought union. One can be entirely derailed from one's goal by simply analyzing and scrutinizing each of one's sins in detail.

c. A splendid rhetorical wording: sin is a *lump*! Sin is a dark, nasty, ugly, formless wad of miserable iniquity. The ME word *lumpe* strongly carries all that meaning (and the sense of "heavy" and "imbecilic" as well). For the author, sin is seen not as an intricate and sophisticated encounter with some elaborate wicked abstraction, but as a dirty dimensionless tumor. And what is the sin-lump made of? Nothing but you yourself! And that earthy assertion leads to the virtual explosion of "Sin! Sin! Sin!" The author is a rhetorical virtuoso to display such stunning literary dynamics.

d. It is clear that the author does not describe a cool, abstract, conceptual process, but one that may well produce such "an abundance of spirit" that it may "burst forth into words."

e. The seven classical heavenly virtues are chastity, temperance, charity, diligence, patience, kindness, humility—promulgated by Prudentius in the fifth century and intended to offset the Seven Mortal Sins. The author also includes the Theological Virtues of faith, hope, and charity and adds the monastic counsel of voluntary poverty.

For as has been said before, prayer is prayed in the extension[a] of the spirit, so that it should never cease until the time comes in which it has fully gained what it longed for. We have an example of this in a fearful man or a woman as we said before. For we see well that they do not cease crying out the little word "Out!" or the little word "Fire!" until such time as they have to a full extent obtained help in their trouble.

∽ HERE BEGINS THE FORTIETH CHAPTER

That during this Work a soul has no special vision of any one vice in itself nor of any one virtue in itself.

So, in the same way, fill your spirit with the spiritual significance of this word "sin" without any special attention to any particular kind of sin (whether venial or mortal) such as pride, anger, or envy, covetousness, sloth, gluttony, or lust. What does it matter to contemplatives what specific sin it might be, or how serious a sin it is? For during the time of this Work all sins seem to them each great in itself, since the least sin separates them from God and deprives them of their spiritual peace.[b]

So feel sin as a lump—of you-know-not-what—but nothing other than yourself.[c] And then always cry spiritually this one: "Sin! Sin! Sin!" and this: "Out! Out! Out!" This spiritual cry is better taught by God through experience than by any person with words, for it is best when it is pure spirit without any particular thought or any pronunciation of words so that the body and the soul are both filled with sorrow and the burden of sin (except occasionally when due to abundance of spirit it bursts forth into words).[d]

In the same way you should do with the little word "God." Fill your spirit with the spiritual significance of it without any special attention to any of His works—whether they are good, better, or best, bodily or spiritual—or to any virtue that may be wrought in a person's soul by any grace, not even trying to discover if it is humility or charity, patience or abstinence, hope, faith, or temperance, chastity or voluntary poverty.[e] What does that matter to contemplatives? For they find and recognize all virtues in God—for in Him is everything, both source and on-going being. For they believe that if

a. An amusing and delicate paradox: the author exhaustively lists all possible virtues—and then counsels his protégé to pay no attention to those specific things he has just named in detail!

b. The Latin translation has *Intende Deum totum, et totum Deum*: "Mean that God is everything [that you want] and that everything [that you want] is God" (Clark, 164). The line has the quality of an adage, a memorable bon mot.

c. Note the suggestion that a contemplative *alternate* between the two mantras—so that one's spiritual orientation is either toward the purgation of the impediments of one's sinful nature or, alternately, toward pure union with God.

d. Another axiom typical of the author: "With God, no sin—if no sin, with God."

e. The ME has *"Ryght none!"* Others have translated it as "None at all" (Walsh and Johnston) or "Right none!" (I Underhill and McCann). My translation is based on the fourteenth-century meaning of *ryght* as "exactly" (Mayhew, 192). It has the flavor of a smart-alecky reply to the set-up question—but rhetorically it makes the point emphatically and undeniably: contemplation is the exception among one's ordinary activities that ought to be practiced extravagantly!

f. The author recognizes that what he is asking of his young protégé is virtually more than a human being can accomplish, given matters of health and physical needs.

g. The ME has *outher in ernest or in game*. In the fourteenth century, *game* meant "play" or "sport." Johnston has "playfully"; curiously, Walsh has "preparing." I have tried to capture the sense of "playfulness" without taking it inappropriately lightly.

h. Even if something happens that "pulls you down from the height of this Work," the author expects his protégé to continue *wanting* to do the contemplative Work—either in doing it "or in wishing it."

i. It is important that care be taken that one is not morally responsible for any situation that might pull one down. Sickness is a valid justification for relaxing the discipline of contemplation, but not if it occurs through one's own carelessness. Here is also evidence that the author does not encourage or tolerate the often extreme ascetic practices that were common in the medieval church, such as starvation, mutilation, intentional physical abuse, and self-inflicted pain.

they had God, they would have all good; and therefore they covet nothing with special attention except that good God alone.[a] Do you in the same manner, as far as you can by grace—and intend that God be everything and everything you intend be God,[b] so that nothing controls your mind and your will except God alone.

And since during all the time you live in this wretched life, you must always feel to some degree this foul, stinking lump of sin—as it were joined and coalesced with the very essence of your being, therefore you shall alternately pay attention to these two words: "sin" and "God"[c]—with this overall awareness: that if you had God, you would be without sin, and if you could be without sin, you would have God.[d]

⤚ HERE BEGINS THE FORTY-FIRST CHAPTER

That in all works other than this one, a person should exercise moderation, but in this Work, none.

And furthermore, if you were to ask me what moderation you should apply in this Work, then I would answer you and say: "Exactly none!"[e] For in all your other activities you ought to apply moderation—in eating and drinking, and in sleeping, and in keeping your body from extreme cold or heat, and in praying long or reading, or in communing in speech with your fellow Christian. In all these you ought to practice moderation so that there is neither too much nor too little. But in this contemplative Work you ought not to hold yourself back, for I would prefer that you should never cease this Work as long as you live.

I do not suggest that you should always be able to persist in the Work as when it was brand new, for that cannot be—because sometimes sickness or other unintended dispositions in body and in soul, with many other needs of nature, will stoutly encumber you and often pull you down from the height of this Work.[f] But I say that you ought always to remain in this Work either earnestly or at least good-naturedly[g]—that is to say, either in doing it or in wishing it.[h] And therefore for the love of God watch out for sickness as diligently as you can, so that as far as you can tell you will not yourself be the cause of your debility.[i] For I tell you truly that this Work demands a truly great serenity and a healthy and pure disposition—in body as well as in soul.

a. Jude 1:21: "Keep yourself in the love of God, waiting for the mercy of our Lord Jesus Christ, in eternal life."

b. 2 Cor. 6:4: "But in all things approving ourselves as the ministers of God, in much patience, in tribulation, in necessities, in distresses."

c. "Without trying to make of the Christian life a cult of suffering for its own sake, we must frankly admit that self-denial and sacrifice are absolutely essential to the life of prayer" (Merton, Thomas; *Contemplative Prayer* [Random House; New York; 2009] 50).

d. The ME has *Gete that you gete mayst.* Four translators make it "Take what comes" (Wolters, 109; Hodgson, 197n.; Cowan, 160; Clark, 167). The interjection carries the sense of "Accept whatever comes" or "Don't worry about these details." Curiously, the Latin has *Tu autem ex dictis meis adquiras aliquid si quid potes*—"Gain something from my words if you can" (McCann, 58 n.).

e. The author has very deep and very strong beliefs that the actual practice of the contemplative way will automatically bear fruit in the rest of one's life, e.g., in reasonable moderation in daily life. There is a sense that if one's every thought is oriented toward God (contemplation), everything else will fall into proper place and perspective.

f. There is almost a wry humor here in describing thoroughgoing and uncompromised contemplative life as "reckless."

g. The ME has *set a merke and a mesure in hem. Merke* meant "price" or "value" in the fourteenth century (Mayhew, 143), and *mesure* meant "amount" (Mayhew, 147), and, because of the context, I have used "quota."

h. The author constantly credits "experience" ahead of theory or speculation, and it is apparent that he has faced opposition for his ideas from some other sources: "Others can say what they say."

i. Here is one of the two or three core concepts that are central to the author's understanding: "a naked intent to God," a "piercing lance of longing love," and this "blind stirring of love."

j. Here are the alternating mantras mentioned in chapter 40: "sin" and "God."

And so, for the love of God, govern yourself carefully in body and soul, and keep yourself healthy as well as you can. And if sickness comes in spite of your effort, have patience and rest humbly in God's mercy[a]—and then all will be good enough. For I tell you truly that often patience in sickness and in other varied tribulations[b] pleases God much more than any pleasing devotion that you might have in good health.[c]

HERE BEGINS THE FORTY-SECOND CHAPTER

That by being excessive in this Work, a person shall maintain moderation in all other things; and assuredly in no other way.

But perhaps you would ask me how you should govern yourself wisely in food and in sleep and in all those others. And to that I would answer you very briefly: "Take whatever you may get."[d] Do this Work always without ceasing and without moderation, and you shall know well how to begin and end all your other activities with a great moderation. For I cannot believe that a soul continuing in this Work night and day without moderation could err in any of these outward activities—or otherwise I think that he would be endlessly in error.[e]

And therefore if I were able to acquire a vigilant and active vision of this spiritual Work within my soul, then I would be oblivious to eating and drinking, to sleeping and speaking, and to all my outward activities. For surely I believe that I would rather attain moderation in those activities by means of such a recklessness[f] in contemplation than by some anxious examination of those same things as though I could by that examination set a value[g] and quota on them. Truly, I would never do like that by anything I could do or say. Others can say what they will say, but let experience be the judge.[h] And therefore lift up your heart with a blind stirring of love[i]; and now mean "sin" and then "God."[j] God is what you want to have and sin is what you want to lack. God wants to have you and you are sure to have sin. At this point, may the good God help you, for now you have need of Him!

a. The ME has *felle* (as in "fell a tree"). I have used "chop down" (Cowan, 163).

b. The ME has *under God*.

c. The ME has *treed alle doun full fer.* That is a very strong statement that I have translated as "trample all of it far down."

d. Most translators move "for God" to the end of the sentence and make it "for God's sake" or "because of God," but they miss the basic idea: that even the very good deeds one has previously done "for God" must be suppressed and hidden from consciousness under "the cloud of forgetting."

e. The ME has *for to hate himself for the thing that he loveth.* Although most translators use it, the direction for one to "hate himself" simply cannot reasonably stand. But there is an extremely rare fourteenth-century meaning of *for* as "in relation to" or "compared to" (ODEE, 368).

f. The ME has *do with thiself. Do with* translates as "get on with" (ODEE, 279).

g. The ME has *worchet in thi witten*—literally, "works in your mind."

h. This is an unusually strong self-condemnation, but for the author there is no middle ground—either a "foul stinking lump of sin" or a "blind stirring of love."

i. The ME has *for in rewarde of it.* In the fourteenth century that meant "compared to" (ODEE, 764 and Gallacher, 70 n.).

j. The author claims that when one has dispensed with the thought of all else that is earthly and of one's own past works (both good and bad), one will finally be left with an unadorned knowledge and awareness of one's own essence.

k. The ME has *distroied*—literally, "destroyed," but that seems too physical a term for a spiritual action—I have chosen "obliterated" as a synonym.

❧ HERE BEGINS THE FORTY-THIRD CHAPTER

That all awareness and feeling of one's own being must necessarily be abandoned if the perfection of this Work is truly to be felt in any soul in this life.

See to it that nothing operates in your mind or in your will except God. And try to chop down[a] all knowledge and feeling of anything less than God,[b] and trample all of it far down[c] under the cloud of forgetting. And you should understand that in this Work you shall not only forget all other creatures than yourself and their deed or yours, but also you shall in this Work forget both yourself and even your deeds done for God,[d] as well as all other creatures and their deeds. For it is the condition of a perfect lover not only to love the thing that one loves more than oneself, but also, in a way, to hate oneself compared to[e] that thing one loves.

Thus shall you get on with[f] yourself: you shall loathe and be fed up with everything that operates[g] in your mind and in your will[h] unless it is God alone. Because surely otherwise—whatever it may be—it is between you and your God. And thus no wonder that you loathe and hate to reflect on yourself, since you shall always consider sin as a foul stinking lump (of you-know-not-what) between you and your God—which lump is nothing other than yourself. For you shall consider it joined and congealed with the essence of your being, yea, as it were, without detaching.[i]

And therefore break down all knowledge and awareness of every kind of created thing—but most especially yourself. For on the knowledge and awareness of yourself depends knowledge and awareness of all other creatures; for compared to[a] the self, all other creatures are easily forgotten. For—if you will vigorously set yourself to the test—you will find that when you have forgotten all other creatures and all their works, yea, and with them all your own works, there shall remain afterward between you and your God a naked knowledge and consciousness of your own being.[j] This knowledge and consciousness must necessarily be obliterated[k] before the time comes when you can truthfully sense the perfection of this Work.

a.   It is not easy for us to comprehend something as intemperate as the obliteration of the "knowledge and consciousness of your own being." But what the author speaks of here as obliterating is one's "*self-consciousness*"—one's continuing awareness of "who I am." This is what some have called the "destruction of the ego," and it leaves the *true* self untrammeled by egocentricity or any notions of self-prominence. As Ruth Burrows has written: "Narrow is the gate, strait the way that leads to life, it allows for no baggage, no spiritual acquisitions and no swollen self-importance" (Burrows, Ruth; *Love Unknown* [Bloomsbury Academic; London; 2012], 152).

b.   The ME word *sorow* means primarily "sorrow" (as it is usually translated), but it has a slightly wider meaning that includes "grief," "regret," and "distress" (ODEE, 847). The author's use of the word means more than just "sadness"—it is something like the recognition of one's ontological limitation, the kind of despair or distress one feels when realizing that one is earthly and sinful and useless and incompetent.

c.   Discretion/moderation is needed because this experience of sorrow is not part of the contemplative way itself—it is part of the preparation, part of the accessibility, part of the preparatory openness to God.

d.   Song of Songs 5:2a: "I sleep, and my heart watches," and one is reminded of Saint Francis de Sales's practice of what he called "spiritual sleep." (John-Julian, ed., *Complete Introduction to the Devout Life*, xiv).

e.   Luke 22:45: "And when [Jesus] rose up from his prayer and had come to his disciples, he found them sleeping out of sorrow."

f.   This sorrow has something of the existentialist's angst about it (Cowan, 166). It is recognition of one's separateness from God and ignites the longing for him.

g.   The ME has a comparison of *gamen to ernest*—"games to earnestness."

h.   "Thus, the dark, penitential night of spiritual angst purges the soul of its own existential awareness in order that the void might be filled by an immediate awareness of God" (Cowan, 167).

i.   The author suggests even an emotionally practical benefit from contemplation: that it makes ordinary earthly life tolerable to the sensitive soul.

⟋ HERE BEGINS THE FORTY-FOURTH CHAPTER

How a soul must dispose itself on its own part so as to
destroy all knowledge and consciousness of one's own being.

But now you will ask me how you can obliterate this naked knowledge and consciousness of your own being. For possibly it seems to you that if it were obliterated, all other hindrances would be obliterated, and if that is how you think, you are exactly right![a] But to this I answer and say that without a very special grace given utterly freely by God and a fully corresponding capacity to receive that grace on your part, this naked awareness and consciousness of your being can in no way be obliterated.

And such a capacity is nothing but a strong and deep spiritual sorrow.[b] However, in this sorrow you must have discretion about this: you must be careful in the time of this sorrow[c] that you violently strain neither your body nor your spirit, but sit very still—as it were in a simulated sleep,[d] all exhausted with sobbing and plunged deeply into sorrow.[e] This is true sorrow. This is perfect sorrow. And fortunate is the one who can acquire this sorrow.

Everyone has cause for sorrow, but the one who has awareness and consciousness that he exists most especially feels himself a subject for sorrow.[f] All other sorrows in comparison to this are as mere sport compared to sincerity.[g] For the one who can feel sorrow earnestly knows and is aware not only of *what* he is, but *that* he exists. And even one who has never felt this sorrow is advised to generate sorrow because he has never yet felt perfect sorrow.

When this sorrow is experienced it cleanses the soul not only of sin, but also of the punishment one has deserved because of one's sin. And thus it makes a soul capable of receiving joy that robs one of all knowledge and consciousness of one's own being.[h] This sorrow—if it is truly understood— is full of holy desire (otherwise no one in this life could either tolerate it or endure it). For if it were not that a soul were somewhat nourished with a kind of comfort from a proper accomplishment of this contemplative Work, one would not be able to bear the pain of knowing and feeling one's own existence.[i] For as often as one would want to have a true awareness and consciousness of one's God in purity of spirit (as much as can be in

a. More clarity about the cause of the sorrow/regret: that one's consciousness is so filled with oneself that there is little room left for God.

b. The condition of the limitations of one's existence and one's distance from God is the root of the sorrow—but that very existence was given by God in one's own creation, so wishing to "un-be" would be disrespectful to God the Creator. (I have chosen to leave the ME form *un-be* for its appealing antiquity. If we can speak of *unknowing*, we can also speak of *un-being*.)

c. The ME has *compleccion.* "In medieval physiology this term was used to refer to the combination of humours or vital juices which a man's body was thought to contain. The four humours—blood, phlegm, black bile, and yellow bile—were assumed to be related to the elements: air, water, earth, and fire, and to the primary qualities of these elements: hot and moist, moist and cold, cold and dry, hot and dry, respectively. These humours, which varied in proportion from individual to individual, determined a person's temperament. According to which humour preponderated, temperaments were classified as sanguine, phlegmatic, melancholic, or choleric—epithets still current though retaining only a part of their original meaning" (Hodgson, in Gallacher, 123).

d. "But the purpose of the spiritual life is that a man should be united to God, which is done through charity" (Aquinas, *Summa Theologica* 2.2.44.1).

e. The ME has *in his goostly wittes*—literally, "in his spiritual intelligence."

f. The ME has *coriousté of witte*—literally, "curiosity of mind" (for *coriousté* as "aberration," see ODEE, 236). This is an extremely common phrase in this book. *Coriousté* challenges a translator and is often translated as "inquisitiveness." In most cases, however, it is better to understand the word as meaning "oddity" or "eccentricity" as in "a collector's curiosity cabinet"—and usually with a somewhat negative or unfavorable tinge.

g. The two following sentences and further material following it must be seen as a clear rebuff to the writings of Richard Rolle, a contemporary of the author of *The Cloud*, who promoted a romantic and passionate "enthusiasm" in which feelings of heat or warmth, sounds of music, and a sweetness were signs of God's favor. Much of our author's warnings in the following chapters seem to be addressed specifically against just such expectations of physical (external) manifestations of the Spirit.

this life), and since one feels that one cannot—for one always finds one's awareness and consciousness as it were already occupied and filled with the foul, stinking lump of oneself[a] (which must always be detested and despised and abandoned if one would be God's perfect disciple, taught by Himself in the mount of perfection)—just as often one goes nearly insane with sorrow, insomuch so that one weeps and wails, struggles, curses, and swears and, to be brief, one thinks that one carries so heavy a burden of one's own self that one cares nothing for one's own honor, as long as God be pleased. And yet in all this sorrow one does not wish to un-be, for that would be the devil's madness and contempt for God.[b] But one desires strongly to exist, and intends very great gratitude to God for the honor and gift of existence—although one longs unceasingly to escape the awareness and consciousness of that existence.

Every soul must have and feel in itself this sorrow and this desire, either in this way or in another, since God is willing to teach his spiritual disciples according to his goodwill and their capability in body and soul, in degree and character[c] before the time that they can be totally one-ed to God in perfect charity[d]—such as can be attained here if God allows it.

⟳ HERE BEGINS THE FORTY-FIFTH CHAPTER

An explanation of some certain deceptions that might occur in this Work.

But one thing I tell you: that in this Work a young disciple who has not yet been accustomed and tested in spiritual works can very easily be deceived. And, unless he is wary early on and has the grace to leave off and submit himself to spiritual direction, his physical power could possibly be damaged and he might succumb to delusion in his spiritual thoughts.[e] And all this on account of pride and sensuality and aberration of mind.[f]

And this is the way that deception can happen: a young man or a woman only begun in the school of devotion hears this sorrow and this desire being read or spoken about—how one shall lift up the heart to God and unceasingly desire to feel the love of one's God.[g] And then, hastily, in an aberration of mind they conceive these words not to be *spiritual*—as they

a. The ME has *travaylen*—literally, "labor" or "toil" or "strain" (ODEE, 938).

b. The ME has *veynes*—literally, "veins." One could legitimately translate it as "hearts" since the veins lead to the heart. Walsh (I 206) has "strain themselves."

c. The ME has *beestly*—literally, "beastly." For "carnally" see Gallacher, 72 n.

d. The ME has *unlisty*—literally, "un-listy" or "un-joyful." For "listless" see Gallacher, 72 n.

e. Throughout the book, the author cautions against the kinds of abusive behavior very commonly commended in the fourteenth century: hair shirts, self-scourging with a "discipline" (whip), drastic fasting, endurance of cold, and the like. Most of his criticisms of false contemplatives have to do with their inclinations to deal with *internal* spiritual matters by *external* physical disciplines and practices.

f. From Walter Hilton's *Scale of Perfection*: "All men who speak of the fire of love do not know well what it is.... It is never physical, nor is it felt bodily. A soul which is in the body may feel it in prayer or in devotion, but feels it by no bodily sense ... the fire of love is not bodily, for it is only in the spiritual desire of the soul" (Hilton, 298). Also, a major book by Richard Rolle was entitled *The Fire of Love*.

g. The ME has *braunches*—literally, "branches" or "twigs" (MED).

h. The ME has *mescheves*—literally, "mischiefs" or "troubles" or "wounds" (MED).

i. This is the author's core message in these middle chapters: that much that passes as true religious practice is the result of pride and individualism detached from the oversight of the church and a spiritual director. The most dangerous aspect of this deception is that it even fools the practitioner who actually thinks that she or he is holy and devout.

j. The ME has *sotyl*—usually translated as "subtle," but in the fourteenth century it came also to mean "oblique" or "devious" (ODEE, 881).

were meant—but *physical* and *literal*, and so they trouble[a] their fleshly hearts outrageously in their breasts. And for the lack of grace (that they deserve!) and their pride and inquisitiveness into themselves, they strain their veins[b] and their bodily strength so carnally[c] and so violently that within a short time they fall either into weariness or into a kind of listless[d] weakness in body and in soul, which makes them go out of themselves and seek some false and vain physical and bodily comfort outside—as it were—for the restoration of their body and spirit. Or else, if they do not fall into this (as they deserve) through their spiritual blindness and the carnal enflaming of their constitution in their bodily breasts during this false physical and un-spiritual operation—in order to have their breasts either enflamed with an unnatural physical fervor caused by abuse of their bodies[e] or by this false exercise, or else by creating an imaginary warmth: the work of the Fiend, their spiritual enemy—it is caused by their pride and their sensuality and their inquisitiveness of mind.

And even then they probably think it is the fire of love,[f] created and kindled by the grace and goodness of the Holy Spirit. Truly from this deception and from the extensions[g] of it spring many misfortunes:[h] much hypocrisy, a lot of heresy, and great error. For just as quickly after such a deceptive experience comes deceptive knowledge in the Fiend's school— equally after a true experience comes true knowledge in God's school. For I tell you truly that the devil has his contemplatives just as God has His.[i] This ruse of a deceptive experience and the illusory knowledge following it has diverse and astonishing variations matching the diversity of states and the devious[j] conditions of those who have been deceived—just as has the true experience and knowledge of those that are preserved from damnation.

But I will not set down here any more of these deceptions except those with which I believe you could be assailed, if ever you propose yourself to undertake this Work. For what would it profit you to know how these great scholars and men and women of other levels than you are have been deceived? Surely, exactly nothing! And therefore I shall tell you no more than those that may happen to you if you labor in this Work. And henceforth I will tell you this so that you may beware of them in your working, if you are assailed by them.

a. The ME has *lither strengthe*—literally, "bad violence." Most make the translation as "evil brute force" (Gallacher, 73 n.; I Walsh, 208; Cowan, 174; Wolters, 114; Johnston, 106).

b. From the thirteenth-century *Ancren Riwle* ("Anchorite's Rule"): "Better is listening than evil force" (cited in Cowan, 175).

c. Quite clearly the author makes reference to Moses's experience at Mount Sinai in Exod. 19:12–13a: "[The Lord told Moses:] 'Set certain limits to the people round about and you shall say to them: "Take heed; do not go up the mountain or even touch the border of it. Whoever touches the mountain in that manner, he shall die. No hands shall touch him, but he shall be stoned to death." ' " And Heb. 12:20b: "If even an animal touches the mountain, it shall be stoned."

d. The ME word is *wetyng of grace*—literally, "a wetting of grace." "'Heavenly dew' as a medieval metaphor for grace is a commonplace, both scripturally and liturgically" (I Walsh, 208 n.). Also see Prov. 19:12b: "[A king's] favor is like dew on the grass."

e. The "f" alliteration is in the original ME.

f. The ME has *rude and the grete steryng*. My translation of "coarse movements" is from ODEE, 412.

g. Certainly an amazing metaphor, unprecedented in Christian literature to my knowledge, that not only characterizes the reader as a "greedy greyhound," suggesting that you not "snatch at the Lord's will," but restrain yourself—as though you didn't want God to know how glad you are to see Him—but subtly suggesting that one can fool God (as a dog might fool its keeper) into not knowing how much one longs for him.

h. The concluding phrase in ME is *that weel were him so*. It is a confusing phrase. Walsh and Cowan omit the phrase altogether; both McCann and Underhill leave it in ME "that well were him so"; Spearing (115) has "and would be glad to have it so."

HERE BEGINS THE FORTY-SIXTH CHAPTER

*An honest teaching on how one should flee these deceptions
and work more with a lightness of spirit than with any
unruliness of body.*

And therefore for the love of God be careful in this Work and do not
strain your heart in your breast too roughly or immoderately—but work
more with a lightness than with any evil brute force.[a] For always the more
lightly, the more humbly and spiritually; and always the more roughly, the
more bodily and beastly.[b] And therefore take care. For surely whatever
beastly heart that presumes to touch the high mountain of this Work will
be driven away with stones.[c] Stones are hard and dry by their nature,
and they hurt sorely where they hit. And surely such rough strainings are
very soon connected to fleshliness and bodily feeling, and very dry from
lacking any dew of grace,[d] and they sorely wound the simple soul and
make it fester in the fantasy fabricated by the Fiends.[e] And therefore be
on guard against this beastly roughness, and teach yourself to love lightly
with a soft and calm demeanor both in body and in soul. And accept the
will of our Lord courteously and humbly, and do not snatch at it hurriedly
like a greedy greyhound (no matter how hungry you are). And as in play
let it be said: I advise that you do what is in you to refrain from the rough
and coarse[f] movements of your spirit—just as though you would not wish
Him to know how glad you would be to see Him and possess Him or be
aware of Him.[g]

Probably you think that this is childishly and playfully spoken. But I
believe that whoever has the grace to do and feel as I say, would notice God
good-naturedly playing with him as the father does with the child, kissing
and embracing, as it would be if it were so.[h]

a. The ME has *certeyn*—literally, "certain." I translate it as "confident" (ODEE, 159).

b. "It would appear from the intimate tone of this passage that the *Cloud* is addressed, as it claims, to one disciple, by a man who enjoys a wide reputation as a spiritual counselor, with many 'spiritual friends in God.' It is equally a 'spiritual letter,' in the accepted sense: having one particular addressee but written in the knowledge that it will become available in the *ex professo* contemplative milieu of the time" (I Walsh, 209). And possible further evidence that the author was indeed a Procurator of lay brothers.

c. "The spiritual knot of burning love" joins the other striking phrases unique to the author of *The Cloud*. Perhaps the most important aspect of the image is not the binding together of the self with God, but the fact that there is no loss of personhood in this binding—while combined, a knot continues to be two distinct ropes.

d. Although it seems odd on the surface, after some thought one can agree with the author that there are definite spiritual (and contemplative) advantages in not parading one's devotion—even before God. It helps keep one humble and it rests on the faith that God already *knows* one's true devotion without having to be overtly shown.

e. Jn. 4:24: "God is spirit: and those who adore him must adore him in spirit and truth."

f. A subtle and interesting note: when one "stretch[es] and strain[s]" one is putting the self farther from God than when one approaches him in tranquility, purity, and spiritual depth. Again the author demonstrates his criticism of an emotional, physical show of devotion—which must be addressing a problem he has seen in his day and age (as do we in ours). One cannot help but be reminded of the devotional extremes of the fourteenth century's Margery Kempe.

g. The author addresses the paradox he has just expressed and explains that he has asked the impossible in order to impress the importance of not mixing the physical with the spiritual or confusing the two.

HERE BEGINS THE FORTY-SEVENTH CHAPTER

A wise teaching on the purity of spirit in this Work, explaining how a soul should show its desire to God in one way, and in the opposite way to humans.

Don't be surprised that I speak so childishly and, as it were, foolishly and lacking in natural discretion, for I do it for fully confident[a] reasons, and since I think I have been directed for many days both to feel this way and think this way and speak this way even to some other of my special friends in God, as I am speaking now to you.[b]

And this is one reason why I bid you hide the desire of your heart from God: because I hope that by such a concealment it would come more clearly to His attention—to your benefit and the fulfilling of your desire—than it would by any other manner of showing I believe you would be able to show. And another reason is this: because I wish by such a concealment to bring you out of the crudeness of *physical* feeling into the purity and depth of *spiritual* feeling, and thus additionally at the end to help you to bind the spiritual knot of burning love[c] between you and your God, in spiritual cohesion and harmony of wills.[d]

You know well that God is a spirit, and whoever would be one-ed to Him must be, in truth and depth of spirit,[e] entirely free of any contrived physical thing. It is true that everything is known by God, and nothing can be hidden from His knowledge—neither a physical nor a spiritual thing. So what is hidden in the depths of one's spirit is known and shown to Him more openly (since it is true that He is a spirit) than is anything that is mixed with any kind of physicality. For every physical thing is farther from God—simply in the course of nature—than any spiritual thing. For this reason it seems that when our desire is mixed with any kind of physicality—as it is when we stretch and strain ourselves in both spirit and body together—just so long is it farther from God than it ought to be if it were done more devoutly and more effectively in tranquility and in purity and in depth of spirit.[f]

And here you can see somewhat and in part the reason that I bid you so childishly to conceal and hide the stirring of your desire from God. And yet I did not bid you wholly to hide it, for that would be the bidding of a fool, because that would be to bid you do wholly what cannot in any way be done. But I bid you do what you can to hide it.[g] And why bid you

a. The author clearly delineates a differentiation between the physical and the spiritual. However, unlike classical dualists or Gnostics, he does not see the physical as evil or malevolent, but merely as an impediment to serious apophatic spiritual growth. It is his commitment that in the highest realms of the contemplative way, every physical impediment or even every memory—be it good or evil—must be cast into the cloud of forgetting and prohibited from contaminating the purely spiritual, non-physical, non-emotional, and non-intellectual activity of the contemplative Work. To put it rather harshly: if one intends to be a reclusive contemplative hermit, one simply cannot feed the hungry and house the homeless—however creditable those pursuits may be for others.

b. Here is another small clue that the author has the expectation that this book will be communicated to other contemplatives as well as to his novice protégé.

c. Even a physical expression or a single external word that endeavors to communicate one's spiritual circumstance—even to Godself—makes the contemplative Work itself "impure."

d. It is interesting that when the author speaks of prayer that breaks out into words, those words are adulation of Jesus rather than of God the Father, since the apophatic contemplative effort is often criticized as involving a "low Christology"—that is, at its rarified height paying relatively little attention to the Incarnation. But we are reminded that the Incarnation, the church, the sacraments, and the Corporal Works of Mercy are all precedent to "the Work"—it is assumed that they have been previously understood and practiced before one begins the contemplative way.

e. An obvious reference to the familiar declaration of Holy Matrimony. The author backsteps slightly from his extreme statements in the previous chapter to make clear that the physical and spiritual are *not* inimical but will be joined eternally in heaven at the last resurrection.

thus? Surely because I want you to cast it into the depths of your spirit, far from any rough interference with any physicality which would make it less spiritual and, to that degree, farther from God—for I am well aware that the more your soul has of spirituality, the less it has of physicality and the nearer it is to God, and the better it pleases Him, and the more clearly it can be seen by Him.[a] (Not that his sight can be at any one time or in respect to any one thing more clear than at another time because it is evermore unchangeable—but because it is more like Him when it is in purity of spirit—for He is a spirit.)

There is another reason why I bid you do what you can to keep Him from knowing: for you and I—and many such as we are[b]—are so able to conceive a thing physically which is spoken spiritually, that possibly if I had bid you show God the stirring of your heart, you would have made some physical display to Him, either in expression or in voice or in word or in some other rough physical exertion as you do when you show something that is hidden in your heart to a physical human—and to that degree your Work would have been impure.[c] For in one manner a thing should be shown to humans, and in another manner to God.

⟋ HERE BEGINS THE FORTY-EIGHTH CHAPTER

How God wishes to be served both with body and with soul,
and rewards us in both; and how we shall know when all
those sounds and sweetness that rise within the body in
the course of prayer are either good or evil.

I say this not because I want you to quit at any time if you are stirred to pray with your lips, or to break out from abundance of devotion in your spirit in order to speak to God as if to a human, and say some good word as you feel yourself stirred, such as "Good Jesus! Fair Jesus! Sweet Jesus!" and any others.[d] No, God forbid you understand it thus! For truly I do not mean it that way. And God forbid that I should separate what God has joined— the body and the spirit—for God wishes to be served with body and with soul, both together—as is seemly—and to give us our reward in bliss both in body and soul.[e]

a. The ME has the *wyndowes of thi wittys*, which one is inclined to leave alone for its literary beauty—except that it would then conflict with the meaning of the sentence. And so *wittys* cannot be "wits" but rather the Old English meaning it still carried in the fourteenth century of "the senses" (ODEE, 1009).

b. These experiences of "comfort" and "sweetness" are gifts from God, arising from within one's spirit (rather than from any external source), and so they should be enjoyed and not held suspect.

c. The author is a churchman of the fourteenth century: i.e., spiritual comforts, sounds, gladness, and sweetness are delivered to us by the actions of angels—either the good angels of heaven or the evil (fallen) angels of hell!

d. There is much speculation about who this nameless "another man" may be. It is apparent that his work is well-known enough that the author feels no need to identify him. Both Hodgson (198 n.) and Walsh (I 213 n.) propose that the book in question is Walter Hilton's *Scale of Perfection*. A marginal note in a mid-fifteenth century manuscript of *The Cloud* (University College, Oxford 14) reads "*hyltons*" (Cowan, 187).

e. The author speaks here with sincere personal interest, not just professional concern. It is likely that he has been with the novice (probably as his Procurator) and has become aware of contemplative growth and development on his part, and now is ready to expand on his earlier instructions.

f. Again the author bids his disciple to pay attention to the "blind, devout, and vigorous stirring of love" without break. Experience is still the best teacher of the contemplative way. One can hark back to the parenthetical expression two paragraphs earlier where the author bids his protégé to follow the advice that he gives "or, better, if you can improve on it"—crediting his student with discovering something of his own way.

g. The ME here is *than I have no doute that it ne wel kun telle thee of hem*. This is an awkward phrase with the strange ME double negative and the dubious pronoun *hem*. I repeated "the sounds and sweetnesses" for clarity.

h. The ME has *astonied*—literally, "astonished," but the sense here is that the protégé may be overwhelmed at first, so I use the synonym "bewildered."

And in anticipation of that reward sometimes He will enflame the body of a devout servant of His here in this life—not once or twice, but possibly very often as He wishes—with very wonderful sweetness and comforts, of which some do not come from outside into the body by the windows of your senses,[a] but from within, rising and springing from an abundance of spiritual joy and true devotion in the spirit. Such a comfort and such a sweetness should not be held suspect, and, to put it briefly, I believe that the one who feels it cannot hold it suspect.[b]

But all such comforts, sounds, and gladness and sweetness that come from *outside* suddenly—and one never knows from whence—I pray you hold them suspect. For they may be either good or evil—wrought by a good angel if they are good and by an evil angel if they are evil.[c] And these can in no way be evil if their deceptions or inquisitiveness of mind and disordered exertions of the physical heart are eliminated, as I taught you (or, better, if you can improve on it). And why is that? Surely because of the cause of this comfort—that is to say, the devout stirring of love that dwells in a pure spirit. It is wrought directly by the hand of Almighty God, and therefore it must always be distant from any delusion or any false judgment that may come to a person in this life.

And about the other comforts and sounds and sweetness and how you should know whether they are good or evil, I think I will not tell you at this time, because I think it unnecessary since you can find it written in another place of another man's work a thousand times better than I can say or write.[d] And so may you find this that I set here far better expressed there than it is here. But what of that? Because of that I shall not desist, nor shall it bother me to fulfill the desire and stirring of your heart that you have demonstrated to me before now through your own words and now in your actions.[e]

But I can say something to you about those sounds and those sweetnesses that come in by the windows of your senses and that may be both good and evil. Devote yourself constantly to this blind, devout, and vigorous stirring of love of which I have been telling you,[f] and then I have no doubt that this will be well able to reveal the sounds and sweetnesses to you.[g] And if you are still partially bewildered[h] by them the first time (and that is because they are strange to you), yet it will do this for you: it will bind your heart so fast that

a.   The author solves the dilemma by assuring his protégé that if he is faithful in his "loving intent to God," the experience will show him which ecstatic dimensions are good and which are bad. This is an accomplished teacher loosening the bands and allowing his student to take tentative steps on his own.

b.   The ME has *substaunce*, which I have translated "essence," and *accidents*, which I have translated "nonessentials." These are technical Scholastic terms that came originally from Aristotle through Thomas Aquinas and whose modern meanings are almost directly opposite to their medieval meanings. "Substance" was the purely *spiritual* aspect of a being that gives it its true nature, and "accidents" were the external *physical* aspects of a being. It is a bit oversimplified, but we might say that the "substance" of a person is the soul and the "accidents" are the body (Gallacher, 77).

c.   It is always a clear sign of maturing spirituality when one stops petitioning God to *change* things and recognizes, accepts, submits, and gladly embraces God's will—no matter what it may be.

d.   This is a crucial sentence, because for the author the human agency that is active in salvation is the will—not the emotions, or the intellect, or tradition, or custom, or practice, or action, but *will*—the element of humanity that makes us human. The will is our human "choosing mechanism"—and the choices we make determine our morality, our fulfillment, and our salvation.

e.   The classic example of perfect submission to God's will: when one can be just as pleased and content to do without any consolations as to have them.

you will not be able in any way to have full confidence in them until they are either verified for you inwardly and wonderfully by the spirit of God, or else externally by the counsel of some discrete spiritual father.[a]

⮸   HERE BEGINS THE FORTY-NINTH CHAPTER

The essence of all perfection is nothing else but a good will; and how all sounds, comforts, and sweetness that may fall into this life is to it only as it were non-essentials.[b]

And therefore I beg you, incline eagerly toward this humble stirring of love in your heart and follow after it, for it will be your guide in this life and bring you to bliss in the other life. It is the essence of all good living and without it no good work can be undertaken or concluded. It is really nothing more than a good will in agreement with God, and a kind of full satisfaction and gladness that you sense in your will about everything God does.[c]

Such a clear will is the essence of all perfection.[d] All sweetness and comforts, physical or spiritual, compared to this are only, as it were, nonessentials— no matter how holy they may be; and they all depend on this clear will. I call them "nonessentials" for they may be either present or absent without shattering the good will. (I mean in this life, for it is not so in the bliss of heaven, for there shall they be one-ed with the essence without distinction, as shall the body in which they work be one-ed with the soul. So the essence of them here is nothing but a good will. And surely I believe that for the person who experiences the perfection of this will (as far as it may be so here) there can be no sweetness nor any comfort which can come to anyone in this life unless one is as willing and as glad to do without it as to sense it and have it, if that is God's will.[e]

a. The ME has *sensible*—but this is always a difficult translation because in common use today "sensible" almost exclusively means "reasonable" instead of its original meaning "able to be sensed"—as applies here. Hence "tangible" (after Cowan, 192).

b. This is the first time the author has spoken of "weepings" as part of one's consolations—referring to the traditional "gift of tears." Saint Augustine: "Inflame my soul with the fire you cast upon the earth, and willed it be kindled, so that with welling tears I may offer you daily the sacrifice of an afflicted spirit, and a contrite heart" (*Book of Meditations* 1. 36.930). On April 2, 2013, in a homily, Pope Francis said: "We too can ask the Lord for the gift of tears…. It is a beautiful grace … to weep praying for everything: for what is good, for our sins, for graces, for joy itself" (Catholic News Agency, April 3, 2013).

c. A strong caution: one can be tempted to love God only because of the blessings and consolations received. This needs to be guarded against strongly because the temptation is very great (and very common) to replace Godself with consolations and good feelings.

d. We see here a typical example of one of the author's frequent pedagogical methods: he will make a bold, unqualified, and categorical statement—and then very gently back off with a reasonable qualification or two. Here he proceeds to describe (1) those who truly *need* spiritual consolation, (2) those who are too physically weak to do penances, and (3) those who are strong enough to do without many spiritual gifts and solaces.

e. It should be particularly noted that the author recognizes that for those who are physically unable to do strong penances, the Lord intervenes and cleanses their souls *without penance* but with "sweet feelings and weeping." Here the "gift of tears" is seen as a kind of ersatz penance for those who can't fast or endure physical stress.

f. The ME has *thei kun pike him counforte inowgh*. The word *pike* is rare and is the etymological source of the modern word "pitch"—as in "pitch a tent."

⟋ HERE BEGINS THE FIFTIETH CHAPTER

What chaste love is, and how in some creatures such
tangible[a] comforts are only rare and in others quite frequent.

And by this you can see that we ought to direct all our attention on this humble stirring of love in our will. And regarding all other sweetness and consolations, physical or spiritual, may they be never so pleasant nor so holy (if it is courteous and seemly to speak thus) that we should not adopt a kind of indifference. If they come, welcome them, but do not rely too much on them for fear of weakness, for it will require all of your willpower to remain any length of time in such sweet feelings and weepings.[b] And perhaps you might be moved to love God simply for their sake.[c] And you will sense that by whether you complain excessively when they are absent—and if it is so, your love is not yet either chaste or perfect. For a love that is chaste and perfect—although it allows that the body be fed and comforted by the presence of such sweet feelings and weepings—it does not complain but is entirely content to do without these comforts, if that is God's will.

And yet such sweet comforts are not usually lacking in some creatures and in some other creatures such sweetness and comforts are only infrequent. And all this is according to the disposition and the ordinance of God, all depending on the benefit and needs of various creatures.[d] For some creatures are so weak and delicate in spirit that unless they are somewhat comforted by the feelings of such sweetness, they could in no way tolerate or bear the diversity of temptations and tribulations that they endure and are burdened with in this life from their physical and spiritual enemies. And some there are who are so weak in body that they can do no great penance with which to cleanse themselves. And these creatures our Lord cleanses most graciously in spirit by such sweet feelings and weepings.[e] And also, on the other hand, there are some creatures so strong in spirit that they can raise[f] for themselves enough comfort within their souls by offering up this reverent and humble stirring of love and submission of will, so that they do not much need to be fed with such sweet comforts in physical feelings. And which of these is holier or more precious to God, one more than another, God knows and I do not.

a. The author starts with a first line similar to the one he used in chapter 49.

b. Once again our author places his emphasis on the action of the *will*! For him an act of the will supersedes all other spiritual activity on the part of a human being. One must indeed understand that there is nothing one can do which will *earn* salvation, but there is one thing one must do to *gain* that salvation: and that is to *will* it—to *want* it—since even God cannot force salvation upon an *un*-willing human. For the author the will is the core implement of the spiritual life—beyond all affect, all emotion, all ecstasy, all intellect, all wisdom, and all ascetical practice. It is the will that mounts the "naked intent unto God." It is into our will that God puts the "blind stirring of love." It is an act of will that puts our past beneath the cloud of forgetting, and it is an act of will that sends our piercing "lance of longing love" into the cloud of unknowing.

c. The author is not creating a paper tiger here, as it may seem. The confusion between the physical and the spiritual is a universal problem and one that often occurs in the devout Christian spirit unknowingly.

d. The "within" and the "above" in this sentence are the references to "in" and "up" mentioned in the epigraph. "These represent spatial determinants which, while marvelous for geography, have little place in the contemplative work" (Cowan, 196).

e. It is curious that the author changes at this point from the singular *he* to the plural *thei* for the rest of this sentence. I have maintained the singular simply for grammatical consistency.

f. The ME has *hid things*. Hodgson (109) convincingly translates it as "mystical."

⤳ HERE BEGINS THE FIFTY-FIRST CHAPTER

That people should have great caution so that they do not understand something as physical that is meant spiritually—and namely, that it is good to be careful in understanding the word "in" and the word "up."

So therefore incline humbly to this blind stirring of love in your heart[a]—I mean not in your bodily heart, but in your spiritual heart, that is, your will.[b] And take great care that you not consider physically that which is spoken spiritually. For truly I tell you that the physical and fleshly fantasies of those who have eager and imaginative wits are the cause of much error.

You can see an example of this in that I bade you hide your desire from God insofar as you could. For, perhaps if I had bidden you to show your desire to God, you would have thought of it more physically than you would when I bade you hide it. For you know well that everything that is hidden is cast into the depths of the spirit.

And thus I think that it is necessary to have great caution in understanding words that are spoken with spiritual intent so that you do not consider them physically, but spiritually, as they are meant.[c] And specifically, it is good to be careful with the word "in" and the word "up," for on the misconception of these two words depends much error and much duplicity in those who intend themselves to be spiritual workers—as it seems to me. I know this partly by experience, and partly by hearsay, and I think I will tell you a little about these frauds.

A young disciple in God's school, newly converted from the world, who supposes that for the short time he has given himself to penance and to prayer and following advice in Confession, that he is therefore able to take upon himself these spiritual exercises which he hears men speak of or reads about or possibly reads himself. Therefore when he reads or hears words about spiritual exercises—and namely of this word: how a man should especially draw all his wits *within* himself or how he shall climb *above* himself[d]—immediately, through blindness of soul and sensuality and natural inquisitiveness of the senses, he[e] misunderstands these words and supposes that because he finds in himself a natural longing for mystical[f] things that he

a. The greatest possible danger in serious contemplative Work is that one disengage or disconnect from a competent spiritual director. The contemplative Work is so intensely internal that one almost inevitably loses all sense of perspective and context, so it is absolutely essential that one be led by a competent and experienced spiritual director who understands "the Work" but can also observe the directee from a necessary spiritual distance. Indeed, it is that perspective and that context—in addition to regular fulfillment of one's ecclesiastical responsibilities (i.e., attending Mass regularly, reciting the Offices, etc.)—that keeps the Work from driving one mad.

b. The deep sorrow here is that the young novice described in the author's example is a very good person, who entirely means well, is truly devout, and sincerely longs for perfect union with God—but has lost his bearings in the wide dark sea of contemplation.

c. "Paradoxically, it is the great longing for God which placed the young disciple in danger" (Cowan, 198).

d. There are at least two records (noted elsewhere) of contemplative novices developing mental illness.

e. "God gives to contemplatives grace sufficient to perform the work to which they have been called. Proper contemplation is, for them, natural; it occurs within the scope of God's purpose for that soul. The human body is not, however, designed to accommodate the kinds of stress which would be imposed upon it by unnatural contemplation—the turning of *theire bodily wittes inwards*" (Cowan, 200). Probably criticism of Richard Rolle's teaching.

f. The ME has *thei turne here brayne in her hedes.* Johnston (115) has "he does violence to his nature and drives his imagination so mercilessly with this stupidity that eventually his mind snaps." A very powerful image!

g. "But sometimes 'miracle' can be taken in a broad sense, for anything that exceeds human power and comprehension. And so demons can work 'miracles,' that is, things that rouse man's astonishment, because they are beyond his power and outside his sphere of knowledge … [It] can occur from within, to the degree that the demon is able to affect a man's imagination or even his bodily senses in such a way that … something appears to be other than it really is" (Aquinas, *Summa Theologica* 1.114.4.5). Likely more criticisms of Rolle.

is therefore called to that Work by grace, to such a degree that if a spiritual director will not agree that he should undertake this Work, immediately he feels some kind of grudge against his director, and believes—yea, and possibly even says to others like himself—that he can find no one that can understand what he means completely.[a] And so, right away, because of arrogance and the presumption of his eager wit, he abandons humble prayer and penance too early and sets himself (so he thinks) to a full spiritual Work within his soul[b]—which Work, if it is actually undertaken, is neither physical work nor spiritual exercise. And, to be brief, it is an unnatural exercise and the devil is the chief worker of it.[c] And it is the quickest way to death of body and of soul, for it is madness and not wisdom, and leads a person even to insanity.[d] And yet that young disciple does not think like this, because he means to offer himself in this Work to think on nothing except God.

❧ HERE BEGINS THE FIFTY-SECOND CHAPTER

How these young, presumptuous disciples misunderstand the word "in," and of the delusions that follow from that.

And here is how this kind of madness that I speak of occurs: they read and hear it often said that they should leave off working with their senses and work inwardly—and because they do not know what inward working is, therefore they work wrongly. For they turn their bodily senses inward to their bodies against the order of nature, and strain themselves as if they could see inward with their bodily eyes, and hear inward with their ears, and so forth with all their senses—smelling, tasting, and touching inward.[e] And thus they reverse themselves against the order of nature, and with this curiosity they burden their imagination so recklessly that finally they turn their brains inside out in their heads.[f] And then immediately the devil has power to concoct some false lights or sounds, sweet smells in their noses, astonishing tastes in their mouths, and many strange fervors and burnings in their physical breasts or in their bowels, in their backs and in their loins, and in their private parts.[g]

And yet in this fantasy they think that they have a restful thought of their God without any hindrance of vain thoughts. And surely so have they, in

a. Those who have undertaken this "false contemplation" may think they have attained "a restful thought of their God"—because the devil who has initiated this false spirituality is not going to hinder their confusion or misunderstanding. So, paradoxically, if one *feels* great comfort and restfulness, with no apparent threat or hindrance, it may well be that one has been deceived by the devil, who is providing those sensations. In a way characterized by C. S. Lewis's "Wormwood" in his *The Screwtape Letters*, the devil would be quite content for the pray-er to think about God—so that then the devil would not be noticed (cited by Cowan, 202).

b. The ME has *sturdy scheep betyn in the heed.* The reference is to a brain disease of sheep that causes them to run in circles. McCann and Cowan appropriately translate *sturdy* as "giddy," but most others translated *betyn* as some form of "beaten" instead of "bitten"—i.e., "bitten by an insect/ worm in the head" that causes the disease. Walsh (I 222) describes it as "vertigo in sheep caused by a tapeworm in the brain." ODEE (878) describes it as a "stupefying brain disease in cattle." Since *The Cloud* was written in sheep-farming country the image was probably very familiar.

c. The ME has *Som pipyn when thei schuld speke as ther were no spirit in theire bodies*—possible translation: "Some play a pipe when they should speak, as though there were no vital power in their bodies" (ODEE, 683). Johnston (116) offers an interesting broad translation: "Others, like ghosts, utter shrill, piping sounds that are supposed to pass for speech." In the Middle Ages, piping was often considered sounds made by demons (Connor, ix–xvi).

d. Cowan (204) perceptively recognizes that "hypocrite" comes from the Greek *hypokrites* and means "a stage actor" who "would be expected to change his voice to suit a part."

e. Proverbs 6:12–14: "A renegade man, a useless man, saunters with a malformed mouth, blinks with his eyes, drags his foot, speaks with his finger; with a wicked heart he concocts evil, and always sows discord."

f. The ME has *brest oute in som partye.* It has been translated variously, but the important sense is that some violence occurs when a fraud is confronted.

g. "One modern parallel which might be drawn are certain pentecostal groups which make glossolalia the benchmark by which one's faith, indeed one's Christianity (and by either implication or explication, one's salvation) is measured" (Cowan, 205).

a way, because they are so filled with falsehood that vanity cannot disturb them. And why? Because he—the same Fiend that ought to deliver vain thoughts to them if they were in a good way, he, the same—is the author of this Work.[a] And you know right well that he does not wish to hinder himself. He will not put from them the thought of God for fear that it might be noticed and he would be suspected.

⮌ HERE BEGINS THE FIFTY-THIRD CHAPTER

Of various inappropriate behaviors that pursue those who are deprived of the Work of this book.

Many astounding behaviors pursue those who are deceived by this false work, or in any variety of it, compared with those who are God's true disciples—for they are always wholly appropriate in all their behaviors, physically or spiritually. But it is not so of these others, for whoever would or could observe them where they sit during this time, if their eyelids were open, he would see them staring as though they were insane, and laughingly staring as though they saw the devil. Surely it is good that they are thus aware, for the Fiend is not far away. Some set their eyes in their heads as if they were giddy sheep bitten on the head[b] and like as though they would die soon. Some hang their heads to one side as though a worm were in their ears. Some squeak when they ought to speak,[c] just as if there were no vitality in their bodies (and this is the ordinary situation of an actor on stage).[d] Some cry and whine in their throat because they are so greedy and hasty to say what they think (and this is the condition of heretics and of those who with presumption and aberration of mind will always sustain error).[e]

Many extravagant and unseemly behaviors follow on this error: anyone could notice them all. Nevertheless, there are some that are so peculiar that they can refrain themselves in great part when they come before others. But were these to be seen in a place where they feel at home, then I swear that they could not be hidden. And still I believe that if anyone were to contradict their opinion, they would see them burst out in some way;[f] and yet they think that everything they ever do is for the love of God and to maintain the truth.[g] Now truly I expect that unless God shows

a. Of course, for the medieval mind, insanity was a certain sign of inhabitance by the devil. "There is no bodily infirmity, not even leprosy or epilepsy, which cannot be caused by witches" (Sprenger and Kramer, *Malleus Maleficarum* [London, The Folio Society; reprint 1969], 115; originally published 1486).

b. It is plain that the author is confused here—the two preceding sentences seem to contradict each other.

c. The ME has *rowyn*—literally, "row" (Mayhew, 191).

d. The ME has *gigelotes*. Gallacher (81) translates this as "flirts." Walsh (I 223) has "girlish gossips." McCann (73) has "giddy girls." Johnston (116) has "giddy school girls." ODEE, 397 has "wanton woman; giddy girl."

e. The ME has *nice japing jogelers*—literally, "wanton/foolish/stupid jesting jugglers/buffoons" (Gallacher, 81). It is interesting to note that the word *nice* has virtually reversed its meaning since the fourteenth century.

f. All of these odd behaviors are not merely from the mind of the author. Although this quotation is from a later date, it reflects the social attitudes of the author's century as well: "For there was neither devil nor urchin nor Elfe but themselves, who did metamorphoze themselves in every scene into the person eyther of the devil himselfe or of his Interpreter; and made the devils name their Puppet, to squeak, pipe, and fume out what they pleased to inspire" (Harsnett, Samuel; *Declaration of Egregious Popish Impostures*; [James Roberts; London; 1603]; reprinted in F. W. Brownlow, *Shakespeare, Harsnett, and the Devils of Denham* [Associated Univ. Press, Plainsboro, NJ, 1996]). The following from an ancient Irish folk tale: "Cries on the air—whirring and wailing and whining, hurtling in as though from a distance and then abruptly borne away as if by a fierce gust of wind: howls, growls, grumbles, snarls, shrieks, grunts rent the air; piping squeaks such as bats might make, rasping noises as of two stones being ground against one another; sounds like something splitting apart" (*Con, Cliona, and the Demon: A Tale from Cork of Oldentime*, 53 [accessed September 2, 2013, at http://tinyurl.com/ogucgwm]).

His merciful miracle to make them soon stop, they shall love God so long in this manner that they shall go stark raving mad to the devil.[a] I do not say that the devil has so perfect a servant in this life that is diseased and infected with *all* these fantasies that I mention here. Yet at the same time it *may* be that one—yea, and many a one—is infected with them all.[b] But what I do say here is that the devil has no perfect hypocrite or heretic on earth who is not guilty of some that I have mentioned (or will mention, if God allows). For some are so burdened with wanton and queer behaviors in their physical bearings that when they want to listen to something, they writhe their heads to one side and raise their chins; they gape with their mouths as if they could hear with them instead of with their ears. Some, when they ought to speak, point with their fingers, or on their fingers, or on their own breasts or on theirs to whom they speak. Some can neither sit still, stand still, nor lie still unless they are swinging their feet or doing something with their hands. Some flail[c] with their arms in time with their speaking (as one would need to do in order to swim over a great water). Some are endlessly smiling and laughing at each other words that they speak as if they were giddy girls[d] and foolish, jesting buffoons[e] who don't know how to behave.[f] Far more seemly would be a sober and demure comportment of the body and a cheerfulness in manner.

I do not say that all these unseemly behaviors are great sins in themselves, nor yet that all those who do them are great sinners themselves, but do I say that if these unseemly and inordinate behaviors control the person that does them so that he cannot stop them when he will, then I say that they are tokens of pride and aberration of mind and of unfitting posturing and a hankering for erudition. And especially they are truly tokens of instability of heart and mental restlessness, and, specifically, a lack of the disciplines described in this book. And this is only the reason why I have put so many of these deceits here in this writing—because a spiritual worker shall be able to test his work by them.

a. "The human spirit walking through the journeys of the contemplative life shall be made beautiful in face." (Rudolph of Biberach, *De Septem Itineribus Aeternitatis* 2:5, cited and translated by Gallacher, 125).

b. Another instance of the author changing from singular to plural in mid-sentence—from *hym* to *hem*—which often happens when he makes a point of inclusion: *man or woman*.

c. This is the first suggestion that there may even be a mild evangelistic nature to the contemplative way—i.e., others would witness the changes in the practitioner and could be drawn to follow the same regimen.

d. The ME has *fire*—literally, "fire" but more commonly used in the fourteenth century to imply "heat of fever" or "passion" (ODEE, 357).

e. The ME has *frute*—literally, "fruit" or "produce" or "product" (ODEE, 379).

f. The ME has *pipynge*—literally, "piping" or "squeaking" (MED). It was commonly used to describe the sound of peeping or cheeping birds, so I have here translated it as "twittering," which also captures the fluttery chattering of busybodies.

g. The ME has *spekyng how they mowe stuffe hem and underput hem. Stuff hem* translates as "reinforce themselves" and *underput* as "support"—I have used "undergird" (Gallacher, 82).

h. The ME has *countenances of devocion*—literally, "face" or "demeanor" or "appearance of devotion" (ODEE, 220).

i. Hodgson (200) notes that the ME word *voided* used here "contains the idea of an unpleasant discharge, and was used in the late fourteenth century with the meaning of 'to spit forth poison' or 'to vomit.'"

j. The author reaches the limits of his toleration with the behavior of the counterfeit contemplatives. This exclamation is a very personal interjection that demonstrates his private exasperation with the frauds.

⤳ HERE BEGINS THE FIFTY-FOURTH CHAPTER

How that by virtue of this Work one is governed very
wisely and made very becoming, in body as well as in soul.

Whoever is engaged in this Work, it ought to govern him very suitably, in body as well as in soul, and make him wholly attractive to every man or woman who looks upon him[a]—to such a degree that the ugliest man or woman that lives this life, if they[b] were to come by grace to practice this Work, their features would rapidly and graciously be changed so that every good person that saw them would be glad and rejoice to have them in their company, and would totally consider themselves spiritually satisfied and guided by grace to God by their very presence.

So obtain this gift—whoever can get it by grace—for whoever has it truly shall well be able to govern himself and all that is his by the power of it. He should easily recognize, if need be, all natures and all dispositions. He should well adapt himself to all who talk with him—whether they are habitual sinners or sinless—yet he would be without sin in himself. To the wonder of all who saw him, and by the help of grace, he would attract others to the Work of that same spirit in which he engages himself.[c]

His looks and his words should be full of spiritual wisdom, full of passion[d] and of results,[e] spoken in solemn truthfulness, without any falsehood, far from any pretense or the twittering[f] of hypocrites. For some there are who with all their might—inner and outer—strive in their speaking to reinforce themselves and undergird themselves[g] on every side (to keep from falling) with many lowly, twittering words and appearances[h] of devotion—trying more to appear holy in the eyes of others than to be truly so in the sight of God and His angels. These people will make more allegations and more grief over a disturbed appearance or unseemly or unbecoming word spoken before people than they will for a thousand idle thoughts and stinking stirrings of sin purposely drawn upon themselves or recklessly vomited forth[i] in the sight of God and the saints and angels in heaven. Ah, Lord God![j] Whether or not there is as much pride within them while such humble twittering words are so plenteous without, I agree that it is becoming and seemly for those who are humble within to show humble and seemly words and appearance without—according to the humility that

a. When a close friend of mine had just professed solemn vows as a monk, I asked him, "What was the last thing you thought of before committing yourself for life to this monastery?" He replied, "Can I tolerate the way Brother Wilfred sings for the rest of my life?" That may sound petty to anyone outside a monastic community, but when one is exposed to such a vexing thing several times daily for a lifetime, it can become a serious irritant. It is clear that the author has had just this kind of experience with people using what we sometimes now call "stained glass voices"—false, unnatural, affected pronunciation and resonance.

b. The ME has *boystous* that usually means "loud" or "rough," but there is a less common meaning of "booming" or "low"—related to *boiste* that means "box" or "coffin"—i.e., a voice speaking in a box (Mossé, 430).

c. The ME has *pipyng*. Wolters (126) has "bleating," which I have followed.

d. The ME has *sely soule*, which usually means "silly" or "simple" soul. McCann (74) suggests "poor, unfortunate, pitiable, *misera anima*."

e. The ME has *sorow* that can translate as "sorrow," but the sense here is a deeper problem than mere sadness, so "distress" or "trouble" (ODEE, 847) seems a more appropriate translation.

f. Cowan (212) provides an appealing description: "This is, as it were, the 'I-have-something-to-tell-you-in-love' chapter."

g. In the fourteenth century, the ME word *feend* ("fiend") inevitably referred to the devil (ODEE, 354)—hence my capitalization of the word. In later years it applied more broadly to any demon or evil spirit.

h. "The devil is very wise: he will never say, 'Be evil!' In almost every instance he will say, 'Be good—but not *too* good'" (unpublished sermon by Edward Caldwell Lewis, ca. 1949).

i. "Prelates" are high-ranking ecclesiastical officials. The ME for the adjective is *besy*—literally, "curiously or officiously active" (ODEE, 130)—a definite derogatory implication which I meant to catch in "bustling."

j. The *cura animarum* ("cure of souls" or "care of souls") has been used since the fourth century to describe the responsibilities of a parish priest. The word *curate* drives from the term. The author may be referring to the wandering self-described "holy men" who exploited simple and trusting people. There was also a problem of wandering Franciscan friars who preached in the open and drew people away from their parish churches.

k. We all recognize this person who delights in pointing out someone else's faults—always "for your own good."

is within the heart. But I do not declare that those words should then be flaunted in cracked or piping voices, contrary to the clear natural voice that speaks them.[a] And if one who has a clear and true low[b] natural voice speaks poorly and pipingly—I mean unless he is sick in body or else that it is between him and his God or his confessor—then it is a true evidence of hypocrisy, whether the hypocrite is young or old.

And what more should I say about these poisonous deceptions? I truly believe that unless these people have the grace to leave off such bleating[c] hypocrisy, in between that private pride in their hearts within and such humble words without, the pitiable[d] soul can very soon sink into trouble.[e]

☜ HERE BEGINS THE FIFTY-FIFTH CHAPTER

How those who follow the zeal of spirit in condemning sin without discretion are deceived.[f]

The Fiend[g] will deceive some this way: very surprisingly he will enflame their brains to maintain God's law and to obliterate sin in all others. He will never tempt them with a thing that is obviously evil.[h] He makes them like bustling prelates[i] watching over every last degree of Christian lives—as an abbot over his monks. They will condemn all others for their faults, just as if they had responsibility for the care of their souls.[j] And yet they think that they dare not do anything else for God's sake. But they tell them their faults that they see—and they say that they are led to do that by the fire of charity and of God's love in their hearts. But truly they are lying, for it is rather with the fire of hell welling up in their brains and in their imaginations.[k]

That this is the truth is shown by the following: the devil is a spirit, and by his own nature, he has no body any more than does an angel. And yet, whenever he or an angel shall take some body (by God's permission) to undertake some ministry to someone in this life—appropriate for the ministry that he shall undertake—thereafter the character of that body retains his appearance to some degree. We have an example of this in Holy Writ: whenever an angel was sent in bodily form in the Old Testament (and in the New also) it was always shown—either by his name or by some

a. "Just as in Sacred Scripture, the properties of intelligible things are described in the likeness of material things" (Aquinas, *Summa Theologica* 1.51.2.2).

b. Etymology: *necro-* is "black"; *-mancy* is "divination" (ODEE, 605, 550).

c. Although the church had consistently "forbidden magical practices to Christians," this was commonly discarded at a popular level and "the growing interest in science led to an increase in the amount of magic practiced and discussed" (Benedicta Ward, 9).

d. The lamprey eel (hagfish)—snakelike (demonic?)—has a single nostril. And the ancient Scottish folklore figure—the *bean nighe*—comes from hell, has webbed feet, one tooth, and also has a single nostril. Gregory the Great, in his exegesis of Job, mentions that the sperm whale has one nostril and is a symbol of the demonic (Green, 26).

e. It seems strange to modern readers that someone as obviously intellectually gifted as the author should be embracing such primitive ideas—but he was very much a man of his time, and magic was common.

f. The ME has *staunson*—literally, "an upright bar, prop, or support" (ODEE, 862). Johnston, McCann, Spearing, Walsh, and Wolters all have "division" or "division in the nose"; Cowan has "septum"; Gallacher has "membrane separating the nostrils, septum." It is an apparently very rare use of the word.

g. It is unusual that the author apparently uses the presence of the nose's septum as a metaphor for discretion or prudence—with two nostrils one can discern what one could not discern with only one. The metaphor seems to carry the idea that one can "smell out" the good and evil and tell the difference. And such discretion precedes the judgment of the will. A possible source: "what is meant by the nose except the prophetic discretion of the saints" (Gregory the Great, *Moralia in Job*, Job 39:25).

h. The author connects "brain" and "imagination" whereas modern use tends to make the connection between "brain" and "reason." It is likely that the author sees "mind" and "reason" as immaterial and so not related to "brain."

measure or aspect of his body—what his spiritual purpose or message was.[a] In the same manner it happens for the Fiend, for when he appears bodily, he betrays in some aspect of his body what his servants are spiritually.

An example of this can be seen in a single instance instead of all these others: for as I have conceived by some disciples of necromancy[b] which has in it the science of making invocation of evil spirits,[c] and by some to whom the Fiend has appeared in bodily likeness, that in whatever likeness the Fiend appears, he always has only one nostril[d]—and that is great and wide. And he will gladly lift it up so that one can see up it to his brain within his head—which is nothing but the fire of hell, for the Fiend could have no other brain. And he values nothing more than if he could make someone look at it, for by that looking one would lose his wits for ever. But a perfect apprentice of necromancy knows this well enough and can well plan for it, so that it does not harm him.[e]

This is why I say (and have said) that whenever the devil takes a body, he betrays in some aspect of his body what his servants are spiritually, for he so enflames the imagination of his contemplatives with the fire of hell that suddenly, without good judgment, they spew out their bizarre opinions, and without any forethought they take it upon themselves at once to point the finger at other people's faults. And this is because they have only one spiritual nostril. The fleshy division[f] in a person's nose which separates one nostril from the other signifies that a person would have spiritual discretion[g] and be able to discern the good from the evil, and the evil from the worse, and the good from the better, before he gives any judgment of anything he has heard or seen or was spoken around him. And by a person's brain is spiritually understood the imagination—for naturally it dwells and works in the head.[h]

a. The author has cautioned against "necromancy and spiritualism as one kind of spiritual deceit to which the unwary contemplative may succumb, the subject of this chapter—heresy—represents quite another" (Cowan, 217).

b. The ME has *letterly kunnyng*—literally, "learned wisdom." It wasn't until the sixteenth century that "cunning" came to mean "sly" or "crafty" (ODEE, 235). Another dig the author takes at formal "scholarship" and its presumptions.

c. The author sees the advantage of commitment to the church's formal doctrines and practice as a protection and restraint against the error that can arise from one's own pride, curiosity, and unguided erudite knowledge.

d. Hodgson (200) perceptibly suggests that this may be an "indirect reference" to the followers of John Wycliff and the Lollards, who were beginning to be noticed in England by the latter half of the fourteenth century when this book was written. They preached against fasting, confession, pilgrimages, monasticism, and many of the church's rules, rituals, and practices.

e. The reference is probably to Matt. 7:13–14: "Enter through the narrow gate: for wide is the gate and broad the road that leads to destruction, and many there are who go in through it. How narrow the gate and restricted the road that leads to life: and few there are who find it."

f. The author spares no invective against these self-indulgent, decadent heretics. It is also very clear that he has some specific individuals in mind and his vituperation is not merely theoretical—almost certainly the Lollards and also the followers of his fellow writer Richard Rolle (who promoted emotion, bodily warmth, music, and ecstatic joy as signs of spiritual validity) or John of Gaunt, who lived with a concubine while supporting Lollardy (McKisack, May; *The Fourteenth Century* [Clarendon; Oxford; 1959], 393).

g. Even the author realizes he has let himself stray a bit in his polemic and now calls himself and his readers back to the subject at hand!

h. A quote from the *Sursum Corda* that introduces the consecration prayer of the Mass: *Priest*: "Lift up your hearts"; *Response*: "We lift them up to the Lord."

HERE BEGINS THE FIFTY-SIXTH CHAPTER

How they are deceived who depend more on the novelty of
natural wit or on scholars trained in worldly schools
than on the common doctrine and counsel of Holy Church.[a]

There are some who, although they are not deceived by this error I have mentioned here, yet because of pride and the curiosity of natural wit and scholarly learning[b] they still depart from the common doctrine and counsel of Holy Church.[c] And these with all their followers depend too much on their own knowledge. And because they are never grounded in this humble blind sense and virtuous living, they deserve to have a false feeling, invented and produced by the spiritual Enemy—to such a degree that finally they burst out and blaspheme all the saints, sacraments, statutes, and ordinance of Holy Church. Carnal worldly people who think the statutes of Holy Church too strict to amend their lives by show a preference for these heretics very promptly and very easily and defend them steadfastly, all because they think they will lead them on an easier way than is ordained by Holy Church.[d]

Now truly I believe that whoever will not walk the difficult way to heaven shall go the easy way to hell—each person must put himself to the test.[e] For I believe if all such heretics and all their followers would plainly be seen as they shall be on Judgment Day, they would immediately be seen to be privately weighed down by great and repulsive sins of the world and their foul flesh—even without their obvious presumption in preserving error. So they are full properly called "disciples of Antichrist," for it is said of them that for all their misleading behavior in public, yet in private they are filthy lechers.[f]

HERE BEGINS THE FIFTY-SEVENTH CHAPTER

How these young presumptuous disciples misunderstand this
other word "up"; and of the deception that follows from this.

Now, no more of this at this time, but on with our subject:[g] how these young presumptuous spiritual disciples misunderstand this other word "up." For if it should happen that they either read or hear read or spoken how people should lift up their hearts to God,[h] right off they peer up at the

a. From Richard Rolle († 1349): "he has mirth and joy and melody in angels' song" and "your thought shall all be on Jesus, and so shall be received above all earthly things, above the firmament and the stars, so that the eye of the heart may look into heaven." Our author is trying to counter a literalist interpretation of Rolle's words (*Ego Dormio*, cited in Hodgson, 200).

b. The author is concerned about those who tend to take spiritual matters in a purely physical sense—and who tend to apply to God, the angels, and saints entirely worldly dimensions and aspects. The problem is not unknown in our own day when God is often spoken of as a big invisible human being.

c. "The Blessed Sacrament is commonly referred to as the 'food of angels' as in the Corpus Christi sequence *Lauda Sion* by St. Thomas Aquinas" (I Clark, 195). And from Ps. 77:25 [78:25]:"Man ate the bread of angels: [God] sent them provisions in abundance"; and Wisd. 16:20: "you gave your people the food of angels and without labor, you supplied them with bread from heaven."

d. An obvious reference to Num. 11:4–9: "And the mixed multitude of people … burned with desire, sitting and weeping, and said, 'Who shall give us flesh to eat? … Our soul is dry, our eyes see nothing except manna.' Now the manna was like coriander seed, of the color of resin. The people went around gathering it, ground it in mills or pounded it in a mortar, and boiled it in a pot, and made cakes of it with the taste like oiled bread. And when the dew fell around the camp at night, the manna also fell with it."

e. Conceivably a literal interpretation of Ps. 50:17 [51:16]: "Lord, open my lips and my mouth will announce your praise"; or Ps. 80:11 [81:10b]: "I am the Lord your God who brought you out of the land of Egypt: open your mouth wide and I will fill it." The Hebrew name for the devil—*Beelzebul*—means "Lord of the Flies."

f. The legend of Saint Martin of Tours († 397) tells of his cutting his cloak in half and giving half to a poor freezing beggar, only to be visited in a dream by the image of Jesus in heaven wearing the half-cloak he had given to the beggar.

g. Saint Stephen was the first Christian martyr. He was stoned to death, and as he was dying, he said: "Look! I see heaven open and the Son of Man standing on the right hand of God!" (Acts 7:55).

stars as though they wished they were above the moon and they listen as though they might hear some angels singing out of heaven.[a] These people would sometimes, with the curiosity of their imagination, pierce the planets and make a hole in the firmament to look through. These people would construct a God as they like—and dress him richly in vestments and set him on a throne far more elaborately than ever He was depicted in paintings on this earth. These people would fabricate angels in bodily likeness, and provide each one with a different musical instrument—far more remarkable than ever as any seen or heard of in this life.[b]

Some of these people the devil will deceive brilliantly. For he will send a kind of dew—angels' food they imagine it is[c]—coming, as it were, out of the air, and softly and sweetly falling into their mouths;[d] and therefore they will take up the habit of sitting with their mouths open as if they were catching flies.[e] Now truly all this is nothing but delusion, no matter how holy it may seem, for at the time they have souls entirely void of any true devotion. Much vanity and falsehood is in their hearts, caused by their bizarre activities, so much so that often the devil produces strange sounds in their ears, peculiar lights and shining in their eyes, and amazing smells in their noses—and all of it is nothing but fabrication.

And yet they do not know it as such, for they think that they have an example of the "upward looking and worshiping" in Saint Martin who by revelation saw God clad in his cloak "up" among his angels[f]—or of Saint Stephen who saw our Lord standing "up" in heaven[g]—and of many others—and even of Christ who ascended bodily "up" into heaven, in the sight of his disciples. And therefore these people say that we should cast our eyes upward. I fully admit that in our bodily observance we should lift up our eyes and our hands if we are moved in spirit, but I say that the Work of our spirit should not be directed either upward or downward nor to one side or another, nor forward or backward—since that would

a. The author's innate neo-Platonism shows—he seriously distrusts and has misgivings about the physical and material—and considers those who depend on the material dimension to be spiritually immature.

b. The phrase is reminiscent of Julian of Norwich's *Revelations of Divine Love* when she refers thirty times to "those who shall be saved" (I Julian, 93 and throughout).

c. "Truly I tell you, as much as you did to one of the least of these my brothers you did to me" (Matt. 25:40); and also "and I live no more, but it is Christ who lives in me" (Gal. 2:20).

d. The ME has *pike* from the verb *picken*—literally, "steal," "peck," or "pick" (Bradley, 474–75).

e. The ME has *kyrnel*—literally, "kernel" (ODEE, 504), but I follow Johnston (123) with "sweet fruit" because it makes a better contrast to "rough husk." In translating Guido II's *Ladder of Four Rungs*, our author uses this same image: "Reading puts, as it were, whole food in the mouth; meditation chews and breaks it up; prayer discovers the taste; contemplation is the pleasant sweetness that gives so much comfort. Reading is outwardly the husk; meditation is inwardly the fruit; prayer is the wishful asking; and contemplation is in the delight of great sweetness" (II Hodgson, from *Deonise Hid Divinite* 101:29–33).

f. The phrase "throw the cup against the wall" has been used literarily as a synonym for "stop hesitating and get on with it" (e.g., in "Sherlock's Surrender," http://tinyurl.com/oqp7eox).

be a physical thing—but our Work should be spiritual, not performed in a physical manner.[a]

⤺ HERE BEGINS THE FIFTY-EIGHTH CHAPTER

*That one should not use the example of Saint Martin
and Saint Stephen in order to stretch one's physical
imaginings upward during the time of prayer.*

For what they say of Saint Martin and Saint Stephen—though they all look upon such things with their bodily eyes—was shown only in a miracle and in confirmation of something that was spiritual. For they know right well that Saint Martin's cloak never appeared on Christ's own body *in reality* (because He had no need of it to keep Him from the cold) but by miracle and in a likeness for all of us who can be saved,[b] who are joined to the body of Christ spiritually. And whoever clothes a poor man and does any other good deed for the sake of God's love—physically or spiritually—to anyone who has need, they can be sure that they do it unto Christ spiritually, and they shall be rewarded as greatly for it as though they had done it to Christ's own body. This He says Himself in the Gospel.[c] And still He thought this was not enough until He had affirmed it later by miracle—and for this reason He showed Himself to Saint Martin by revelation.

All the revelations that any person ever saw in bodily likeness in this life have spiritual significances. And I believe that if they to whom these revelations were shown (or we *for* whom they were shown) had been spiritual enough, or could have perceived their significance spiritually, then they would never have been shown bodily. And therefore, let us pick off[d] the rough husk and feed ourselves on the sweet fruit.[e]

But how? Not as these heretics do who can well be compared to mad men who have the custom that whenever they have drunken from a beautiful cup, always throw it against the wall and break it![f] This we contemplatives ought not to do, if we wish to do well. For we ought not so to feed ourselves with the fruit that we despise the tree—nor so to drink that we would break the cup when we have drunk. The tree and the cup I call "visible miracles"—and all those seemly physical practices that are in accord with

a. *"Kiss the cup* arose in the fifteenth century, meaning *to take a drink."* (Morton, Mark; *The Lover's Tongue* [Insomniac Press; London, ON; 2003], 165). The phrase is used as this idiom in the poem "A Merry Jest" by Sir Thomas More († 1535) and in "The Deserted Village" by Oliver Goldsmith († 1774).

b. Lk. 24:50–53: "And [Jesus] led [his disciples] out into Bethany, and, lifting up his hands, he blessed them. And it was while he blessed them, he withdrew from them and was carried into heaven." It is a curious and very early tradition (with absolutely no support in Scripture) that the Blessed Virgin Mary was present at Jesus's ascension. Also there is no scriptural mention of Jesus going "into the clouds." That idea may well have been founded in the author's own ideas of "the cloud."

c. The author certainly refers to the only scriptural reference to Jesus's being *seated* in heaven: Heb. 1:3b: "When [the Son] had made purification for sins, he sat down on the right hand of the Majesty on high." There is also the phrase in the Nicene Creed: "and is seated at the right hand of the Father." (See previous note on Saint Stephen's vision of Christ standing.)

d. The author stretches his point into foolishness to illustrate the absurdity of any concern with Christ's heavenly posture. Again, the author's point is to ridicule those who take mystical truths literally or spiritual realities physically—a concern that remains among some Christians to our day.

e. The author makes a clear statement of the orthodox Christological doctrine that (a) Jesus had an entirely human body and an entirely human soul, and (b) was also entirely divine. The Monophysite heresy had claimed that Christ has only one nature that was either divine or human or a mixture of the two.

and do not hinder the Work of the spirit. The fruit and the drink I call the "spiritual significance" of these visible miracles, and of these seemly physical practices, like lifting up our eyes and hands to heaven. But if they are done by the stirring of the spirit, then they are well done—otherwise, they are hypocrisy and in that case they are false. If they are true and contain spiritual fruit within them, why should they then be despised? For people will kiss the cup on account of the wine in it.[a]

And what of our Lord, when He ascended bodily into heaven, and made his way upward into the clouds, being seen by his mother and his disciples with their bodily eyes?[b] Should we therefore in our spiritual Work always stare upward with our bodily eyes, to look for Him as though we might see Him sitting bodily in heaven,[c] or else standing (as Saint Stephen saw Him)? Now, surely He showed Himself not to Saint Stephen bodily in heaven so that He could leave us an example that we should in our spiritual Work look bodily up into heaven, as though we might see Him as Saint Stephen did, either standing or sitting or lying down.[d] For no one knows how His body is in heaven—standing, sitting, or lying down. And there is no need to know—no more than that His body is ascended with his soul, without the two being separated. His body and soul—which is His humanity—is joined with the divinity also without any separation.[e] There is no need to know about His sitting, His standing, or His lying down—except that He is there as He wishes, and has Himself in body as it is most seemly for Him to be. For if He showed Himself lying down or standing or sitting by bodily revelation to any creature in this life, it is done for some spiritual significance, and not for any kind of bodily posture that He has in heaven.

Look at an example: by "standing" is understood "a readiness to help." So it is commonly said by one friend to another who is about to enter bodily battle: "Bear yourself well, friend, and fight hard, and do not give up the battle too easily, for I shall stand by you." He does not mean just "bodily standing," for perhaps this battle is on horseback and not on foot, and perhaps it is shifting about and not staying in one place. But when he says that he will "stand by him," he means that he will be ready to help him.

For this reason it was that our Lord showed Himself bodily in heaven to Saint Stephen when Stephen was suffering his martyrdom—and not to give

a. In order to make his point, the author presumes to put words into the Lord's mouth in this imaginary address to Stephen. In his words he refers indirectly to two biblical passages: (1) James 1:12: "Blessed is the man who endures temptation, for when he has been proved, he will receive the crown of life, which God has promised to them that love him"; and (2) James 1:112: "Blessed is the man who endures temptation: for when he has been tested, he will receive the crown of life which the Lord has promised to those who love him."

b. It is interesting that the author refers to "the physical firmament that is called heaven." It is unlikely that the author believed in anything like a "physical heaven," but was speaking as part of his putative comment of Christ to Stephen. The word *firmament* in the Old Testament referred to what the early Jews believed to be the solid ceiling dome of the sky that covered the earth. Our author is saying: "I let you see what looked physical to you in order to convey something spiritual."

c. The ME has *stiffly*—literally, "stiffly," "strongly," or "valiantly" (Bradley, 578).

d. A reassertion of orthodox Christology as above: Christ was both truly and completely divine and also truly and completely human.

e. The ME has the wonderful word *undeedliness*—literally, "undeadliness," the quality of being "undead"—hence "immortality." And the author uses the biblical metaphor of "clothing," for which see 1 Corinthians 15:53: "For this corruptible must be clothed with incorruption and this mortal must be clothed with immortality."

f. The ME has *sotyl*—literally, "subtly" or "craftily." I have followed Mayhew (210) with "finely." (The word also carries overtones of "skillfully" or "cunningly.") It is interesting that Aquinas also uses the Latin word *subtilitas* ("subtlety") to describe the resurrected human body (*Summa Theologica* 83.1).

g. The author describes the heavenly state as the freedom to "go wherever we wish"—that is, with spiritual and heavenly resurrected bodies, we will no longer be limited by geography.

h. The ME has *as clerkes seyne*. The word *clerkes* can be translated accurately as either "clerics" or "clergy" or "scholars"—since in the fourteenth century all scholars were clergy, and by and large the clergy were the only ones who had a university education and could write and do accounts. In this place I think that the author refers to sermons and preachments, so I translate the word as "clergy" here.

us an exemplar to look up to heaven. It is as if He had said thus to Saint Stephen (who represented all those who suffer persecution for His love's sake):[a] "Behold, Stephen! As truly as I open this physical firmament that is called heaven,[b] and let you see me standing bodily, so trust stalwartly that just as truly do I stand beside you spiritually, by the power of my Divinity. And I am ready to help you. And therefore, stand valiantly[c] in the faith, and suffer bravely the cruel blows of those hard stones for I shall crown you in bliss for your reward—and not only you, but all those who suffer any kind of persecution for me."

And thus you can see that these bodily showings were presented for their spiritual significance.

⤐ HERE BEGINS THE FIFTY-NINTH CHAPTER

That a person shall not take the exemplar of the bodily ascension of Christ in order to strain one's aspirations physically upward in the time of prayer; and that time, place, and body, these three should be forgotten in all spiritual labor.

And if you say anything regarding the ascension of our Lord because it was done bodily and for a bodily significance as well as for a spiritual one, because He ascended both as truly divine and truly human,[d] to this I will answer you: that He had been dead, and was clothed with immortality,[e] and so shall we be at Judgment Day. And then we shall be made so finely[f] in body and soul together that we shall then go wherever we wish to be bodily, just as now we do in our thoughts spiritually—whether it be up or down, or to one side or another, or behind or before.[g] Everything I long for shall then be invariably good, as the clergy tell us.[h]

But now you cannot come to heaven bodily, but spiritually. And still it will be so spiritual that it shall not be bodily in any manner—neither upward nor downward, nor to one side or the other, behind or before.

And know well that all those who set themselves to be spiritual workers—and specifically in the Work of this book—that although they all read "lift up" or "go in" and although all the Work of this book is called a "stirring," nevertheless, they must take very careful notice, that this stirring reaches

a. Matt. 11:28: "Come to me all you that labor and are burdened, and I will give you rest."

b. In these paragraphs, the author speaks almost at an elementary school level—attempting to break his protégé free from literalism and teach him the necessity of understanding spiritual metaphor. (Indeed, if his protégé were a lay brother, he may well have had natural intelligence, but may not have been highly educated.)

c. Jn. 3:13: "And no one has ascended into heaven except the one who descended from heaven, the Son of Man who is in heaven." Note the author's variation and addition to the biblical verse: *bycome man for the love of man*—"and became human for the love of humanity."

d. This is one of the passages in the book in which one suspects that the author wrote himself beyond his own reach, as it were, and then had to backtrack to clean up the language a bit. Here, for instance, he first makes the uncompromised statement: "No one can ascend bodily into heaven except Christ" and then qualifies it: "But if it were possible...." And then he reasserts his original statement: "which it isn't" and then doubles back again: "it would be accomplished only by the power of the spirit." It is interesting that he makes no reference to the two biblical instances of people who *were* taken bodily into heaven: Enoch (Gen. 5:24: "[Enoch] walked with God, and was seen no more, for God took him") and Elijah (4 Kgs. 2:11 [2 Kgs. 2:11]: "Elias went up by a whirlwind into heaven"). These omissions are more evidence that the author is not closely tied to Scripture as source, proof, or validation.

e. Once again we see the author discrediting physical stress and strain as part of spiritual maturation—no emphasis on fasting, self-flagellation, bodily contortions, etc. This is radically atypical of late-medieval ascetical practice.

f. The ME has *heighe*—literally, "high," but "principal" is a less common variation (Mayhew, 111). Mossé (450) also suggests "celestial."

g. The ME has *pases of feet*—literally, "passage of feet." Cowan (235) has "footsteps." "The soul is not moved by feet, but by affections" (Augustine, *Tr. in Joannes Ev.* 48.3).

h. Acts 2:3–4: "And there appeared to them cloven tongues like as of fire, and settled on each of them. And all were all filled with the Holy Ghost."

i. The ME has *febly*—literally, "feebly," but that meaning of the word used in this sentence makes no sense. "Delicately" or "precisely" are more appropriate synonyms of "feebly."

neither physically upward nor physically inward, nor yet that there is any such movement as is from one place to another. And although it is sometimes called a "rest,"[a] nonetheless they should not think that it is any such "rest" as if it meant "remaining in one place without moving on." For the perfection of this Work is so pure and so spiritual in itself that if it is well and truly understood, it will be seen to be far from any movement or from any place.[b]

And it should reasonably rather be called a sudden "transformation" rather than any steady "movement." For time, place, and body—these three should be forgotten in all spiritual labor. And therefore beware in this Work that you do not follow the exemplar of the bodily ascension of Christ, in order to strain your aspirations physically upward in the time of your prayer as though you would climb above the moon. For it could never be that way spiritually. Still, if you *were* going to ascend into heaven bodily as Christ did, then you can take it as an exemplar—but none can do that except God, as He Himself witnessed, saying, "No one can ascend into heaven except only He that descended from heaven and became human for the love of humanity."[c] And if it *were* possible[d]—as it no way can be—still it would be from an abundance of *spiritual* effort, solely by the power of the spirit—far distant from any bodily stressing or straining of our imaginings physically,[e] whether "up," or "in," or "to one side or another." And therefore drop such falsehood: it ought never to be so.

HERE BEGINS THE SIXTIETH CHAPTER

That the principal[f] and nearest way to heaven is measured by longings and not by footsteps.[g]

But now, perhaps, you say: How should it be then? For you think that you have genuine evidence that heaven is *upward*—for Christ ascended there bodily upward, and sent the Holy Ghost, as He promised, coming *from above* physically in the sight of all His disciples.[h] And this is our belief. And therefore you think that since you have this genuine evidence, why should you not direct your mind upward physically in the time of your prayer?

And to this I shall answer you as precisely[i] as I can, and say: since it was so that Christ should ascend bodily and afterward send the Holy Ghost

a. Finally the author makes the simple orthodox declaration: that heaven is not a geographical place! "If you love God, you are in heaven, even though you are standing on the earth" (Augustine, *Enarr. in Psalmos* 85.6). Note: It is wanting (i.e., "willing") to be in heaven that puts one there spiritually.

b. Phil. 3:20: "For our residence is in heaven, from whence we also look for the Savior, our Lord Jesus Christ."

c. Jn. 17:1a: "These things Jesus said and lifting up his eyes toward heaven, he said...."

d. 1 Tim. 2:8a: "Therefore, I want men to pray in every place, lifting up pure hands, without anger and disputation."

e. The ME has *in whiche the elementes ben fastnid*—Hodgson (201) maintains that ME *elementes* usually referred to the heavens or the concentric spherical shells that comprised the heavens. One must remember that astrology was closely mixed with religion in the fourteenth century, so that there still exist medieval chancel arches and mosaic floors decorated with the signs of the zodiac (Lilly, William; *Christian Astrology*, vol. 1 [Astrology Center of America; Belair, MD; 2005]; reprint of 1647 edition).

f. The author makes another qualification: in spite of the last chapter's strong condemnation of "aiming" one's prayers, here he declares one *should* lift hands and eyes upward—but only "if we are led by the work of the spirit."

g. John 13:1: "Now before the feast of the Passover, when Jesus knew that his time had come that he should go out of this world to the Father, having loved his own who were in the world, he loved them to the end."

h. Another reaffirmation of the doctrine of the hypostatic union of human and divine in the person of Christ. The author's reiteration of this theological concept suggests that his prejudice for the mystical may have inclined some to be suspicious of this aspect of his theology.

i. The ME has *onheed*—literally, "one-hood" or "unity."

physically, then it was more fitting that it were "upward" and "from above," rather than "downward" and "from beneath, behind, or before," or "on one side or the other." But aside from this stateliness, He needed no more to have gone upward than downward—I mean for the shortness of the trip— because spiritual heaven is just as near "down" as it is "up" and "up" as it is "down," "behind" as it is "before," "before" as it is "behind," on one side as it is the other, since whoever has a true longing to be in heaven, then at that very moment, he is in heaven spiritually.[a] For the principal and nearest way there is measured by longings and not by footsteps. And so Saint Paul says about himself and many others thus: "Although our bodies are presently here on earth, nevertheless our life is in heaven."[b] (He meant their love and their longings which spiritually constitute their life.) And surely as truly a soul is wherever it loves, just as so it is in the body that lives by it and to which it gives life. And so if we wish to go to heaven spiritually, we need not strain our spirit either up or down, nor on one side or the other.

☞ HERE BEGINS THE SIXTY-FIRST CHAPTER

That by the course of nature everything physical is subject to something spiritual; and is ruled by it, and not vice versa.

Nevertheless it is necessary to lift up our physical eyes[c] and our hands[d] as if to the distant physical heaven in which the heavenly bodies[e] are fixed. I mean if we are led by the work of our spirit—otherwise not.[f] For every physical thing is subject to something spiritual and is governed by it—and not vice versa.

An example of this may be seen by the ascension of our Lord, for when the time appointed had come that it pleased Him to go to his Father[g] bodily in his Manhood—which was never, nor ever could be, separate from his Divinity[h]—then mightily, by the power of the spirit of God, the Manhood with its body followed in unity[i] of the Person. The visible appearance of this was most seemly and most fittingly upward.

This same subjection of the body to the spirit can in a way be truly understood in the proof of the spiritual Work of this book by those who undertake it. For at the time that a soul disposes itself effectively to this

a. The author describes a peculiar phenomenon that tends to mystify commentators. It is true that most spiritual directors advise an upright, seated position (on the floor or in a chair) for contemplative practice, but that is not universal. The most devout contemplative I have ever known frequently prayed lying face down on the floor (which disquieted a visitor who thought she saw a dead body in the chapel!). Another person uses a lounge chair. And still another sits and kneels on a kneeling stool.

b. The ME has *seemliest creature in body.* I follow Cowan (241) with "most physically attractive."

c. Ecclesiastes 7:29: "Only this have I found: that God made man upright"; and "We are not prone, but erect ... the body is naturally raised upright toward those bodily things which are most elevated, that is, toward celestial things" (Augustine, *De Trinitate* 12.1.1).

d. The ME has *figure*—translated as "mark" or "symbolize" in ODEE, 355.

e. In a few words the author sums up the apophatic challenge: there simply are no physical words that can do complete justice in describing spiritual realities.

f. The author tries to make clear the difference between words used in ordinary conversation and those same words used to discuss spiritual realities. This chapter is a kind of kindergarten presentation of the language of the *via negativa.*

Work, then suddenly—unbeknownst to the one who is working—the body (that perhaps before one began was somewhat leaning downward on one side or the other for comfort of the flesh) by virtue of the spirit shall straighten itself upright, following physically in manner and appearance the work of the spirit that is being done spiritually. And thus it is most fitting.[a]

And it is for this suitability that a human—who is the most physically attractive creature[b] that ever God made—is not made bent over toward the earth as are all other beasts, but upright toward heaven[c]—in order that it should symbolize[d] in bodily likeness the Work of the spiritual soul which should be spiritually upright, and not crooked physically. Take notice that I say *spiritually* upright and not bodily. For how could a soul—which by its nature has no kind of physicality—be stretched upright bodily? No, it cannot be.

And so beware that you consider physically that which is meant spiritually, although it be spoken of in physical words such as these: "up" and "down," "in" or "out," "behind" or "before," "on one side" or "on the other." For although a thing is entirely spiritual in itself, nevertheless, if it is to be spoken of, since speech is a physical thing wrought with the tongue (which is an instrument of the body), it is necessary always to be speak of it in physical words. But what of it? Shall it therefore be taken and thought of physically? No, spiritually instead.[e]

≈ HERE BEGINS THE SIXTY-SECOND CHAPTER

How one can know when one's spiritual work is below or outside oneself, and when it is equal with or within oneself, and when it is beyond oneself but under one's God.

So that you may learn better how these words that are spoken physically should be regarded spiritually, I intend to point out to you the spiritual significance of some words that pertain to spiritual work[f]—so that you can understand clearly without error when your spiritual work involves what is lower than you and outside of yourself, and when it involves what is within you and equal with yourself, and when it involves what is beyond you but beneath your God.

a.   The first classification involves all physical and material things. They
     are all to be understood as external to the soul and below the soul in
     value or worth. It is certainly the author's neo-Platonic bent that has him
     classifying all material things as inferior to and subordinate to the soul
     (Cowan, 243).

b.   All spiritual beings—i.e., angels and other souls, in heaven or on earth—
     are of equal worth and value compared to one's own soul. It is of interest
     that in his spiritual cosmology even souls particularly enhanced by grace
     and virtue (which are thus more *pure* than one's own) are still no greater
     by their nature than one's own soul.

c.   It is helpful here to recognize again the two separate sets of actors in
     the Work of soul—first: mind, reason, and will; and second: imagination
     and sensuality. In most classical divisions (e.g., Saint Augustine; see
     Lacoste, 574), the soul is constituted of memory, intelligence, and will.
     Consequently, wherever I have translated "mind" one can properly read
     "memory"—and wherever I have translated "reason" one can properly
     read "intelligence." Note also that the ME *sensualite* ("sensuality")
     refers to the five bodily senses—seeing, touching, smelling, hearing,
     and tasting—and has none of the sexual overtones it tends to have in
     modern use.

d.   The only place in which a contemplative finds the self inferior or
     subordinate is in its relationship with God.

e.   The classical identification of the "soul" with the "self."

f.   The concluding lesson: how one's soul relates to what is below, to what
     is within, and to what is beyond oneself determines the worth of one's
     work. These matters will now be dealt with in greater detail in the next
     three chapters.

g.   In all instances, the words "memory" and "mind" and "consciousness" are
     interchangeable—they refer to the same dimension of the soul. Mind is
     "the form or superstructure of which the content or substructure is the
     other four faculties. Reason and will, imagination and sensuality are the
     working faculties" (Cowan, 245). A person processes the data of reality
     through reason, will, imagination, and sensuality—then mind receives
     and retains all that input. So mind's activity of sorting and saving is not
     considered to be a work in itself.

Every kind of physical thing is outside your soul and below it in nature. Yea, the sun and the moon and all the stars—although they may be higher than your body, nevertheless they are lower than your soul.[a]

All angels and all other souls—even though they are enhanced and adorned with grace and virtues (for which they are beyond you in purity) still they are only equal with you in nature.[b]

Within yourself in nature are these powers of your soul: mind, reason, and will; and secondarily, imagination and sensuality.[c]

Beyond yourself in nature there is nothing except God alone.[d]

Wherever you find the word "yourself" in spiritual writings, your soul is meant, and not your body.[e] And then everything after that is what the powers of your soul work with, and based on that the quality and the suitability of your work will be judged—whether it is below you, within you, or beyond you.[f]

⤚ HERE BEGINS THE SIXTY-THIRD CHAPTER

Of the powers of a soul in general, and how mind in particular is a primary power, including within it all the other powers and everything in which they work.

Mind is such a power in itself that strictly speaking and in a way it does not do the work itself. But reason and will are the two working powers, and so are imagination and sensuality as well. Mind contains and encompasses all these four powers and their works. And in no other way can it be said that the mind works unless that inclusion itself is considered a work.[g]

And so it is that I refer to the powers of a soul: some principal and some secondary. Not because a soul is divisible—because that simply cannot be— but because all those objects on which the soul's parts work are divisible. And some objects of work are principal (as are all spiritual matters) and some are secondary (as are all physical matters). The two principal working powers—reason and will—work solely in all the *spiritual* matters, without help from the other two secondary powers. Imagination and sensuality work carnally in all *physical* matters (whether they are bodily present or absent) and with the physical senses. Only by them—without the help of reason

a. The classical Scholastic understanding of the role of the senses: they alone are the "bridge" by which we can know anything about the physical world in which we live.

b. The ME has *bodelines*—literally, "bodiliness" or "physicality." I have used "brutishness" in parallel to the *beestly* reference in the previous paragraph.

c. The identity between "mind" and "memory"—it is the mind that contains within itself (i.e., remembers) all the matters the soul works with.

d. That is, reason is the faculty by which one interprets incoming data from the imagination and the senses and makes a value judgment about it. Reason is the "sorting" or "selecting" faculty.

e. A simpler way of saying this is that before humanity was contaminated by original sin, human reason was able to make accurate value judgments by itself ("naturally")—but now it requires the infusion of grace to guarantee that its judgments are right.

f. Will takes the results of reason's working on the imagination and the senses, and based on reason's estimation of moral value, the will acts—to choose what the reason tells it is good, to love that good, to desire and seek that good, and finally to rest in God. It is important for modern Christians to understand this function of the will—for us too often morality is merely what "feels good," rather than what has been evaluated by reason and chosen freely by will. It is also important to notice the author's association of "love" with "will"—they are the same faculty. For the author (and for most theologians before modern times) the theological virtue of "love" had nothing whatsoever to do with "feeling" anything. Aquinas defined love as "willing the good for another"—an action of will, not of emotion.

g. Like reason, will made reliably accurate choices before humanity was tainted by sin—now it requires the illumination of grace to see clearly what the proper choice would be.

h. The great theologians have always maintained that the human soul naturally seeks the good—but is often perverted from that seeking by confusion about *what the good is*. The drug addict believes the drug high is "good" and so chooses it. The liar believes is it "good" to lie for one's own benefit. In all these cases there is a repudiation of reason and a refusal of grace, and so the will is misled in its choices.

and will—can a soul ever come to know the virtue and the conditions of physical creatures and the origin of their being and their creation.[a]

And for this cause reason and will are called "the principal powers": because they work in the realm of pure spirit without any kind of brutishness[b]— and imagination and sensuality are called "secondary powers" because they work within the body with physical agents (which are our five senses). Mind is called "a principal power" because spiritually it contains within it not only all the other powers but also all the objects with which those powers work.[c] See here the proof:

 ## HERE BEGINS THE SIXTY-FOURTH CHAPTER

Of the other two principal powers—reason and will—and of their work before original sin and afterward.

Reason is a power by means of which we separate the evil from the good, the bad from the worse, the good from the better, the worse from the worst, and the better from the best.[d] Before ever humans sinned, reason could do all this naturally. But now it is so blinded by original sin that it cannot know how to carry out this work unless it is illumined by grace.[e] And both reason itself and the object it works on are contained and encompassed in the mind.

Will is a power through which we choose the good (after it has been determined to be good by reason) and through which we love the good, we desire the good, and finally rest with full gratification and accord in God.[f] Before ever humans sinned, will could not be deceived in its choice, in its loving, nor in any of its works, because it could then naturally cherish each thing as it was. But now it cannot do so unless it is anointed with grace.[g] For often—because of the infection of original sin—it cherishes a thing as good that is full evil and has only the appearance of good.[h] And the mind contains and encompasses the will and the thing that it wills.

a. The ME has *mynystrid*—literally, "ministered to" or "administered to."

b. The ME has *conseyte*—literally, "conception," "thought," or "personal opinion" (ODEE, 200).

c. The ME has *anexte unto errour*. I use "affixed to error" (ODEE, 38).

d. The ME has *kyndenes*—literally, "lawfulness," "benevolence," or "good-naturedness" (ODEE, 506).

e. The ME has *pyne*—literally, "pain" or "torture" or "penalty" (Bradley, 471, 475).

f. This is perhaps a place to extend an explanation of "original sin." This is the teaching that the taint of the sin of disobedience committed by Adam and Eve in the Garden of Eden is passed on to all human beings since then, so all human beings are tainted with sin at birth although they have never committed any actual sin. An explanation of the means of transmission of this sin has always been a problem. Saint Thomas Aquinas solved it by saying that the original sin of Adam is passed on to every human being in the semen of the father: "the movement of the semen is in the nature of a transmission of the rational soul: so that the semen by its own power conveys the human nature from parent to child, and with that nature, the stain which infects it" (Aquinas, *Summa Theologica* 2.1.81.1.2). This "stain" of original sin is removed in Holy Baptism, but concupiscence or the "tendency to sin" remains in all human beings— hence the author's frequent comment about the need for grace. And my own simple definition of "grace" is "God's own life shared with us."

g. The ME has *rechyng*—literally, "ranging" or "reaching" (Gallacher, 92) or "attaining" (Mayhew, 184).

h. The ME has *gruchyng*—literally, "displeasing" (Gallacher, 92). Sensuality is the bridge that exists between the physical world and the human mind— the experience of the senses is necessary for intellectual comprehension.

i. Another way to understand the word *sensuality* would be to think of it as "appetite"—it is the important and valuable appetite that signals to us our need for food, rest, warmth, etc. Its darker side, on the other hand, is that it can also involve a hungering for more than we need, or for bodily gratifications that are distorted, or for bodily satisfactions that are lustful and overpowering.

HERE BEGINS THE SIXTY-FIFTH CHAPTER

*Of the first secondary power—imagination, by name—
and of its works and its obedience to reason before original
sin and afterward.*

Imagination is a power through which we picture all images of absent and present things. And both it and the objects it works on are contained in the mind. Before ever humans sinned, imagination was so obedient to reason—to which it was, as it were, a servant—that it never supplied[a] the reason with any inordinate image of any physical creature or any illusion of any spiritual creature. But now it is not so, for unless it is restrained by the light of grace in the reason, it will never cease, sleeping or waking, to portray diverse distorted images of bodily creatures or else some illusion that is nothing but a bodily conception[b] of a spiritual thing, or else a spiritual conception of a bodily thing. And this is always feigned and false and affixed to error.[c]

This disobedience of the imagination can clearly be perceived in those who have recently turned from the world to devotion in the time of their prayer. For before the time comes that the imagination is in great part restrained by the light of grace in the reason—as it is in continual meditation on spiritual things such as one's wretchedness, the Passion, and the benevolence[d] of our Lord God, with many other such—they can in no way cast off the shocking and varied thoughts, illusions, and images which are dispensed and printed on their minds by the light and the aberration of imagination. And all this disobedience is the penalty[e] of original sin.[f]

HERE BEGINS THE SIXTY-SIXTH CHAPTER

*Of the other secondary power—sensuality, by name—and of its
works, and of its obedience to reason before original sin and after.*

Sensuality is a power of our soul, ranging[g] and reigning in the bodily senses, through which we have physical knowledge and feeling of all bodily creatures—whether they are pleasing or offensive.[h] And it has two parts: one through which it looks after the needs of our body, and another through which it serves the lusts of the bodily senses.[i] For this is the same power

a. A point must be made clear: the author does *not* think all physicality is evil and wrong. He is critical of our appetites and sensuality only when they escape the control of the will—that is, when they become addictions that are beyond restraint and seize the reins from the will. For him this is *dis*-order. It must also be clear that when he speaks of the contemplative Work itself, he excludes the function of sensuality because it relates to the physical world and that can only be an impediment to the contemplative.

b. "The work of apophatic contemplative prayer must have nothing to do with the material universe" (Cowan, 257). This stance of the author is frequently misunderstood as a Gnostic aversion to the material world, but it is not that. It is only when a person has made the choice to set aside all physical matters in order to undertake serious and committed contemplative prayer that the material world becomes a potential impediment. An example: it is a good and kind thing to take one's dog out for a daily walk around the neighborhood—it is good for the dog and good for the master. But if one decides to attend the performance of an opera, it is not good to bring one's dog along. That is not because there is anything "wrong" with the dog—it is just that a dog is an inappropriate companion in a concert hall. So, the material world is a good and fine thing—unless one chooses to be a serious apophatic contemplative, in which case, the physical world is only an impediment.

that grumbles when the body lacks necessary things, and that in the filling of the need directs us to take more than we require in feeding and fostering our lusts. It complains of the absence of pleasing creatures, and is pleasurably delighted in their presence. It complains in the presence of created things we dislike, and is heartily delighted when they are not there. Both this power and the effect it has are contained in the mind.

Before ever humans sinned, sensuality was so obedient to the will—to which it was, as it were, a servant—that it never supplied to the will any offensive pleasure or revulsion for any created thing, or in any spiritual illusion of pleasure or repugnance created by any spiritual enemy through the bodily senses. But now it is not so, for unless it is governed by grace in the will (so that it can accept humbly and in proportion the pain of original sin which it feels in the absence of needed pleasures and in the presence of beneficial irritations) and also restrains itself from lust in the presence of necessary comforts, and from lusty pleasure in the absence of beneficial discomforts, it will so wretchedly and wantonly wallow—like a pig in the mud—in the good things of this world and so much in the foul flesh that our entire life would be more beastly and carnal than either human or spiritual.[a]

⤳ HERE BEGINS THE SIXTY-SEVENTH CHAPTER

That whoever does not know the powers of a soul and the way they work may easily be deceived in the understanding of spiritual words and spiritual works; and how a soul is made into a God through grace.

Look, my spiritual friend, and you can see here into what wretchedness we are fallen because of sin! And therefore what wonder is it that we are blindly and easily deceived in the understanding of spiritual words and of spiritual works—and specifically those who do not yet know the powers of their souls and the ways they work?

For whenever the mind is occupied with any bodily thing—no matter how good an intention it may have—yet you are still below yourself in this working, and outside of your soul.[b] And whenever you are aware of your

a. Here is the spiritual "midpoint." One's concern is not with strictly material things, but with one's spiritual realities, one's virtues or vices or those of others. In this case one is dealing with the spiritual world and is a step above the physical.

b. But one comes to the peak when one realizes that everything else has been abandoned and that the only thing in one's mind is a longing for Godself.

c. Phil. 3:13–15: "Brothers, I do not consider myself to have grasped it yet, but this one thing I do: forgetting what is behind and reaching forth for what is ahead, I pursue the destination, the prize of the upward call of God in Christ Jesus. Let us therefore—as many as are perfect—be thus inclined; and if in anything you are otherwise inclined, God shall also reveal this to you."

d. 1 Cor. 6:17: "But he who is united to the Lord becomes one spirit with him."

e. Ps. 81:6 [82:6]: "I have said, 'You are gods and all of you sons of the Most High.'" (Also quoted by Jesus in Jn. 10:34.)

f. It should be noted that in the ME text, the word "God" is capitalized here. "If we have been made sons of God, we have also been made gods; but this is the effect of Grace adopting, not of nature penetrating" (Augustine, *On the Psalms* 1.2, cited in Cowan, 259).

g. This is the utter peak of the contemplative way—to be perfectly one with God in his grace and will—and yet to maintain one's individual personhood within that union with the Divine. "In the moment of communion there is no distinction between the love, spirit, and will of the contingent being and those of the essential Being ... the [contingent] being is not absorbed by the [essential] Being: the contingent and conditional does not cease to exist in the face of the essential and unconditional" (Cowan, 258).

h. See chapters 46–51 above where even the expressed desire for God can be turned against the contemplative.

mind being occupied with the subtle aspects of the powers of your soul
and their workings in spiritual things—such as your own vices or virtues or
those of anyone who is spiritual and equal with you in nature, to the end
that you might by this Work learn to know yourself in the advancement
of perfection—then you are within yourself and equal with yourself.[a] But
whenever you are aware of your mind being occupied with nothing that
is either bodily or spiritual, but only with the essence of Godself—as the
mind is and can be in exhibiting the Work of this book, then you are above
yourself and beneath your God.[b]

You are above yourself—because you are able to come by grace to where
you cannot come by nature—that is to say—to be one-ed to God in spirit
and in love and in congruence of will.[c] You are beneath your God—for
although it may be said in a way that at this time God and you are not two
but one in spirit[d] to such a degree that you (or anyone else who because
of such oneness feels the perfection of this Work) may truly, by witness of
Scripture, be called a god[e]—nevertheless you are still beneath Him, because
He is God by nature without beginning, and you that once were nothing
in essence and after that when you were made something by His power
and His love, willfully with sin you made yourself worse than nothing: only
by His mercy—without your deserving it—you are made a God[f] by grace,
one-ed with Him in spirit without any separation both here and in the bliss
of heaven without end. So that though you are all one with Him in grace,
yet you are very far beneath Him in your human nature.[g]

Look, my spiritual friend! By this you can see at least to some degree that
those who do not recognize the powers of their own souls and the way they
work can very easily be deceived in understanding words that are written
for a spiritual purpose. And here also you can see something of the reason
why I dared not openly tell you to show your desire to God, but I told you
to do what you can to hide it and conceal it like a child.[h] And this I do for
fear lest you should understand physically that which is intended spiritually.

a. Quite amazingly the author takes on some very familiar spiritual leaders who do, indeed, recommend that one look inward. Hodgson (202) quotes Walter Hilton's *The Scale of Perfection*: "And that is for a man to enter into himself, to know his own soul and the mights thereof." Walsh (I 251) cites Augustine: "Too late have I loved thee … and behold, thou wert within" (*Confessions*, 10); and Gregory the Great: "The first step is for the soul to collect itself within itself" (*Homilies on Ezekiel* 2.5.9).

b. A delightful anticipated statement put in the mouth of the protégé: "If I am not to look within for my self, I will be nowhere!" as a ploy to extract the author's own statement: "Right! 'Nowhere' is just where you ought to be."

c. "If the contemplative is careful neither to locate nor confine his or her efforts to the material world, then where the object upon which s/he set his/her soul and his/her contemplation is, there too will s/he be in spirit" (McCann, 263).

d. McCann (91) quotes the Latin annotator: "*O Nihilum, quam pretiosum!*" "O, Nothing, how precious!" In his postscript (217) McCann quotes an essay by Father Augustine Baker: "For when the soul hath cast out of her understanding all natural images and apprehensions, and out of her will all loves and affections to creatures, then is she become, as to all natural things, as if she were nothing: being free, naked, and clean from them all…. But when she, being in such case of nothing, apprehendith God also as nothing, that is to say, as no imaginable or intelligible thing, but as another thing that is above all images and species, but as it were nothing—as being none of those things which may be understood or conceived by any image or species—and that she doth further apply and add her own aforesaid nothing to the said nothing of God.…"

e. The author does not mean that God is "totally unknowable" but rather that God is not "totally knowable"; that is, a created being can never fully comprehend the uncreated Creator.

f. "God is 'nowhere' because He is omnipresent and cannot to be localized; He is 'nothing,' because by the transcendence of his being He is of a different order to all created things" (Clark, 210). He means that God is no-thing.

g. It should be noted that the word "God" is capitalized in the Middle English.

h. "The author has, at this point, reached what will be called two centuries later 'the dark night of the soul' or a 'dark night of the senses'" (Cowan, 264).

⟿ HERE BEGINS THE SIXTY-EIGHTH CHAPTER

That "nowhere" physically is "everywhere" spiritually; and how our outer person refers to the Work of this book as "nothing."

And in the same manner, where another man might bid you gather yourself and your faculties wholly within yourself, and worship God there[a]—although he speaks full well and full truly, yea, and no man more true if he is well regarded—yet for fear of deceit and conceiving his words physically, it does not please me to bid you do so. But this I will bid you: See to it that you are no way "within yourself"—nor yet above, nor behind, nor on one side, nor on the other.

"Where then," say you, "shall I be? Nowhere, by your reckoning!"[b] Ah, now truly you say well: for that is where I would have you be. Because "nowhere" physically is "everywhere" spiritually. See to it vigorously that your spiritual Work be nowhere physically—and then wherever that thing is on which you Work willingly in your mind in essence, oh, then surely that is where you will be in spirit just as truly as your body is in that place where you are bodily.[c] And although all your bodily wits can find nothing there to feed on—because they think that you are doing nothing—yea, go on then doing this "nothing"[d] (as long as you are doing it for the love of God). And do not depart from "nothing," therefore, but labor vigorously in that "nothing" with a vigilant desire to will to have God, whom no one can know.[e] For I tell you truly that I would rather be thus "nowhere" bodily, wrestling with that unseen "nothing"[f] than to be so great a lord that I could when I wished be everywhere physically, merrily playing with all this "something" as a lord does with his own.

Leave aside this "everywhere" and this "something" in favor of this "nowhere" and this "nothing."[g] Do not care at all if your wits cannot discern any of this "nothing," because that is why I like it much better. It is so precious a thing in itself that they cannot discern anything there. This "nothing" can better be sensed than seen, for it is completely unseen and entirely dark to those who have only briefly looked upon it.[h] Nevertheless, if I were to speak more truthfully, a soul is more blinded in sensing it by

a. "The mind, passing beyond the confinement of the semi-dark room of earthly knowledge, is dazzled by the bright light of supernatural wisdom without. Though there is still the same light as ever within the room, the mind cannot perceive it at all" (Hodgson, 203).

b. When a contemplative encounters with the inner self this sense of "All" or "Everything," the small distinction of an individual, single thing is lost.

c. Perhaps the strangest phenomenon of reaching this level of contemplation is the sudden and vivid recall of almost every sinful inclination, thought, or act of one's entire life—albeit all are forgiven. It is an overwhelming and massively humbling experience, and makes one intensely aware of one's own categorically unspeakable inadequacy, that one deserves absolutely nothing that is in any way good, and finally the dazzling reality of the silent, invisible personhood of divine Mercy.

d. This dark display of one's own profanity and sinfulness "wears off" without any effort or intention—it gradually fades to shadows and then the day comes when one discovers that it has disappeared.

e. It is a massive undertaking of sheer faith to sense intuitively that this vision of wickedness is just that—a vision—and that it is part of the essential sheering away of the world and the past. But the unknowability and the uncertainty of the future and of the "nothing" one faces is a powerful temptation to retreat to the familiar comfort of the world and the flesh.

f. The author makes it very clear that there is great pain and anguish in this Work—and early on the consolations are miserably few. But one stays with it because of an entirely irrational (or even anti-rational) conviction that beyond the pain and the cloud is that thin, filmy, indescribable essence for which one's soul hungers and yearns with the very fiber of one's spiritual being—with a *nakid intent to God*. (Note: In some manuscripts *ellys* mistakenly replaces *helle* so it reads "nothing else but purgatory.")

g. The experience of the recall of all one's sins is so overwhelming that the sins themselves seem to lose their individual characteristics and become simply that "lump"—that "wad" of blackness that is partially the spiritual baggage that comes from the persistent stains of original sin. The up-and-down, light-and-dark, joy-and-sorrow fluctuations are also a characteristic of serious spiritual growth.

the abundance of spiritual light, than any darkness or lack of physical light.[a] Who is this person who calls it "nothing"? Surely, it is our outer self, and not our inner self. Our inner self calls it "All" for because of it he is well taught to be able to understand all things—physical or spiritual—without any specific insight into any one thing alone.[b]

✍ HERE BEGINS THE SIXTY-NINTH CHAPTER

How a person's disposition is marvelously changed by the spiritual sensing of this "nothing" when it is occurs "nowhere."

A person's disposition is wonderfully changed by the spiritual experience of this "nothing" when it occurs "nowhere." For the first time that a soul looks at this "nothing" that is "nowhere," it will find all the particular deeds of sin that it ever did since birth—physically or spiritually—secretly or darkly portrayed upon it.[c] And however one twists it around, they will always appear before one's eyes, until the time that with much hard labor, many painful regrets, and many bitter tears, one will have mostly rubbed them away.[d]

Sometimes during this labor it may seem to him that to look on that is like looking on hell, because he thinks that he despairs of gaining the perfection of spiritual relief from that pain. Many come this far, but because of the magnitude of pain that they feel and for the lack of consolation, they go back to looking at physical things, seeking external fleshly comfort, since they are lacking any spiritual comfort that they have not yet deserved (and they would if they had remained).[e]

For the person who remains sometimes feels some consolation and has some hope of perfection because one feels and sees that many of the previous particular sins are mostly rubbed away by the help of grace. Nonetheless, all along one feels pain, but one thinks that it shall have an end because it is growing less and less. And therefore one calls it not "hell," but "purgatory."[f] Sometimes one can find no particular sin portrayed there, but it still seems that sin is a "lump"—one knows not what of—nothing else but oneself—and then it can be called the root and torment of the original sin.[g] Sometimes it seems that it is paradise or heaven, because of the many wonderful sweetnesses

a.   Julian of Norwich recorded such fluctuations: "And in the times of joy,
      I could have said with Saint Paul: "Nothing shall separate me from the
      love of Christ." And in the pain I could have said with Peter: "Lord, save
      me, I perish." This vision was shown me, for my understanding, that it
      is advantageous for some souls to feel this way—sometimes to be in
      comfort, and sometimes to fail and to be left by themselves" (I Julian,
      115).

b.   The physical senses are capable of a great many things—but the one
      thing that is beyond even their strongest endeavors is the comprehension
      of God, so the author advises fast and vigorous abandonment of the
      bodily senses as useless in the search for God.

c.   The author lists all the things that are accessible to the bodily senses—
      and concludes, of course, that they include neither God nor any spiritual
      things.

d.   The author is clear: nothing that is physical or can be perceived by the
      senses has anything to do with spiritual realities. This harsh opinion was
      relevant in his day because there were teachers and religious communities
      who taught that it was specifically in physical ways that God *could* be
      known—in emotional charismatic eruptions, in tit-for-tat external
      bargains with God, in belief in what we now call "prosperity sects," and
      the like.

e.   It is when our physical senses demonstrate failure or inadequacy that we
      can be assured that the matter at hand is actually a spiritual matter that
      cannot be dealt with physically. The author works with the analogy of
      the physical senses of hearing, smelling, seeing, tasting, and touching with
      the spiritual senses of the soul: mind, reason, and will.

and comforts, joys and blessed virtues, that one finds there. Sometimes it seems it is God, because of the peace and rest one finds there.[a]

Yea! think whatever you will, because you will evermore find it a cloud of unknowing that is between yourself and God.

⌒ HERE BEGINS THE SEVENTIETH CHAPTER

That just as by the failure of our bodily senses we begin most readily to come to the knowledge of spiritual things, so by the failure of our spiritual functions we begin most readily to come to the knowledge of God (inasmuch as that can be had here by grace).

And therefore, work vigorously in this "nothing" and this "nowhere," and abandon your bodily senses and all that they work with, for I tell you truly that this Work cannot even be imagined by them.[b]

For by your eye you cannot comprehend any thing except by the length and the breadth, the smallness and the greatness, the roundness and the squareness, the distance and the nearness, and the color of it. And by your ear, nothing but noise or some kind of sound. By your nose, nothing except stench or aroma. And by your taste nothing except sour or sweet, salty or fresh, bitter or pleasant. And by your touching, nothing except whether hot or cold, hard or tender, soft or sharp.[c] And truly neither God nor spiritual things have any of these qualities or quantities. And therefore abandon those outward senses and do not do your Work with them—neither within nor without. For all those who set out to be spiritual Workers within, and still believe that they shall either hear, smell, or see, taste, or touch spiritual things, either within them or without, surely they are deceived and wrongly against the course of nature. For by nature it is ordained that by the senses people should have knowledge of all outward *physical* things, but in no way by those senses come to the knowledge of *spiritual* things. I mean gaining by their actual works.[d]

By their failings, on the other hand, we can—thus: when we read or hear spoken of some particular things, and from that realize that our outward senses cannot tell us what those things are by any of their qualities, then we must be truly assured that those things are spiritual things, and not physical things.[e]

a. But the application of our spiritual senses can also fail when we encounter a spiritual reality that cannot be explained by mind, reason, or will—and then we can be assured that it must be the incomprehensible God.

b. The first and only explicit reference to Pseudo-Dionysius—although the entire book is based on his ideas. (Dionysius, *Divine Names*, in P. Chevalier, ed., *Dionysiaca* [Bruges: 1937]). My translation: "On the other hand, the most divinely inspired knowledge of God is that he is known by unknowing."

c. The ME has *doctour*—literally, in the fourteenth century, either "medical doctor" or "one with a doctor's degree (authorizing one to teach)," or, thus, "teacher." The author obviously refers to earlier spiritual writers, so I use "teacher" here and "Fathers" in the next sentence.

d. In effect the author is telling his protégé that he could cite all sorts of experts and authorities, but that would only be *corioustee and schewyng of kunnyng*—and he doesn't need that! The ME word *corioustee*—"curiosity"—developed from an original innocent "inquisitiveness" to an unsavory "prurience" or "meddlesomeness" by the fifteenth century—some of which is captured by our author.

e. Matthew 13:9: "Who has ears to hear, let him hear."

f. The ending is both abrupt and has a quality of intolerant judgment: "If you don't believe what I have written without references and citations, then you simply won't believe it." The ME verb for "shall" here—*scholen*—is strong enough when used with the third person to carry the sense of "even if they wish it otherwise, they *shall* not believe."

g. Chapters 71–73 are "little more than a translation of passages from *Benjamin Major* [by Richard of St. Victor]" (Hodgson, lxxiii).

h. The ME has *tyme of ravisching*—often taken as "time of rapture"—but Walsh properly points out that the author means "mystical trance" (I Walsh, 257 n.).

i. Perhaps the core dynamic of contemplative Work: that it comes *only* as a gift of insight at the "dictate and disposition of God" and can never be earned, merited, or deserved.

In this same manner, spiritually it works within our spiritual abilities, when we labor over the knowledge of God Himself—for no matter how much spiritual understanding a person has in the knowledge of every *created* spiritual thing, still one can never by the efforts of one's understanding come to the knowledge of an *un*created spiritual thing, which is nothing but God.ª But by the failure of such spiritual understanding, one can do so, because that in which it fails is nothing else but God alone. And for this it was that Saint Denis said, "The most godly knowledge of God is that which is known by unknowing."ᵇ

And truly, those who read Saint Denis's books will find that his words will clearly affirm all that I have said or shall say, from the beginning of this treatise to the end. Otherwise than this I care not to cite him, nor any other teacherᶜ for me at this time. For at one time people thought it humility to say nothing out of their own heads unless they affirmed it by Scripture and sayings of the Fathers—and now this practice has turned into idiosyncrasy and the flaunting of cleverness. You do not need it and therefore I do not do it.ᵈ For whoever has ears, let them hear,ᵉ and whoever is stirred to believe, let them believe—otherwise they shall not.ᶠ

☞ HERE BEGINS THE SEVENTY-FIRST CHAPTERᵍ

That some may not find the perfection of this Work except during ecstasy and some may find it when they wish, in the ordinary state of one's soul.

Some think that this matter is so difficult and so terrifying that they say it cannot be undertaken without much fervent effort preceding it, nor achieved only seldom, and then in the time of ecstasy.ʰ And to these I will answer as delicately as I can, and say that it is all at the dictate and disposition of God—depending on the fitness of their soul—that this grace of contemplation and of spiritual working is given.ⁱ

For some there are who without extensive or long spiritual exercises may not come to contemplation—and even then it shall be both very seldom and by special vocation from our Lord that they shall experience the perfection of this Work—which vocation is called "ecstasy." And there are some who

a. The ME has *sotyl in grace*—literally, "subtle" (Bradley, 592). ODEE (881) has "of fine consistency or fine discrimination." Cowan (274) translates it as "refined"; OAD (1688) has "delicate" or "precise."

b. The ME has *homely*—literally, "familiar." I tried to capture the "home-ishness" by using "at home with."

c. Although the author speaks of two ways the contemplative state is discovered—some by hard and arduous work, and others very effortlessly—his choice of language certainly suggests that the latter is superior. (Note: the phrase "but without very much" was inserted in the MS in a different hand.)

d. The ME has *Arke of the Testament*. I have chosen the more modern terminology: "Ark of the Covenant."

e. This same set of metaphors of the Ark, Moses, and Aaron are used by Saint Augustine, Richard of St. Victor, and Saint John of the Cross (cited by Cowan, 274). The references are, of course, to the accounts in Exod. 24:15 and the following chapters concerning the intricate design and construction of the Ark.

f. This surely is a very peculiar exegesis of the story of Moses on Mount Sinai. Elsewhere it is universally understood that the purpose for Moses's extended time on Mount Sinai was to receive the Ten Commandments, but here the author suggests that Moses was going through a strenuous struggle on the mountain in order to convince God to give him instructions on how to build the Ark. The author warps the story a bit to make his metaphorical point.

g. This paragraph is almost word for word from Richard of St. Victor's treatise *Benjamin Major*.

h. It is telling that our author has a broad enough experience with the contemplative way that he would know of people who had struggled with the experience as well as those for whom it came quickly and easily. Having done spiritual direction with contemplatives for over thirty years, I can testify to the accuracy of this distinction. It is also of some interest that the author sees Aaron's contemplative facility as related to his priestly office in the Temple—possibly a subtle extension of the metaphor to suggest that the ordained have an easier time of it.

are so temperate[a] in grace and in spirit, and so at home[b] with God in this grace of contemplation, that they may have it when they remain in the ordinary state of their soul—as in sitting, moving, standing, or kneeling. And yet in this time they have full use of all their senses, bodily or spiritually, and may use them if they wish (not without some difficulty, but without very much).[c] An example of the first we have in Moses, and of the other in Aaron, the priest of the Temple, because this grace of contemplation is signified by the Ark of the Covenant[d] of the Old Law, and the workers in this grace are signified by those that most assembled themselves around this Ark (as the story will witness).[e] And this grace and this Work are well-linked to that Ark. For just as in that Ark were contained all the jewels and relics of the Temple, just so in this little offered love which is the *spiritual* Temple of God are contained all the virtues of one's soul.

Moses, before he could come to see this Ark, and before he knew how it ought to be made, with great long effort climbed up to the top of the mountain and dwelled there and toiled within a cloud for six days (remaining until the seventh day) so that our Lord would consent to show him the method of Ark-building.[f] By Moses's long struggle and his delayed showing are understood those that may not come to the perfection of this spiritual Work without long struggle preceding it, and even then only very seldom, and when God may consent to show it.[g]

But what Moses could not come to see (except seldom and that not without great long struggle), Aaron had in his power (because of his office) to see it in the temple within the veil as often as he wished to enter. And by this Aaron is understood as all those whom I spoke of above, who by their spiritual skills with the help of grace may arrogate to themselves the perfection of this Work as often as they like.[h]

⟡ HERE BEGINS THE SEVENTY-SECOND CHAPTER

That one who undertakes this Work should not judge or evaluate another contemplative on the basis of one's own experience.

Look! By this you can see that someone who cannot attain and experience the perfection of this Work except with great struggle, and then only seldom,

a. The author's prohibition of one's comparing one's contemplative experience with that of others is extremely fervent—including the terse ME injunction *Lat be this* (literally, "Let this be!") and the use of the ME *he may not think thus*, when in ME *may* paradoxically means "can." Some even translate it as "must" (I Walsh, 259; Walters, 147; Butcher, 159); and some as "should" (Cowan, 276; Spearing, 98). And I second the author's caution against comparisons between the two styles based on my experience as spiritual director.

b. The author holds out hope that one's "contemplative style" may change over time and with practice so that the one who struggles early in the Work may find it easier later on.

c. An interesting textual issue: several early manuscripts of the book have the ME words *in the veyle* ("within the veil") here, and one of the Latin translations has *intra velum* ("within the veil"). This would refer to the veil of the Temple that separated the Holy of Holies where the Ark lay. But the manuscript we have been following has the ME *in the vaale* ("in the valley"), which makes an appropriate contrast for Moses between "on the mountain" where he had to struggle and "in the valley" where no struggle was needed. Note: In the third sentence of the next paragraph the word *vaale* clearly means "valley."

d. *Beseleel* is the Vulgate's Latin spelling of the name "Bezalel." He was the craftsman whom God appointed to construct the Ark under Moses's direction. He is described as "the son of Uri, the son of Hur, of the tribe of Juda." The Lord tells Moses: "I have filled him [Beseleel] with the spirit of God, with wisdom and intelligence, and knowledge in all manner of workmanship" (Exod. 31:2).

e. The author knows a good metaphor when he has one, and he presses forward now with Moses as the example of our benefiting from spiritual growth "by grace alone"; Beseleel as our benefiting from our own spiritual skill and resourcefulness developed from practice (and from the "spiritual direction" of Moses); and Aaron as our spiritual growth that comes from the teachings of others. Cowan (280) suggests that Aaron is presented as "the official spiritual director."

may be easily deceived if one speaks, thinks, and judges others on the basis of one's own experience. In the same way, one can also be deceived who can have the contemplative experience whenever one wishes, if that person judges all others based on that, saying that they, too, can have it whenever they wish. Leave this alone: no, assuredly one simply cannot think this way.[a] For possibly, when it is pleasing to God, those who at first can have it only seldom and not without great struggle, later on may come to have it whenever they wish, as often as they like.[b] As an example of this we have Moses who at first could see the design of the Ark only seldom and not without great labor on the mountain, but later on, as often as he wished, he saw it in the valley.[c]

HERE BEGINS THE SEVENTY-THIRD CHAPTER

How by following the examples of Moses, of Beseleel, and of Aaron as they concerned themselves with the Ark of the Covenant, we benefit in three ways in this grace of contemplation, for that grace is represented by the Ark.

Three men there were who primarily concerned themselves with this Ark of the Old Covenant: Moses, Beseleel,[d] and Aaron. Moses learned on the mountain of our Lord how the Ark should be made. Beseleel constructed and built it in the valley, following the example that had been shown on the mountain. And Aaron had the Ark in his care in the Temple, to touch it and see it as often as he liked.

Based on the similarity of these three, we benefit in three ways in this grace of contemplation.[e] Sometimes we benefit by grace alone, and then we are similar to Moses who for all the climbing and the labors that he has on the mountain, could not come to see it except rarely—and even then that vision was only by our Lord's showing it to him when it pleased Him to show it, and not because Moses deserved it for his labors. Sometimes we benefit in this grace by our own spiritual skill, aided by grace, and then we are similar to Beseleel who could not see the Ark before the time that he built it by his own labor, aided by the example that had been shown to Moses on the mountain. And sometimes we benefit in this grace by others'

a.   All humble protestations notwithstanding, the author *does* see himself as the prime constructor of his protégé's spiritual and contemplative life. It is also clear that when writing this the author had a very specific individual reader in mind. However, his recommendation is that his protégé can do most to advance spiritually by practicing contemplation "constantly." If the author sees himself as Beseleel, he wants his protégé to be Aaron.

b.   Here the author suggests that the task of a contemplative is not merely to achieve personal union with God, but to do so on behalf of the Church. He speaks of his protégé and himself as "both called by God to undertake this Work"—which distinguishes this call to contemplation as clearly distinct from the call of other Christians. The contemplative call, in a very real sense, is not unlike that of the *Lamed Vav Tzadikim*—the "righteous ones" in the mystical Judaic tradition—who are the thirty-six men whose righteousness keeps God from destroying the world. They serve for the sake and the benefit of the many. Also, the line may be evidence that both author and protégé are in the same spiritual (monastic?) community.

c.   The author is very careful here near the end to remind both himself and his reader that the true contemplative way requires a calling from God—a sense that one's temperament has been divinely attuned to and attracted by this Work. And if one does not sense this call or one's temperament seems not in harmony with it, one ought to drop it and move in another spiritual direction.

d.   If the reader does not feel drawn to "the Work," the author asks to be excused. The ME *haue me excusid* in the fourteenth century did not mean "pardon me" (as some have it); it meant "release me [from responsibility]."

e.   This advice for the book to be read two or three times before being rejected is as valid today as it was then. It is not an "easy" book, and repetitive exposure makes it ultimately much clearer and less obstructed.

f.   The ME has *the effecte of this werk*. In the fourteenth century *effecte* meant "result" or "outcome" (MED).

g.   The author is still dealing with the question of the suitability of this book for a contemplative seeker—and here he states his strong opinion that anyone who is truly called and inclined to contemplation would feel attracted to this book. I know from experience that this is absolutely true given the reactions of readers. Only those with a natural contemplative bent (or "disposition") find it at all appealing.

teaching. And then we are similar to Aaron who had the Ark in his keeping and regularly could see and touch the Ark whenever he liked after Beseleel had built it and made it ready for his hands.

See, my spiritual friend, in this Work—although it may seem childish and crudely spoken and though I am a wretch unworthy to teach any creature—I have the task of Beseleel—making and in a way placing in your hands the pattern of this spiritual Ark.[a] But you can work far better and more worthily than I if you will be Aaron—that is to say, constantly working in contemplation for you and for me. Do so then, I beg you, for the love of God Almighty. And since we are both called by God to undertake this Work,[b] I beseech you for the love of God, fulfill on your part what is lacking in mine.

✎ HERE BEGINS THE SEVENTY-FOURTH CHAPTER

How the subject of this book is never read or spoken, nor heard read or spoken of, by a soul inclined to contemplation without that soul feeling a true harmony with the effect of the same work; and of repeating the same charge that is written in the prologue.

And if you think that this way of Working does not agree with your temperament in body and in soul, you can leave it and with good spiritual advice take up another safely without liability.[c] And then I beseech you that you have me excused, for truly I wanted to have benefited you in this writing out of my humble wisdom, and that was my intent.[d] So read it over twice or thrice—and always the more often the better, and the more you will understand about it, so much so that, perhaps, some article that was very difficult for you at the first or second reading, afterward you shall consider very easy.[e]

Yea! and it seems impossible to my understanding that any soul that is disposed to this Work should read it, or speak it, or else hear it read or spoken, but that that same soul should feel then a true attraction to the outcome[f] of this Work.[g] And then, if you think it does you good, thank God heartily, and for God's love, pray for me.

Do so then! Also I beg you for the love of God that you let none see this book unless it be such a person as you think is amenable to the book—

a. Basically this is a paraphrase of the opening lines in the prologue to the book. "This recapitulation produces an 'envelope' effect for the work as a whole. The reader is not left hanging in the cloud of unknowing, but is explicitly brought back to the point at which s/he began" (Cowan, 282).

b. This order to "read it all the way through" was not uncommon in medieval spiritual writing. Note the colophon to Julian's *Revelations*: "I pray Almighty God that this book does not come into the hands of anyone except those who are His faithful lovers, and those that will submit themselves to the Faith of Holy Church.... And beware that thou not accept one thing after thine own inclination and preference and omit another, for that is the situation of an heretic. But accept each thing with the other and truly understand that all is in agreement with Holy Scripture and grounded in the same" (II Julian, 375).

c. And *The Letter of Privy Counsel* is precisely what he promises.

d. The ME list of ne'er-do-wells—*fleschley jangelers, glosers and blamers, roukers and rounders, and alle maner of pynchers*—can be translated in dozens of ways. *Jangelers* are "babblers" or "prattlers"; *glosers* are "flatterers" or "perverts"; *blamers* are "fault-finders" or "carpers"; *roukers* are "cowards" or "crouchers" (the word is Scottish); *rounders* are "whisperers" or "rumor-mongers"; and *pynchers* are "fault-finders" or "complainers."

e. The ME has *never the rather*—literally, "no matter the more" or almost "nevertheless." The sense is "in spite of that."

f. The author is clear that there is no point in even wondering if one is called to contemplation without having one's conscience cleared by auricular confession. The author is not guilty (as some critics have claimed) of bypassing the rites and functions of the Church, but rather sees them as essential.

g. The presence of a competent and experienced spiritual director in all aspects of the contemplative life—from entry to ecstasy—is absolutely essential. Perhaps the greatest challenge to a modern-day aspiring contemplative is to find such a director. They are rare in today's church. And, notice that he speaks of the director in the third person, i.e., he himself is *not* the protégé's formal spiritual director. Further evidence that they are separated.

h. The ME has *Yif it be thus, weel is inasmoche*—"So far, so good" (I Walsh, 264; Wolters, 150). "If it be thus, it is so far well" (McCann, 98). "When this is done, that much is well" (Butcher, 165). "If so, it is well so far" (Spearing, 100).

according to what you find written in the book above where it tells who and when they should undertake this Work.[a] And if you shall allow any such person to see it, then I beg you that you bid the person to take time to read it all the way through. For possibly there may be some matter in it— in the beginning or in the middle—which is left hanging and not clearly explained there as it stands, but if not there, then soon after or else in the end. And thus if a person saw one part and not another, possibly he could easily be led into error. And therefore I beg you to do as I tell you.[b]

And if you think that there is any matter in it that you would like more clearly explained than it is, let me know what it is and your concept of it, and by my humble wisdom it shall be amended if I can.[c]

Worldly prattlers, flatterers and hecklers, sneaks and gossips, and all kind of detractors[d]—I never cared that they saw this book. For my intention was never to write such a thing for them. And therefore I prefer that they not hear it, neither they nor any of these merely curious educated or unlettered people. Yea! even if they may be truly good people who live active lives— for this offers nothing to them.

HERE BEGINS THE SEVENTY-FIFTH CHAPTER

Of some specific signs by which one can confirm whether one is called by God to this Work.

All those who read or hear the contents of this book read or spoken, and in this reading or hearing think it a good and pleasing thing, are by no means actually[e] called by God to undertake this Work only because of this pleasing stirring they feel while reading this. For possibly the stirring comes more from a natural curiosity of mind than of any calling of grace.

But if they wish to discover where this feeling comes from, they may test this if they wish. First let them see if they have done all they can beforehand, making themselves adequate for that by the cleansing of their conscience at the judgment of Holy Church,[f] with the agreement of their spiritual director.[g] If that be so, then so far all is well.[h] But if they wish to know more closely, let them see if it always presses on their mind more regularly than any other spiritual exercise. And if they think that there is nothing

a. The ME has *put be*—"pushed by" or "put by."

b. The ME has *cheef*—literally, "chief" or "head man" or "top" (ODEE, 168).

c. "For the contemplative to think that s/he had anything to do with the grace, in terms of desert, is simply pride. Whenever the feeling of grace is withdrawn, pride is the cause" (Cowan, 286).

d. An unusual concept: that God withdraws grace to protect the apprentice not just from being prideful at the moment, but also as protection against a future pride that would result if the grace were not withdrawn. Note: The author subtly demonstrates God's freedom from the limitations of time and place in his knowing "what would happen if...."

e. How often is heard something like: "I hate you, God, for letting my loved one die"? The author wants his readers to know that the temporary withdrawal of grace must not be seen to mean God is one's enemy.

f. The ME has *cauteel*—literally, "deceit" (Mayhew, 40).

g. The ME has in *deintee*—literally, "importance" or "dignity" (Bradley, 157).

h. The ME has *sovereynist*—literally, "supreme" or "paramount." "Authoritative" is from Cowan (286).

i. The ME word *love-longing* is of such beauty that I choose not to translate it.

j. The surest evidence that one has a calling to the contemplative way is the joy and overweening fervor when the "sense of vocation" returns after being temporarily withheld by God.

k. One of the best of the many adages in the book. Walsh (I 265 n.) reminds us of the phrase from the writings of Margery Kempe († 1438): "I take no heed of what a man has been, but I take heed of what he will be."

l. Found in Gregory the Great, *Homilia in Evangelia* 2.25 (I Walsh, 265 n.).

that they do, physically or spiritually, that is adequately done according to the witness of their conscience, unless this secret little love is pushed forth[a] spiritually as the head[b] of all their work, and if they experience this it is a sign that they are called by God to this Work—otherwise, surely not.

I do not say that it shall always last and dwell in all their minds continually who are called to undertake this Work. No, it is not so. For from a young spiritual apprentice in this Work, the actual feeling of it is often withdrawn for various reasons—sometimes so that he shall not become over-familiar with it and imagine that it is in a large measure in his own power to have it when he wishes and as he wishes it. And such a belief would be pride.[c] And always when the feeling of grace is withdrawn, pride is the cause—not only the pride that exists, but the pride that would be if the feeling of grace were withdrawn.[d] And often some young fools believe that God is their enemy—when He is their true friend.[e]

Sometimes the feeling is withdrawn because of their carelessness, and when it is thus, they feel soon after a very bitter pain that strikes them profoundly. Sometimes our Lord will delay it by a deception,[f] for He wishes by such a delay to make it grow and be more in value[g] when it is newfound and felt again after having been lost. And this is one of the surest and most authoritative[h] signs that a soul can have to know whether it is called or not to undertake this Work—if one feels after such a delay and long absence of this Work that when it comes as unexpectedly as it does, not acquired by any means, that one has then a greater fervor of desire and a greater love-longing[i] to undertake this Work than one ever had before, so much so that I believe one has more joy finding it than ever one had sorrow in losing it.[j] And if it is so, surely it is a strong sign without doubt that he is called by God to undertake this Work—whatever he is now or has been in the past.

For with His merciful eye God looks upon neither what you are, nor what you have been, but what you wish to be.[k] And Saint Gregory is witness that "all holy desires grow by delays; and if they fade by delays, then they were never holy desires."[l] For the one who experiences less and less joy in the new discoveries and sudden presentations of one's old intended desires (even though they all may be called "natural desires for the good") nevertheless they were never "holy desires." Of this holy desire Saint Augustine speaks

a. Found in Augustine, *In Epistolam Joannis at Parthos* 4.6 (I Walsh, 266 n.).

b. It is nice to use *farewell* in its ME sense: "Fare well" ("Journey well").

and says that "All the life of a good Christian person is nothing except holy desire."[a]

Fare well,[b] my spiritual friend, with God's blessing and mine! And I beseech Almighty God that true peace, holy counsel, and spiritual comfort in God with plenteous grace may evermore be with you and all God's lovers on earth. Amen.

HERE ENDS THE CLOUD OF UNKNOWING.

THE LETTER
OF PRIVY
COUNSEL

a. The title of this piece has varied among manuscripts. It has been called *The Book of Priue Counseling* (MS Harleian 674); *A Tretyse of Priue Counceile* (MS Harleian 2373); *An Epistle of Priuate Counsell* (MS Ff. vi. 41); *The Pystle of Pryuate Cownsell* (MS Ii. vi. 31); *A Tretyse of Pryuey Conseylle* (MS Kk. vi. 26); *The Pystelle of Priuat Councelle* (MS Douce 262); *The Pystell of Pryvate Cownsell* (MS Bodleian 576); *The Pistle of Pryuate Cownsell* (Parkminster MS). I have chosen to use "The Letter of Privy Counsel" because (1) the writing is too brief to be called a "book"; (2) it is too personal to be called a "treatise"; (3) I think the meaning of the ME *privy* is clear even to modern readers who know no Middle English; and (4) it really is a letter—an epistle addressed to one person—probably the last thing written by the author.

b. The ME has *here*—literally, "hear" but also "get to know," "hear of," or "be told of" (ODEE, 433).

c. By "this time" is mean to contrast with "last time"—i.e., in *The Cloud*.

d. The ME has *prik*—literally, "prick" or "spike" or "spur"—but with the narrower sense of "mark on a target" (Bradley, 484).

e. The chapter headings and their epigrams do not appear in the original manuscripts. They were composed and inserted in 1924 by Abbot Justin McCann (101) and have been modernized for this book.

f. In the phrase "by yourself" the author means "when you go apart for contemplative prayer". Butcher (172) has "when you withdraw from the world for prayer." It presumes the reader is a practicing contemplative.

g. The ME has *ne charge not*. *Charge* is translated as "put load on" or "care for" (Mayhew, 527).

h. The ME has *bemenith*—literally, "signifies" (Mossé, 427) or "means."

i. The ME has *enditid*—literally, "composed," "written," "indicted," or "accused" (Mayhew, 73).

j. The ME has *make*—literally, "create" or "build" (Burrow, 286). This is a challenge because in modern English "make" can also carry the sense of "force" or "present as" or "characterize as," as I use it here (OAD, 1023).

THE LETTER OF PRIVY COUNSEL[a]

Spiritual friend in God, regarding your inner Work to which I believe you are predisposed, I speak at this time in particular to yourself and not to all those in general who might be told of[b] this writing. For if I were to write for everyone, then I would have to write something that was widely agreeable to all. But since this time I shall be writing to you in particular, therefore I shall write nothing except what I think it most beneficial and suited to your disposition alone. If any other is as predisposed as you are— whom this writing can benefit as it does you—so much the better, for I am well satisfied. At this time,[c] however, your own inner disposition by itself, as I can understand it, is the only point and the target[d] of my consideration. And therefore to you—representing all others like you—I say thus:

THE FIRST CHAPTER

That this Work is a striving toward God, wherein one offers oneself to God, being-to-being, without unusual questioning about the attributes of one's own being or of God's.[e]

When you come to be by yourself[f] do not plan beforehand what you shall do afterward, but abandon both good thoughts as well as evil thoughts. And do not pray with your mouth unless that pleases you a lot; and then, if you do say anything, pay no attention to how much or how little it may be— and pay no attention to[g] what it seems to be or what it signifies,[h] whether it is a prayer or a psalm, hymn, or antiphon, or any other prayer, general or specific, mental (composed[i] inwardly by thought) or vocal (outwardly by speaking words). And see to it that nothing remains in your working mind except a naked intent reaching toward God, not wrapped in any particular thought about God in Himself—what He is in his own nature or in any of His works—but only that He is as He is. Let Him be so, I beg you, and make Him out[j] to be in no other way. Look no further into Him by cleverness of wit. Let that belief be your foundation. The naked intent, freely fixed and grounded in true belief, shall be nothing more to your thought and to your

a. "The external world seems to get further and further away, till at last nothing but the paramount fact of his own existence remains" (Underhill, cited by Hodgson, 205 n.). The feeling becomes "more particularly an imageless awareness of God (and of oneself)" (III Clark, 2).

b. The ME has *mynde*—literally, "mind," but fourteenth-century use has "memory," "love," and "desire" as alternative meanings (ODEE, 577).

c. The ME has *ferther*—literally, "further" or "to an advanced point" (ODEE, 382).

d. The ME has *departyng*—literally, "departure" or "separation" (ODEE, 257).

e. The ME has *scatering*—literally, "squandering" or "dispersal" (ODEE, 795).

f. The ME has *bi cause & bi being*. Since these are technical theological terms from the Scholastic tradition, in order to avoid confusion I have translated them as "by creation" and "by essence."

g. Reminiscent of Julian of Norwich's words: "It is an exalted understanding inwardly to see and to know that God who is our Creator dwells in our soul, and it is a more exalted understanding inwardly to see and to know that our soul, which is created, dwells in God's essence—from which essence, by God, we are what we are. I saw no difference between God and our essence, but just as if it were all God, and yet my understanding accepted that our essence is in God—that is to say, that God is God, and our essence is a creation of God" (I Julian, 263).

h. "For our soul is so completely one-ed to God by His own goodness, that there can be absolutely nothing at all separating God and soul" (I Julian, 213).

i. The ME has *corious sechinges*—literally, "curious seekings," but there is a negative sense of "nosy snooping" that I translate as "inquisitive scrutiny."

j. The ME has *queinte*—literally, "quaint," but with a negative sense of "odd" or even "bizarre" that I translate as "peculiar."

k. The ME has *blinde*—literally, "blind" but here takes the sense of "unseen" or "obscure." In most cases I have left "blind" when it implies "unseeing."

l. The ME *nakid* and *touching* are among the author's favorite words—*nakid* with the implications of "unadorned," "unprotected," "vulnerable"; and *touching* describing the gentle trace of contact with grace/God.

m. The ME has *boistously*—literally, "sturdily," "loudly," "violently," "roughly," or "stiffly" (ODEE, 105).

n. The ME has *coriouste*—literally, "curiosity," but the author uses the word in an edgy kind of way, usually with some negative implications. (See "d" above.) Here I chose to use "speculation" (Burrow, 272).

feeling than a naked thought and a blind feeling of your own being[a]—as if you said thus to God inwardly in your meaning: "What I am, Lord, I offer to you, without any analysis of any aspect of your being except simply that you are as you are—without anything more."

Let that humble darkness be your vision and your whole desire.[b] Think no differently[c] of yourself than I bade you think of your God, so that in this way you may be one with Him in spirit, without any separation[d] or diffusion[e] of mind—for He is your being, and in Him you are what you are, not only generally by creating and by being, but also He is within you as both your own creator and your own being.

And therefore think of God in this Work as you think of yourself, and think of yourself as you do of God—that He is as He is and you are as you are—so that your thought is not dispersed or diffused, but united within Him who is all (always excepting this difference between you and Him: that He is your essence and you are not his). For, although it is true that all things are in Him as their cause and their essence[f] and He is in all things as their cause and their essence, yet in Himself He alone is His own cause and His own essence. For just as nothing can exist without Him, so He cannot exist without Himself. He is essence both of Himself and of all things. And in that alone He is different from all else in that He is essence both of Himself and of all things, and that He is one in all things, and that in Him all things have their essence and He is the essence of all.[g]

Thus shall your thoughts and your feelings be one-ed with Him in grace without separation,[h] with all inquisitive scrutiny[i] into the peculiar[j] qualities of your obscure[k] essence (or of His) pushed far back, so that your thought may be naked and your affections in no way befouled, and so you—naked as you are with the touching of grace[l]—may be secretly nourished in your affections only by Him as He is (both blindly and partially as it can be here in this life) so that your longing desire may be constantly working.

Look up then lightly and say to the Lord (either with your mouth or the meaning of your heart): "What I am, Lord, I offer to you, for you are it," and think nakedly, plainly, and firmly[m] that you are as you are, without any kind of speculation.[n]

There is little skill in considering this, it seems to me, even if it were asked of the most ignorant man or woman that lives in the most ordinary natural

a. The ME has *heigh*—literally, "high," but it also carries the sense of "impressive" or even "celestial." I chose "imposing" (Mayhew, 111).

b. The ME has *curious* (once again). In this case the context requires less common meanings. Mayhew (57) gives "dainty" and "refined."

c. The ME has *clergie*. Mayhew (46) gives us a variety of translations:"clergy," or "the clerical profession," or "book-learning." The strange combination derives from the fact that generally the people who had university degrees and could read and write were clergy. So, for instance, the ME word *cleric* in the fourteenth century primarily meant "scholar." In the eleventh century it meant primarily "clergyman," but by the sixteenth century the word became "clerk," lost its ecclesiastical origins completely, and came to mean an accountant or a secretary or bookkeeper.

d. This is linguistically and grammatically the most complicated sentence in the entire book. Forty-two words and at least six dependent clauses!

e. The author's claim of simplicity notwithstanding, the distinction he makes is not easy or self-evident. He differentiates between what the Scholastics of the previous century called "substance" (or "essence" or "being" or "personhood"—who a person *is*) and "accidents" (or "qualities" or "attributes" or "characteristics"—what a person *has*). This is important to the author because in the course of his radical spirituality he aims to have one's actual *essence* one-ed to the *essence* of God—and one's external attributes are at least irrelevant if not an impediment to that union. He wants one to think of one's *states*: human, rational, sinful—rather than one's *traits*: tall or short, fat or thin, talented or unskilled, etc. It is one's "is-ness" that is to relate to God's "is-ness"—since they are both essences, alike and shared by God and human.

f. The author speaks with cutting vitriol—what you and I consider the lowest of human potential is seen by some as their greatest achievement; what you and I see as stupidity is seen by some as wisdom!

wit in this life. And because of that I sometimes marvel quietly, sadly, and amusedly, when I hear people say (I do not mean simple unlettered men and women, but clerics and those of great learning) that my writing to you and to others is so difficult and so imposing[a] and so refined[b] and so bizarre that it can scarcely be understood by the shrewdest scholar or sensible man or woman in this life, as they say. But to these I must answer and say that it is a matter to be greatly regretted and mercifully scorned and bitterly condemned by God and his lovers, that nowadays not only a few people, but generally nearly all (except perhaps for one or two in a country among the specially chosen of God), are so blinded by their ingenious cleverness of book-learning[c] and the likes that the true conception of this easy work, through which the rudeness of man's or woman's soul in this life is truly in loving humility one-ed to God in perfect charity, can no more (nor yet even as much) be understood by them in truthfulness of spirit (because of their blindness and their eccentricity) than can a young child that is at his ABCs understand the intelligence of the greatest scholar in the schools.[d] And because of this blindness they falsely call such simple teaching "ingenuity of wit," when, if it were intelligently examined, it would be only a simple and easy lesson for an unlettered person.

For I hold one to be ignorant and coarse who cannot recognize and be aware that he IS—not WHAT he himself is but THAT he himself is—that he exists.[e] For this is plainly appropriate for the most ignorant cow or for the most irrational beast (in case it were to be said—as it cannot—that one was more ignorant or more irrational than another) to be aware of one's own personal existence. Much more, then, is it appropriate for human beings who are singularly endowed with reason above all other beasts, in order to think and to be aware of their own proper existence.

And therefore, come down into the lowest point of your wit (which some men hold by true experience to be the highest)[f] and think in the most stupid way (which is held by some to be the wisest) not WHAT you yourself are, but THAT you yourself are. Because for you to think WHAT you are in all your idiosyncrasies requires much expertise in learning and in cleverness and much subtle searching in your natural intelligence—and this you have done now for many a day with the help of grace, so that you know now partially (and as I suppose is beneficial to you for the time

a. Like most Christian mystics, the author expends very little energy over sins. Of course, he sees sins as foul, wretched, putrid garbage, but he is also clearly aware that particular sins are absolved in the confessional, and that in general one comes to "this Work" already having been cleansed of actual sin. So, he recognizes sin for what it is and then pays very little attention to it once it has been purged according to the rules of the church.

b. The ME has *caas*—literally, "case" or "circumstance." It also shares with its modern cognate the definition of a "container" (and it can even mean a "quiver") (Mayhew, 37).

c. The author's clear statement about one of the essential preparatory steps before beginning the Work of contemplation: full absolution of all sins. Indeed, much of his writing presumes more fundamental Christian responsibilities—presence at Mass, works of mercy, practice of the virtues, and such like—have already been accomplished before beginning on contemplation.

d. The ME has *a plastre*—literally, a "poultice" or "compress"—"usually made from herbs, meal, or other substance, often applied on a cloth to the affected area" (MED).

e. An atypical (and almost humorous) simplistic statement from the author: "Of course you are a mess, but just stick God on over it all like a Band-Aid and it will be okay!" Or just spiritually lift yourself up and reach out spiritually to "touch" God. It is quite amazing how the author makes the deepest ascetic practices sound so utterly simple.

f. Matt. 9:21 in the Latin Vulgate Bible (which was the "official" Bible during the fourteenth century) has "*Si tetigero tantum vestimentum ejus, salva ero*": "If I can touch only his garment, I shall be healed." The author's ME has *If I touché bot the hemme of his clothing, I schal be saaf.* The slight variation in wording (which does not change the meaning!) is evidence that the author wrote the quotation from memory—and brought in the "hem" from Matt. 14:36 where "[They] begged him to touch even the hem of his cloak, and all who touched it were healed."

g. The ME has *triacle*—literally, "treacle." Today that refers to molasses—the uncrystallized syrup produced in refining sugar—but in the fourteenth century it referred to an antidote for venomous bites and other illnesses composed of many ingredients and also called *theriaca* (ODEE, 939).

being) WHAT you are: a person by nature, and a foul stinking wretch by sin. How well you know it! Indeed, probably you know *too* well all the filths that follow and fall upon a sinner. Fie on them! Let them go, I beg you! Don't stir them up any further for fear of the stench.[a] But to know THAT you exist—that ability you can have merely from your own ignorance and simplicity without any great cleverness from book-learning or from natural wisdom.

THE SECOND CHAPTER

In what way a person should offer one's being to God; and in particular, that one ought to cease from busy meditation.

And therefore, I beg you, do no more now in this situation[b] except to think bluntly that you are as you are—no matter how foul or how wretched—so long as you have beforehand (as I assume you have) been formally absolved of all your sins in particular and in general, following the true counsel of Holy Church—otherwise neither you nor anyone else, by my consent, should ever be so bold as to take upon you this Work.[c] But if you feel that you have done all you can, then you should commit yourself to this Work. And even though you may feel yourself still so vile and so wretched that since you are such burden to yourself you do not yourself know what is best for you to do with yourself, then you shall do as I tell you:

Take the good gracious God as He is, flat and plain as a bandage,[d] and apply it on your sick self just as you are.[e] Or, to say it in another way, bear up your sick self as you are and try by longing for it to touch the good gracious God as He is. That touching of God is limitless help as is witnessed by the woman in the Gospel:

"*Si tetigero vel fimbriam vestimenti eius, salua ero*"[f]—"If I touch only the hem of his clothing, I shall be healed." Much more, then, will *you* be healed of your sickness by this noble heavenly touching of His own essence, His own dear self. Step up stoutly, then, and try that medicine[g]; lift up your sick self (just as you are) unto gracious God (just as He is) without any peculiar or particular examination of any of all the attributes that are part of your essence or of God's—whether they are pure or wretched, divine or human,

a. The ME has beholding—literally, "seeing," "observing," or "comprehending" (MED). I have chosen "vision" as a synonym for "seeing." It produces the paradox "blind vision," which is what I think the author intended (and which is so characteristic of the great mystics).

b. The ME has *listines*, which means "receptivity" or "readiness."

c. This sentence is the kernel, the essence, and the central core of the entire contemplative tradition: an unseeing, unadorned, joyful spirit swept up in love to be melded with the reality that is God.

d. The author is under no false illusions that the contemplative way will be easily acceptable—indeed, he knows that it will be criticized and judged and belittled and even condemned, not only by others, but by one's own rational and practical senses, since it may well seem incomprehensible and purposeless.

e. Once again we need to realize that the author does not condemn "lesser meditation"—but he recognizes that when one comes to true contemplation, such meditations are bypassed and must be put away (III Clark, 13).

f. From the beginning the author has warned that the Work is neither intellectual nor emotional. Therefore one's intellect will want to reject it because it makes no sense; and one's affections and emotions will want to reject it because it doesn't make one feel good. Were he present today, the author would note that most functioning religions tend to appeal either to the mind with beliefs, dogmas, and the like or to the emotions with "conversion experiences" and a sentimental "love for Jesus."

g. Prov. 3:9–10. The Latin Vulgate Bible has: "*Honora Dominum de tua substantia et de primitiis omnium frugum tuarum da ei: et inplebuntur horrea tua saturitate et vino torcularia redundabunt*"—"Honor the Lord with your substance, and give him the first of all your fruits: and your barns will be filled with abundance and your presses shall run over with wine."

from grace or nature. Nothing matters in you now except that your blind vision[a] of your naked being be gladly borne upward in the eagerness[b] of love, to be knitted and one-ed in grace and in spirit to the precious essence of God in Himself as He alone is, without anything more.[c]

And although your wanton searching wits can find no sustenance for themselves in this kind of activity, therefore they will complain and demand in every way that you give up that Work and do some good in their odd routines (for it seems to them that what you are doing is worth nothing—all because they can see no reason for it),[d] but I would then even love it the better, because from that it appears that it is more honorable than they are. And why should I not then love it the better—especially when there is no work that I can do or that can be wrought there in the inquisitiveness of any of my wits, physically or spiritually, that could bring me so near to God and so far from the world as this naked little awareness and offering up of my own blind being would do?

So, although your wits can find no sustenance for themselves in this Work and therefore they would have you leave it, yet see to it that you do not abandon it on their account, but be their master! And do not go back to feeding them, no matter how much they rage. You go back to feeding your wits when you allow them to rummage about among the various odd meditations on your own attributes. Those meditations—although they may be very good and very beneficial[e]—nevertheless, in comparison with this blind awareness and the offering up of your own self, they are entirely alien and break away the perfection of one-ness that should be between God and your soul. And therefore, stay with the first peak of your spirit, which is your own being, and do not turn back for any thing—no matter how good or how holy that thing seems to which your wits would lead you.[f]

THE THIRD CHAPTER

That this Work is ordered by Scripture and that in it all
duties (especially that of charity) should be fully performed.

Fulfill the counsel and the teaching of Solomon who said thus to his son: "*Honora Dominum de tua substancia et de primiciis frugum tuarum da pauperibus: et inplebuntur horrea tua saturitate et vino torcularia redundabunt*"[g]—"Honor the

a. Note that the mandate to "feed the poor" is not in the original Latin text from Proverbs but is probably imported from 1 Cor. 13:3—"And if I should distribute all my goods to feed the poor." Another slip of the author's scriptural memory (III, Clark 13).

b. The ME has *substaunce*: an interesting continuing play on the double (and almost opposite) meanings of the word. "Substance" can mean "physical and material things" (as in the Solomon quote) or, in its theological and Scholastic sense, it can mean "spiritual being" or "essence."

c. The author cautions once again against paying attention to one's qualities or characteristics.

d. "First fruits" is a technical ecclesiastical term referring to the first ten percent of one's income/harvest/wealth, which is the "tithe" that in England (until 1836) was legally mandated to be paid to the local parish priest.

e. Another caution (of the many) to keep one's essence and one's attributes separate and not to allow them to be confused or conflated in the Work. Note: If in true contemplation one concerned oneself with one's body, one's feelings, one's physical desires, it would dissolve the entire contemplative consciousness.

f. The ME has *breide oute*—literally, "pull out" or "draw tight" (MED). Note: The word *breide* was used for the gruesome execution process of "hanging, *drawing*, and quartering" and "drawing" a sword (Bradley, 88).

g. In spite of all the error, sins, and misprisions humans are susceptible to, the author still sees a human as "the noblest being."

Lord with your substance and with your first fruits feed the poor: and your
barns shall be filled with plenty and your grape presses shall run over with
wine."[a]

This is the text that Solomon spoke to his son literally, as if he had said to
your understanding spiritually (as I shall say in person to you): "My spiritual
friend in God, see to it that abandoning all curious seeking in your natural
wits, you do complete honor to your Lord God with your essence,[b] offering
up to Him plainly and simply your own self, all that you are and such as you
are (but in general and not in specifics—that is, without particular attention
to *what* you are[c]—that your vision may not be distracted nor your affection
befouled—which would make you less one-ed with God in purity of spirit)
and with the first of your fruits feed the poor—that is, with the first of
your spiritual or bodily aspects that have grown up with you from the first
beginning of your creation until this day."

All the gifts of nature and grace that ever God gave you, I call them "the
fruits" with which you are bound to foster and nourish in this life—both
physically and spiritually—all your brothers and sisters in nature and in
grace just as you are to nourish your very own self. The first of these gifts
I call your "first fruits."[d] The first gift to every created thing is merely the
simple existence of that creature. For though it is true that the attributes of
your existence are so closely joined to your existing self that they cannot be
separated,[e] yet because they all depend on it, truly that being may be called,
just as it is, your "first fruits," and so it is your existence alone that is *your*
"first fruits." For if you draw out[f] the peculiar concern of your heart for any
or all the subtle attributes and the honorable conditions that relate to the
existence of humanity—which is the noblest being of all created things[g]—
you will always find that the first objective and goal for your consideration
(whatsoever it may be) is your own naked being. As if you said thus within
yourself in every one of your visions, directing yourself by means of this
contemplation to the love and the praise of your Lord God who not only
created you (gave you to be) but so *nobly* made you (as the attributes of
your being will witness in that vision), saying thus: "I exist and I see and
feel that I exist, and not only do I exist, but also I am so and so and so and
so" (counting up in your contemplation all the particular attributes of your
existence). And then (what is more than all this) wrap up all this in general

a. The ME has *thou it arte*. See Julian of Norwich: "And that shewed he in the hey, marvelous words wher he seyd: 'I it am that is heyest; I it am that is lowest; I it am that is all'" (II Julian, 116).

b. One is reminded of the famous *Suscipe* prayer of Saint Ignatius Loyola: "Accept, O Lord, all my liberty. Take my memory, my understanding, and my will. Whatsoever I am or have you have given me, and I give it all back to you to be disposed of at your will. Give me only love for you and your grace, and I shall be more than rich and shall desire nothing more."

c. The ME has *the first & the poynte*. My translation is from Hodgson, 207.

d. In its simplest: "All that you *are* is what you have to offer."

e. The ME has *hangyn*—literally, "suspend" or "hang" or "depend" (eleventh definition, MED). One is tempted in this metaphor of fruit to use "hang"—as an apple on a bough.

f. Hebrews 13:15: "Through him then let us offer a sacrifice of praise to God continually, that is, the fruit of our lips giving thanks to his name." The phrase "sacrifice of praise" also appears in the consecration prayer of *The Book of Common Prayer* of the Church of England: "And we earnestly desire thy fatherly goodness mercifully to accept this our sacrifice of praise and thanksgiving."

g. This very confusing paragraph merely counsels the reader not to tie his contemplative self-offering to any particular cause or private purpose, but to undertake it as an act of Christian charity for the benefit of all Christians.

h. Another reference to the doctrine of original sin in which all of humanity lost its primal unity with God when Adam sinned.

i. The ME has *not in special*. Spearing (154) suggests that this means that Christ's humanity and divinity were not divided.

j. The author uses Christ's universal sacrifice for all humanity as the example for a contemplative who by offering one's own self-sacrifice for all humanity benefits everyone and mystically brings others into union with God as well as oneself. This is a frequent and cogent application among contemplatives of the concept of the vicarious benefits of prayer. The notion is primarily based on a vision of mystical solidarity in which each Christian is seen as spiritually linked and bound with every other Christian by their mutual membership within the mystical Body of Christ so that the prayers and virtues of one benefit all.

k. John 15:13: "Greater love than this no one has, that one lays down one's life for one's friends."

and say this: "What I am and how I am—in nature and by grace—I have received all of it from you, Lord, and you are it.[a] And I offer all of it to you[b] primarily by praising you for the help of all my fellow-Christians and for myself." And thus can you see that the highest reach and ultimate end[c] of your contemplation is truly essentially set in the naked vision and blind awareness of your own being. And thus it is merely your existence that is your "first fruits."[d]

But although it is the first of all of your fruits, and although all the other fruits depend[e] upon it, yet it is of no advantage in this situation to wrap or swathe your vision of it in any one or all of its peculiar attributes (which I call your fruits and with which you have been concerned up till now). But it is enough now for you to do complete honor to God with your very being and to offer up that naked being (which is your "first fruits") in continual sacrifice of praise[f] to God both for yourself and for all others as charity demands—with it being stripped of any attribute or particular aspect that in any way refers (or could refer) to your own outward existence or that of any other (as though you could by that attribute relieve the need, further the fortune, or increase the advantage in the direction of the perfection of yourself or of any other). Let this alone: it will certainly not be true in this case. For such a blind *general* regard benefits the need, the fortune, and the perfection of yourself and of all others in purity of spirit more than any *specific* contemplation that anyone could have, no matter how holy it may seem.[g]

This is so—by witness of Scripture, by example of Christ, and by lively reason. For just as all humans were lost in Adam[h] (for he fell from this love that united him to God) so too all who—by the work appropriate to their calling will testify to their desire for salvation—are saved and shall be saved by virtue of the Passion of Christ alone, offering up in the truest sacrifice all that He was—in general and undivided[i] without particular regard for any one living person, but generally for all in common:[j] just so, a true and perfect sacrifice of oneself in contemplation by an intention for all in common does the best one can to knit all humanity to God as effectively as oneself is thus knit. And more charity can no one show than thus to sacrifice oneself for all one's brothers and sisters[k]—in grace and in nature.

a. The ME has *as the soule is more worthi then the body*. In ME *worthi* means "valued," "precious," "honorable," "splendid," or "noble" (MED).

b. In modern terms we might say that for the soul to be together with God is better than "keeping body and soul together."

c. Spearing (154) suggests: "The implication is that contemplation is of higher value than the corporal works of mercy (which include feeding the hungry), good though the latter are in themselves."

d. It is probably more helpful to think of the word *perfection* in this book as carrying the sense of "completedness" or "success" rather than "flawlessness" (MED).

e. The ME has *poynte*—literally, "point" but also, more rarely, "condition" (Bradley, 480). I use the synonym "state." The word can also mean "a small portion" or "a bit" (Mayhew, 175).

f. Again the author refers to the offering of "that naked, blind sense of your own being"—with an almost childlike naiveté in describing what is probably the most spiritually complex undertaking in all practical mystical theology.

g. The ME has *ransakyng*—literally, "ransacking" or "scrutinizing" or "searching through" (MED and Spearing, 110).

h. This is an immeasurably profound grasp of the nature of God—i.e., that God is not only "everlasting" but God is "everlastingness" *itself*—so that whatever can be described as "everlasting" is divine. See Julian of Norwich for a similar insight: "His goodness fills all His creatures and all His blessed works, and surpasses them without end, for He is the endlessness" (I Julian, 79).

For as the soul is more noble than the body,[a] so the knitting of the soul to God (who is its life) by the heavenly food of charity is better than the knitting of the body to the soul (which is its life) by any earthly food in this life.[b] This last is good to do by itself, but without the former it is never well done. Both this *and* the other together is better, but the knitting of the soul to God by itself is best. For knitting of the body to the soul by itself never deserves salvation, but the other by itself (where there is little of the soul-body union) not only deserves salvation, but leads to the greatest perfection.[c]

THE FOURTH CHAPTER

That one who is engaged in this Work need not consider one's own qualities or those of God.

In order to increase your perfection,[d] you need not now go back to nourishing your intellect (as you would do by thinking about the attributes of your being) as though by such attention you could feed and fill your affections with loving and delightful feelings for God and spiritual things, and feed and fill your understanding with the spiritual wisdom of holy meditations that search for knowledge of God. For if you would keep yourself vigorously—as you can by grace—always and constantly in the first state[e] of your spirit, offering up to God that naked, blind sense of your own being[f] (which I call your "first fruits"), you can be certain that the other latter portion of Solomon's teaching will be completely and truly fulfilled as he promised, without your busying yourself in inquisitive scrutiny and rummaging[g] around with your spiritual wits among any of the attributes that are part of your being or also part of God's.

For you must know well that in this Work you shall have no more awareness of the *attributes* of God's essence than of the *attributes* of your own essence. For there is neither name, nor feeling, nor awareness more fitting—or even equally fitting—to the everlastingness[h] that is God than what can be had, seen, and felt in the blind and loving awareness of this word IS. For if you say "Good" or "Fair Lord" or "Sweet," "Merciful" or "Righteous," "Wise" or "Omniscient," "Mighty" or "Omnipotent," "Thought" or

a. From Saint Augustine of Hippo: "And, far off, I heard your voice saying, 'I am the God who IS…'" (*Confessions*, 147).

b. Notice that the long catalogue of words describe God's nature, God's being, not God's functions. It is not easy for a modern Christian to understand that God has no "attributes" separate from God's own being. Hence, God is not "wise" but God is Wisdom itself; God is not "loving" but God is Love itself. This is part of the author's constant harping on the difference between "being" or "essence" and "attributes" or "qualities." McCann (111 n.) quotes the Latin: "*Eo quod est, est omne quod est*" ("For who he is, is all that he is") and adds: "The attributes of God are identical with his essence."

c. One of the central understandings of the contemplative way is that one's contemplation in no way asks anything of God and expects nothing from God—only the love-longing to be one-ed with God, which longs for God alone. See the prayer of Julian of Norwich: "God of Thy goodness, give me Thyself; for Thou art enough to me, and I can ask nothing that is less that can be full honor to Thee. And if I ask anything that is less, ever shall I be in want, for only in Thee have I all" (I Julian, 79).

d. The ME has *knittingly*—literally, "as in union with" (MED).

e. 2 Peter 1:4: "most great and precious promises have been given so that through them … you are partakers of the divine nature."

f. Another deep grasp of theological ontology: it predicates the pre-existence of one's own essence within God—that is, it declares that before one was created on earth one spiritually already existed in God. I have often tried to express this by saying that the "idea" of me was in the mind of God before I was born.

g. The ME has only *oft*—which I have translated as "over and over again."

h. The ME has *crie*—literally, "cry," but there is also a sense of "announce" or "proclaim" (Mossé, 435).

i. The ME has *mistily*—which can mean "symbolically" or "mystically" (McCann, 111 n.).

j. The ME has *savour*. Bradley (521) has "smell." Spearing (111) has "tasting" (which maintains the metaphor of wine).

"Wisdom," "Power" or "Strength," "Love" or "Charity," or whatever other such thing that you say about God—all of that is hidden and gathered up in this little word IS.[a] For all of that is for Him only "to be"—that is, all these are simply *ways for God to be*.[b] And if you were to add a hundred thousand such sweet words as these are—"good," "fair," and all the others—yet you would not have said anything beyond this word IS. And if you say them all, you have not added to it, and if you say absolutely none, you have not taken away anything from it. Therefore continue to be just as blind in your loving awareness of the being of God as in the naked awareness of your own being—without any inquisitive examination of your wits to search for any attribute that is part of His being or yours.[c] But with all your curiosity abandoned and left far behind, honor your God with your *being*—with all that you *are* (just as you are) unto Him who is just as He is, who alone, with nothing more, is both His own blessed being and yours.

And thus shall you—bound with Him[d] as you are and in a manner that is wondrous—bring honor to God with Himself: for what you are you have from Him and it is His.[e] And although you (who once were nothing) had a beginning in the creation of your being, yet has your essence been always in Him without beginning and shall be without ending[f]—just as He Himself is. And therefore over and over again[g] I proclaim[h] and always on one thing: "Do honor to God with your substance, and benefit all people in common with your 'first fruits'; and then shall your barns be filled with abundance"—that is, then shall your spiritual affection be filled with an abundance of love and virtuous life in God, your ground and your purity of spirit—"And your presses shall run over with wine"—that is, your inner spiritual wits (which you usually strain and press together with diverse curious meditations and rational investigations regarding the spiritual knowledge of God and yourself, regarding His attributes and yours) shall run over with wine (by which wine in Holy Scripture is truly and mystically[i] understood as "spiritual wisdom in true contemplation and exalted flavor[j] of the Godhead").

a. A charming (and theologically precise) conceit: that in one's contemplation one is aided by the ministration of angels (who give it "special service")!

b. Psalm 122:2 [123:2]: "Behold, as the eyes of servants are on the hands of their masters, as the eyes of the handmaid are on the hands of her mistress, so are our eyes unto the Lord our God, until he have mercy on us."

c. The ME has *listi*—literally, either "adroit" or "vigorous" (MED) or "light" or "bright" (Mayhew, 137).

d. The ME has *sleigt*—literally, "cunning" (Mayhew, 207) or "clever" (MED).

e. The ME has *brestith up*—literally, "bursts out" (Mayhew, 34).

f. *The Letter of Privy Counsel* has both the Latin and its full translation.

g. Proverbs 3:13 and 21:26. The author translates and expands on the biblical verses (which he has slightly rewritten), giving his own allegorical interpretation to the words of Solomon. This may be another clue that this protégé is not as highly educated as the author.

h. The ME has *all curious kunnyng of clergie*—literally, "eccentric scholarship of the learned" (MED).

i. The ME has *sleig*—literally, "wise," "clever," "ingenious," "skillful," or "prudent" (MED).

j. Spearing (154) has: "That is, according to the moral or tropological level of interpretation, which related the text of the Bible to the human soul and its virtues."

k. The ME has *curious seching*—literally, "abstruse seeking."

l. The ME has *riftid*—literally, "belched" (MED) or "vomited" (Mayhew, 189). The Latin translation of this book uses the word *eructo*—"to discharge noisily" or "discharge violently" (Lewis, 658), but the Hebrew source has *ratash*—literally, "boil" or "bubble up," as it appears in Psalm 44:1 [45:1]: "My heart throws up your word" (Gesenius, 782).

m. The ME has *to falle under*. I have translated it as "pressed under" to make it parallel to the wine press metaphor in chapter 4.

And all this shall be done swiftly, joyfully, and graciously without any activity or labor on your part—solely by the ministration of angels by virtue of this loving blind Work.[a] For all the angels, knowing of this Work, give it special service—as a handmaid does to her lady.[b]

THE FIFTH CHAPTER

That in this Work the eternal Wisdom—the Word of God—descends into one's soul and unites it to Himself; and of the good effects that follow.

In great commendation of this vigorous[c] clever[d] Work—which in itself is the celestial Wisdom of the Godhead graciously descending into one's soul, knitting it and one-ing it unto Himself in spiritual wisdom and discretion of spirit—the wise man Solomon bursts out[e] and says:[f] "*Beatus hom qui inuenit sapienciam et qui affluit prudencia. Melior est adquisicio eius negociacione auri et argenti. Primi et purissimi fructus eius. Custodi, fili mi, legem atque consilium; et erit vita anime tue et gracia faucibus tuis. Tunc ambulabis fiducialiter in via tua, et pes tuus non inpinget. Si dornieris, non timebis; quiesces et suauis erit sompnus tuus. Ne paueas repentino terrore, et irruentes tibi potencias impriorum, quia Dominus erit in latere tuo et custodiet pedem tuum ne capiaris.*"[g] All this is to your understanding thus: He is a blessed man that can find his one-ing wisdom and that can abound in his spiritual working with this loving dexterity and prudence of spirit, in offering up his own blind affection for his own being, all curious sophisticated erudition of the learned[h] and of nature put far back. The purchasing of this spiritual wisdom and this prudent[i] Work is better than getting gold or silver. By which gold and silver is morally[j] understood all other bodily and spiritual knowledge which is obtained by obscure searching[k] and laboring in our natural wits, beneath ourselves, within ourselves, or even beside ourselves in observing any of the attributes that are part of the being of God or of any created thing. And why is it better? He adds the reason and says: because "*primi et purissimi fructus eius*"—that is, because "the first and purest are the fruits of it," and no wonder, because the fruit of this Work is exalted spiritual wisdom, swiftly and freely brought forth[l] from within one's spirit itself, and uncreated, very far from imaginary, unable to be strained or to be pressed under[m] the activity of natural intellect—which

a. The "four f" alliteration exists in the original ME: *bot feynid foly foryd in fantome.*

b. The reference is to "Midwinter Night," which is the winter solstice—i.e., the coldest, most sunless day in the year.

c. The reference is to "Midsummer Day," which is the summer solstice (also known as Saint John's Day, since the feast of John the Baptist falls on June 24) and is the brightest, most sun-filled day of the year.

d. Proverbs 3:21: "My son, let not these things depart from your eyes. Keep the law and the counsel."

e. The traditional monastic vows of poverty, chastity, and obedience are referred as "the Evangelical Counsels" (i.e., "the advice from the Gospels") or "the Dominical Counsels" ("the advice from the Lord")—meaning that while they are not part of any *commandments* as such, they are gleaned from the "advice" or "recommendations" (counsels) of Jesus in the Gospels. And we should be reminded that this letter is from one monastic writing to another, so it is likely that the word "counsels" would refer, at least obliquely, to monastic vows.

f. The ME has *beholdyng.* This is one of the rare instances when that word does not mean "seeing" or "observing," but "being beholden" or "obligated" (ODEE, 86).

g. The ME has *fullheed*—literally, "fullness" (MED) but here intended as "fulfillment."

h. Romans 13:10b: "*Plenitudo ergo legis est dilectio*"—"Therefore love is the fulfillment of the law."

i. The ME refers to Proverbs 3:22a: "*et erit vita animæ tuæ*"—"and it will be life to your soul."

j. The ME has *softnes*—literally, "softness," "warmth," "mildness," or "gentleness" (Mayhew, 209).

k. The ME refers to Proverbs 3:22b: "*grace to thy chekes.*" *Grace* can mean "adornment" (ODEE, 408), and *chekes* means literally "cheeks" or "side of the face" but is taken figuratively to refer to the neck or throat (ODEE, 166). Here it refers to a necklace.

l. Matthew 22:40: "For on these two hang all the law and the prophets," and the author adds a gloss to clarify: "namely, the love of God and of one's neighbor." It is curious that the author should write out this quotation in English and then *add* the Latin version afterward.

wit, no matter how subtle nor how holy, in comparison to this can be called nothing but feigned folly formed in fantasy[a]—as far from the actual truth when the spiritual sun shines as is the darkness of the moonlight in a mist on Midwinter Night[b] from the brightness of the sunbeam in the fairest minute of Midsummer Day.[c]

"My son," Solomon says, "keep this law and this counsel"[d] in which all the commandments and counsels[e] of the Old Testament as well as the New are truly and perfectly fulfilled, without any particular obligation[f] to any one individually. And in other ways this manner of Working would not be called a "law" except that it contains within it completely all the branches and fruits of the law. For if it is wisely understood, the ground and the strength of this Working shall be seen as nothing else but the glorious gift of love, in which, according to the teaching of the Apostle, all the law is fulfilled: "*Plenitude legis est dilectio*"—"The fulfilling[g] of the law is love."[h]

And this loving law and this living counsel, if you keep it, as Solomon says, "shall be life to your soul"[i] inwardly in the tenderness[j] of love to your God, and outwardly "an adornment to your throat"[k] in the truest teaching and the proper governance of your bodily behavior to your fellow Christians in the outward form of living. "And on these two—the one within and the other without—by the teaching of Christ, hang all the law and the prophets"—"*In hiis enim duobus tota lex pendet et prophete: scilicet dilectio dei et proximi*".[l]

a. The ME has *tristely*—literally, "safely" or "confidently" (III Clark, 31).

b. Proverbs 3:23: "Then you shall walk safely in your way, and your foot will not stumble."

c. The ME has *then arte thou awey*—my translation as "then you are turned away" (ODEE, 65).

d. The ME has *sleigh*—literally, "guile" (MED).

e. The ME has *coriouste*—literally, "ingenuity" (ODEE, 236).

f. The ME has *vnscattered*—literally, "unscattered" or "focused" (OAD, 1514).

g. The ME has *sleigt*—literally, "prudence," "cleverness," or "wisdom" (MED).

h. Proverbs 3:24: "If you sleep, you will not fear; rest, and your sleep will be sweet."

i. The ME has the familiar mystical paradox *blynde beholdyng*—literally, "blind seeing."

j. In many mystical writers, "noise" means "distractions," rather than physical sounds. For Richard Rolle, for instance, "noise" includes "covetings, vanities, and earthly thoughts" (Hodgson, 210 n.).

k. We might be reminded that the three great temptations against which one vows to be on guard in baptism are the world, the flesh, and the devil.

l. The ME has *deceyte*—literally, "deceit" or "deception" (Bradley, 155). "The gift of strictly supernatural contemplation is seen as conferring protection against diabolical delusion, because it means one is made willing to receive God's self-disclosure, to receive him as he wills to reveal himself rather than according to one's own ideas" (III Clark, 34).

m. The ME has *gracyously*—literally, "of a pleasing quality" (ODEE, 408). Notice that again the author has added "sweetly" as a gloss to the actual quotation from Proverbs—see note "a" above.

n. The ME has *softe*—literally "sweet" or "gentle" (MED).

And therefore when you are thus made perfect in your Work both within and without, then you shall go confidently,[a] grounded in grace—the guide of your spiritual way—lovingly lifting up your naked blind being to the blessed being of your God, which beings are one in grace although they are different in nature. "And the foot of your love shall not stumble."[b] That is to say, when you have proof of your spiritual Work in persistence of spirit, then you shall not be as easily hindered and drawn back by the weird questions of your clever wits, as you are now in the beginning. Or else thus: then shall the foot of your love neither trip nor stumble on any kind of illusion caused by the eccentric probing in your thoughts. Because in this Work—as it has been said before—all odd exploring in any of your natural wits is pushed far away and completely forgotten for fear of illusion or some feigned falsehood that can occur in this life which in this Work could befoul the naked affection of your blind being and draw you away from the dignity of this Work.

For if any kind of particular thought of anything besides your naked blind being (which is your God and your objective) comes into your mind, then you are turned away[c] and drawn back to work in the treachery[d] and ingenuity[e] of wits, in dispersal and separation of yourself and of your mind from both yourself and from God. And therefore keep yourself whole and focused[f] as far as you can by grace and by the prudence[g] of spiritual determination. For in this blind awareness of your naked being, thus one-ed to God, as I am telling you, you must do everything that you are going to do—eat and drink; sleep and wake; walk and sit; speak and be still; lie down and get up; stand and kneel; run and ride; labor and rest. Each day you must offer this up to God as the most precious offering that you can make. And it must be the chief of all your deeds in all the things you do, whether they are active or contemplative.

For, as Solomon says in his passage: "if you sleep…"[h] in this blind vision,[i] away from all the noise[j] and the stirring of the fierce Fiend, the false world and the frail flesh,[k] "…you shall not fear any peril" nor any treachery[l] of the Fiend. Because in this Work he is utterly confused and blinded in a painful ignorance and a mad amazement to know what you are doing. But no matter that, for "you shall sweetly[m] rest" in this solitary one-ness of God and your soul; "and your sleep shall be very sweet,"[n] for it shall be spiritual

a. Proverbs 4:22: "For they [Solomon's words] are life to all who find them and healing to all flesh." Once again the author glosses the passage to fit his metaphor.

b. The author reminds us that Adam lost the practice of contemplation in the Fall and the goal is for Christians to regain that lost practice (III Clark, 34).

c. The ME has *listines*—literally, "receptivity" (MED). There is a significant point hidden in this phrase: the way to overcome the sickness and corruption of the fallen soul is to consent to "the acceptance of love"— to agree to receive the love of Jesus!

d. Proverbs 3:25: "Do not fear any sudden terror falling upon you or the power of the wicked."

e. The ME has *lemys*—literally, "limbs" but when related to the devil, "mischievous persons" (ODEE, 528) or "agents" (McCann, 15 n.). As "agents of the devil" I have used "demons."

f. The ME again has *listines* (see note "j" above). This time I have chosen to translate it as "embrace," rather than merely "acceptance."

g. Proverbs 3:26: "For the Lord will be at your side, and shall keep your foot from being taken."

h. The ME has *fautours*—literally, "adherents," "supporters," or "followers" (MED).

i. The ME has *kepyng of him-self*—literally, "keeping" or "defending" (MED).

j. The ME has *noughtyng of it-self*—literally, "making nothing of the self."

sustenance and inner strength, as well for your body as for your soul. As this same Solomon says soon after: "*Universe carni sanitas est.*"[a] "It is a help to all the frailty and the sickness of flesh," and worthily so, since all sickness and corruption fell into the flesh when the soul fell from this Work, then shall all health return to the flesh when the soul (by the grace of Jesus who is the chief Worker) rises to this same Work again.[b] And this you shall hope to have only by the mercy of Jesus and your loving consent. And therefore I beg you—with Solomon here in his passage—that you stand firmly in this Work, evermore lifting up to Him your loving consent in the acceptance[c] of love. *Et ne paveas repentino terrore et irruentes tibi potencias impiorum.*[d] "And be not amazed" with any disturbing fear, even though the Fiend comes (as he will) "with a sudden terror," prodding and beating on the walls of your house where you are sitting, or though he stir any of his powerful demons[e] to rise and "to rush in upon you" suddenly, without any warning. Thus shall it be, know right well, whoever you are that sets yourself to labor truly in this Work, you shall truly see and feel, or else smell, taste, or hear some astonishing things made by the Fiend in one or more of your five bodily senses. And it is all done in order to draw you down from the height of this precious Work. And therefore take good care of your heart in the time of this torment, and rely with a confident embrace[f] on the love of our Lord.

Quia Dominus erit in latere tuo, et custodiet pedem tuum ne capiaris.[g] That is, "for our Lord will be at your side," ready and near for your help, "and He shall keep your foot," that is, the staying up of your love by which you go to God, "so that you shall not be taken" by any trick or guile of your enemies, the Fiend and his followers,[h] the world, and the flesh. Lo! Friend, thus shall our Lord and our love mightily, wisely, and goodly help, keep, and defend all those who—for the loving trust they feel in Him—are willing utterly to abandon their own self-preservation.[i]

THE SIXTH CHAPTER

That the soul must give itself wholly to God who will provide for it; with a warning to those who would criticize this Work.

But where shall a soul be found, so willingly bound and founded in the faith, so fully humbled in self-abnegation,[j] and so lovingly led and fed by the

a.   The ME has *unwetyn*—literally, "unknown," or "unguarded," or "hidden" (Bradley, 689). McCann offers: "The knowledge which God has of existing things is not gathered, as ours is, from their natures and forms, but he knows them by knowing himself, the eternal cause of all things" (Hodgson, 210 n.).

b.   Some of the author's "difficult" ontology: "God is one in all" can mean "God is the same in all things" or "… in all persons." It is part of the author's "panentheism"—the belief that there is a divine presence in all created things (by virtue of their being created). God's presence in human beings is predicated on the biblical "to the image of God he made him" (Gen. 1:27b). The second clause is "and all [humans/things] exist in him" and is predicated on the words "In him we live and move and exist" (Acts 17:28a).

c.   The ME has *this hyge allyng of God*—literally and awkwardly, "this high all-ing of God." My translation is a rare one from the verb *allen* in MED.

d.   The ME has *rewarde*—"regard" is from ODEE, 764.

e.   The ME has *avisement*—literally, "examination" or "consideration" (ODEE, 15).

f.   We learn two things from this apostrophic passage: that the author knew his letter would be read by others, and that he has obviously encountered some nasty criticism for his ideas by those not called to the contemplative way.

g.   The ME has *resonable trasing*—literally, "rational procedure" (MED and Hodgson, 210 n.). *Trasing* suggests a scornful sense—as if to say "your so-called intellectual fussing around."

h.   The ME has *cours*—"extent" is from Bradley, 137. The author reprimands those who criticize conservatives but are unable to take the risks themselves.

i.   The ME has *se*—literally, "see," but "grasp" is an MED option.

j.   The ME has *spice*—Mayhew (213) offers "kind" as a translation, but "flavor" or "savor" would be as valid.

love of our Lord with full knowledge and awareness of his omnipotence, his unfathomable[a] wisdom, and his glorious goodness? A soul who understands how God is one in all and all exist in Him,[b] so that without fully yielding up all there is of oneself to Him, by Him, and in Him, a loving soul is never truly humbled in self-abnegation. So that because of this noble self-abnegation in true humility and this high recognition of God as the one-and-all[c] in perfect charity, that soul deserves to have God (in whose love it is deeply drenched in complete and final abandonment of self as though it were nothing—or less, if less could be) powerfully, wisely, and goodly securing it and keeping it and defending it from all adversities, physical or spiritual, without effort or labor, regard[d] or consideration,[e] of itself.

So let be your human objections, you half-humbled souls,[f] and do not say (in your rational procedure)[g] that such a humble and utter abandonment of one's self-preservation—when one feels oneself thus touched by grace—is any tempting of God, just because you suspect in your reason that you would not dare do the same thing yourself. No, consider yourself satisfied with your role because it is enough to save your soul in the active state, and leave other contemplative souls alone who do dare to do this. And do not wonder and marvel at their words and their works, although it seems to you that they surpass the extent[h] and the familiar judgment of your reason.

O, for shame! How often must you read and hear and yet give neither faith nor credence?—I mean belief in what all our ancient Fathers have written and taught before us, and in what is the fruit and the flower of all Holy Scripture. Either it seems that you are blind and cannot grasp[i] with belief what you read or hear—or else you are touched with some secret kind[j] of envy, that you cannot trust so great good to fall to your brothers because you lack it yourself. It would be good to be careful, because your enemy is subtle and plans to make you to give more faith to your own wit than to ancient teaching of dedicated Fathers or to the working of grace and the will of our Lord.

a. "The allegory of Jacob's wives and children was traditional. Its chief features were introduced by St. Augustine in *Contra Faustum* ... reiterated by St. Gregory in his *Homilies in Ezechiel* ... and *Morals on Job* ... and again by St. Bernard in his *Sermons on the Canticle of Canticles* ... and by many others" (Hodgson, 210–11).

b. "[Jacob] went out from there, and came in the springtime to the land of Ephratah: where Rachel was in travail, on account of her hard labor, and began to be in danger. The midwife said to her: 'Fear not, for you will have this son also.' And when her life was departing because the pain, and death was now at hand, she called the name of her son 'Benoni,' that is, the 'son of my pain,' but his father called him 'Benjamin,' that is, 'son of the right hand.' So Rachel died, and was buried in the highway that leads to Ephratah, which is Bethlehem" (Gen. 35:16–19).

c. The ME has *ravischid*—literally, "seized and carried off" (ODEE, 742).

d. Psalm 67:28a [68:27a]: The Vulgate alone has the unusual and inexplicable *in mentis excessu*. Richard of St. Victor († 1173) translates the words into ME as *in ravisching of mynde*—literally, "in transport of mind" (Oakley, 80). The original Hebrew has "There is the little tribe of Benjamin leading them."

e. A curious statement: such mothers who killed their newborns are not identified. The author may have had in mind a social evil: William Langer claimed that infanticide was still practiced "on a gigantic scale" in medieval Europe (William Langer, "Infanticide: A Historical Survey," in *History of Childhood Quarterly* 1 (3): 253–366).

f. The ME has *stifly in that that in you is*. The meaning of the phrase is not entirely clear. Spearing has "with what boldness you can" and Wolters has "however confident you may be of your own ability." My sense of it is "as boldly as what is in you" (*stifly*—literally, "staunchly" or "boldly" [MED].

g. Apparently the author addresses himself to those who condemn or attack the contemplative way thinking that they are doing God's will in doing so.

h. Possibly a reference to Saints Crispin and Crispinian—extremely popular in England—who were cobblers and evangelists, preaching by day and shoemaking by night. They were martyred ca. 286. (See the King's Crispin Day speech in Shakespeare's *Henry V*.)

i. "Cf. *Martylogium Romanum*, 6 August, Justin and Pastor, brothers and schoolboys in Alcalá, fired by zeal to share the fate of their fellow Christians, cast away their school-books and ran to the place of martyrdom. They we scourged and beheaded" (McCann, 117 n.).

How often have you read and heard, and from how many holy, wise, and faithful persons,[a] that as soon as Benjamin was born, his mother Rachel died?[b] By "Benjamin" we understand "contemplation" and by "Rachel" we understand "Reason." And as soon as a soul is touched with true contemplation—as it is in this noble self-abnegation and this high recognition of God as the one-and-all—then certainly and rightly all human reason dies. And since you read this so frequently, in the words not only one or two but from very many truly holy and fully worthy writers, why do you not believe it? And if you believe it, how dare you then rummage around and scrounge with your reason through the words and deeds of Benjamin—by which Benjamin is understood all those who in an ecstasy of love are transported[c] beyond intellect, as the prophet says: "*Ibi Beniamyn adolescentulus in mentis excessu*"—that is to say, "There is Benjamin, a young child, in ecstasy of mind."[d] Look out, therefore, that you not be like those wretched women that bodily slay their own children when they are newborn.[e] It would be good for you to beware, and not to aim the point of your presumptuous spear against the might, the wisdom, and will of our Lord as boldly as you can,[f] and, because of blindness and lack of experience, not to act as though you would bring our Lord down when you actually believe it better to hold Him up.[g]

Since in the first beginning of Holy Church in the age of persecution, many and diverse souls were so marvelously touched by the unexpectedness of grace that suddenly, without the mediation of any other preparation coming before, craftsmen threw down their tools,[h] children their tablets[i] in the school, and ran without rational fumbling to martyrdom with

a. "I stoutly maintain that martyrdom is good, as required by the God"
and "they who were wont to be led by the Spirit of God used to
be guided by Himself to martyrdoms" (Tertullian [† 225], *Scorpiace*,
chapters 5 and 8).

b. Julian of Norwich: "som of us leven that God is almyty and *may* don all,
and that he is al wisdom and *can* don all, but that he is all love and *will*
don all there we astynten" (italics mine) (II Julian, 118).

c. The ME has *beines*—literally, "preparation" (MED).

d. The ME has *revith*—literally, "plunder" or "snatch" (MED).

e. The ME has *loue-trist*, and I thought the word so utterly perfect in
meaning that I merely modernized the spelling.

f. The ME has *weel-wilnes*—literally, "well-willingness." "Good will" is the
translation from Hodgson (211).

g. Proverbs 3:26: "For the Lord … shall keep your foot from being taken."

h. Saint Francis de Sales († 1622) probably borrowed from *Privy Counsel*
when he called his early practice of mental prayer "spiritual sleep" (de
Sales, xiv).

i. It seems almost a compulsion with the author, who many times repeats
the caution about not confusing one's being (essence) with one's
attributes (qualities)—hence his constant use of the adjective "naked" to
drive home the fundamental prerequisite that in the contemplative Work
the essence, the personhood, must not be screened or masked by any
aspects of the self.

j. The ME has *forby*—literally, "beside" (Bradley, 233). The context needs
the sense of "other than."

the saints[a]—why should people not believe that now, in the time of peace, God may, can, and will and, yes, does touch[b] different souls just as unexpectedly with the grace of contemplation? And this I believe He will do wholly graciously in chosen souls. For He would wish to be honorably known in the end to the wonder of all the world. For such a soul—thus lovingly denying itself and raising its God on high—shall most graciously be protected from all defeat by its spiritual or bodily enemies, without its own effort[c] and exertion, but only by the goodness of God—for godly reason demands that He truly protect all those that because of actions concerning His love abandon themselves and do not care about protecting themselves. And no wonder that they are marvelously protected, for they are so fully humbled in the courage and depth of love.

And whoever dares not do this (and speaks against this), either the devil is in his breast and robs[d] him of the love-trust[e] that he ought to have for his God and the goodwill[f] that he ought to have for his fellow Christian; or else, he is not yet as perfectly humbled as he needs to be— that is, if he aims at that life that is truly contemplative. And therefore do not be ashamed to be humbled in this way toward your Lord, nor to sleep like this in this blind vision of God as He is, away from all the noise of this wicked world, the false Fiend, and your frail flesh; for our Lord will be ready to help you and protect your foot so that you are not taken.[g]

And well is this Work compared to a sleep, for as in sleep the use of the earthly wits is halted, so that the body can take a complete rest in nourishing and strengthening its physical nature—just so in this spiritual sleep[h] the capricious questions of the wayward spiritual wits and illusory motivations are firmly bound and utterly voided, so that the blessed soul can softly sleep and rest in the loving vision of God as He is, in total nourishing and strengthening of its spiritual nature.

And therefore rein in your thoughts when offering up this naked blind sense of your own being, and always see to it, as I often say, that it is naked and not cloaked in any attribute of your being.[i] For if you cover it with any attribute—such as the dignity of your being or with any other private condition that pertains to the being of humanity (rather than[j] the being of any other creature)—then you immediately give food

a. The author warns that the moment one begins to try to understand human or divine attributes, one's intellect will immediately (and almost automatically) be diverted into dealing with small variables, preferences, and trivialities.

b. The ME has *kun no skyle in*—literally, "know no reason in."

c. The ME has *hedirtoward*—literally, "hithertofore" (Mossé, 451).

d. The author recognizes that the intellectual curiosity of critics of the Work will not be satisfied by mystical or unworldly explanations and justifications, but will demand convincing and rational explanations— the author offers to put himself in the place of the critic and respond in the critic's terms.

e. One recognizes parallels to Saint Paul's claims: "And unto the Jews I became as a Jew, that I might gain the Jews; to those who are under the law ... I became as one under the law (though I was not under the law) so that I might redeem those who were under the law; to those that are outside the law, I became as one who was outside the law (being I would not be without God's law, but under Christ's law), so that I might gain them that are outside the law. To the weak I became weak, that I might gain the weak. I have become all things to all, that I might by all means save some. And this I do for the sake of the gospel, so that even I might be a partaker of it with you" (1 Cor. 9:20–23).

f. The author is quoting from memory with a minor variation. The original from Saint Bernard is "For perfect obedience knows no law and is confined by no limits" (*On Precept and Dispensation* 6:12, cited in Spearing, 155 n.).

g. The ME has *sovereyn*—literally, "sovereign" or "ruler" or "superior" (Mayhew, 211). I have chosen "master" (after Spearing, 118).

h. It is possible—as Spearing suggests (155 n. 24)—that this reference might mean that the author is the spiritual director of his protégé, but I think it unlikely because in many places he refers to a spiritual director in the third person. However, the author certainly outranks his protégé monastically.

i. 1 Corinthians 13:9–10: "For we know only in part, and we prophesy in part. But when that which is perfect is come, that which is in part will be emptied."

j. The ME has *to make aseeth to*—literally, "make satisfaction" (Mayhew, 14).

to your wits, by which they gain the chance and the strength to draw you away toward many trivialities, and so you are diverted, even without your knowing it.[a] Beware of this trickery, I beg you.

THE SEVENTH CHAPTER

That this Work is perfection as witnessed by the virtues which accompany it; and that we pursue it at the call and with the grace of God.

But now, perhaps, after the devious judgment of your prying wits—because they make no sense of[b] this Work—you wonder about the method of this Work and are suspicious of it. And no wonder! For up till now[c] you have been too much in your wits to make sense of any such activity. And perhaps you are asking in your heart how you could know whether this Work was pleasing to God or not—or, if it is pleasing, how it could be as pleasant as I say that it is. To this I answer and say that this question is moved by a prying mind that will in no way allow your consent to this Work before the time comes that its curiosity is satisfied by some reasonable logic.[d]

And therefore I shall not stop, but I shall up to a point make myself like you, approving your proud wit, so that afterward you may be able to become like me, following my counsel without setting limits to your humility.[e]

For as Saint Bernard witnesses: "Perfect humility sets no limits."[f] Then you set limits to your humility when you will not fulfill the counsel of your spiritual master[g] unless your wit sees that it should be done. Lo, here you can see that I wish for mastery over you. And truly so I do—and I will have it.[h] I believe that love moves me to it more than any ability that I sense in myself of any height of learning, or even of contemplation, or competence in my own living. God amend what is amiss, for He knows fully, and I only in part.[i]

But now (to gratify[j] your proud wit) in commendation of this Work, truly I tell you that if a soul that is thus occupied had tongue and language to speak as it felt, then all the scholars of Christendom would wonder at that wisdom. Yea! and in comparison with it, all their great book-learning would seem palpable foolishness. And so no wonder that I cannot tell you

a. The ME has *defoulid*—literally, "dishonored" or "despoiled" (MED).

b. The ME has *steringes*—literally, "movement" or "stirring" (Bradley, 578). I have "wagging" from Spearing (119).

c. The end and purpose of humanity—the intention in the mind of God in creating humans—was that human beings would ultimately be perfectly and entirely united (one-ed) with God. That is the reason human beings exist. God shared the divine being with humanity; that is, the "being-ness" that previously had been a property of God alone was, in creation, poured out and shared by the Godhead with another entity—humanity. And the motive for that pouring out was that humanity—using its unique divine gift of free will—would choose to be "poured back again" into God in a perfect union of love and mutual gifting.

d. "The journey to God is an ascent to a divine insight that is beyond ordinary ways of knowing. Characteristically Dionysius described this insight as an entrance into silence or darkness, pointing to the resounding silence of the divine Word and the bright darkness of the divine light. Clearly, in a phrase such as 'brilliant darkness,' Dionysius tested the limits of language to evoke a divine reality beyond sense perception or mental concepts … abandoning language, concepts, and perceptions, the ascent toward God was a plunge into the 'truly mysterious darkness of unknowing'" (Chidester, 237).

e. The ME has *nobilte*—literally, "nobility" or "splendor" (Mossé 464).

f. The ME has *goostly*—literally, "spiritual" (Mossé, 446). I have used "contemplative" to designate the particular exercise alluded to by the author.

g. The ME has *crokyng*—literally, "curving" or "bending" (Bradley, 141).

h. *An Epistle on Prayer* is another short essay by the author—one of seven manuscripts ascribed to him from the second part of the fourteenth century. The remainder of this paragraph contains some of the author's most poetic and most succinct expressions of the deep nature of contemplation.

i. See reference to the Ark of the Covenant in *The Cloud*, chapters 3, 4, and 71.

j. The ME has *drewry*—literally, "darling" or "jewel" (Mayhew, 68).

k. "In his *Mystical Theology*, Dionysius advised, 'Leave behind you everything perceived and understood, everything perceptible and understandable, all that is not and all that is, and, with your understanding laid aside, strive upwards as much as you can toward union with him who is beyond all being and knowledge.' By renouncing everything, especially any sense of self, he promised, 'you will be uplifted to the ray of the divine shadow which is above everything that is'" (Chidester, 237).

the worthiness of this Work with my crude beastly tongue. And God forbid that the Work should be so degraded[a] that it could be constrained under the wagging[b] of a fleshly tongue! Nay, it cannot be, and surely it will not be—and God forbid that I should want it! For everything that is spoken of it is not the Work itself, but is only *about* it. But now, since we cannot speak directly of it, let us speak *about* it, to the confounding of proud wits—and, specifically, of yours—which is at least the one occasion and the cause of this writing at this time.

At the first, I ask you what is the perfection of a human soul, and what are the characteristics that belong to this perfection? I answer on your behalf and I say that the perfection of a human soul is nothing but a one-ing formed between God and the soul in perfect charity.[c] This perfection is so lofty and so pure in itself—beyond human understanding—that it cannot be known or seen in itself.[d] But where the *properties* that belong to this perfection are actually seen and perceived, there it is likely that the actual *being* of it is present. And so one must understand here what the characteristics are that pertain to perfection in order to assert the excellence[e] of this contemplative[f] exercise above all others.

The characteristics that apply to perfection (which each perfect soul must have) are virtues. And then, if you will truly observe this Work in your soul, and the characteristic and the condition of each separate virtue, you will find that all virtues are clearly and totally contained within it, without any twisting[g] or corruption of the intention.

I touch on no particular virtue here, because it is not necessary: you have found them mentioned similarly in other various places in my own writings. For this same Work, if it is properly understood, is that reverent affection and the fruit picked from the tree that I spoke of in your little *Epistle on Prayer*.[h] This is *The Cloud of Unknowing*; this is that secret thrust of love in purity of spirit; this is the Ark of the Covenant;[i] this is Denis's *Divinity*, his wisdom and his jewel,[j] his bright darkness and his unknown knowledge; this is what puts you into silence as well from thoughts as from words; this makes your prayer extremely short. In this you are taught to forsake the world and to despise it.[k]

a. Matthew 16:24: "Then Jesus said to his disciples, If anyone wants to come after me let him deny himself, and take up his cross, and follow me."

b. For the reference to "the mount of perfection" see *The Cloud*, chapter 44. Note that the author is careful to demonstrate that Christ *precedes* a soul into God's perfect presence—since being "with God" is part of Christ's own nature itself, whereas human presence with God comes only from grace.

c. The ME of this brief phrase is pleasingly firm and resolute: *& that is full sothe*.

d. The ME has *disposid*—literally, "disposed" or "inclined" (ODEE, 275). "Receptive" is from Spearing (201).

e. The ME has *ablid*—literally, "made able" or "enabled." "Qualified" is from Spearing (201).

f. The author repeats and underlines the point that the contemplative stance is ultimately a passive one—even though there are things one can do to make oneself receptive and prepared for the potential and desired action of God.

g. The ME has the familiar *mene*—literally, "intermediary," but in this case Hodgson (212) suggests the sense of "something to use" or "instrument" as playing off against the ME word *me* (translated here as "myself").

h. The ME has *sauyng*—literally, "saving." In the context it has the sense of "setting aside," so I have used "reserving" and added "of course."

i. The author has offered to explain the Work intellectually, but, finding that unattainable, he falls back on the statement that says in essence, "Once you have experienced it, you will know how good it is."

j. The ME has *dedein for to*—literally, "disdain" or "scorn" (Mossé, 435). I have used a slightly more active synonym.

k. Again the author cautions about the consideration of any "attribute" or "external aspect" of the self or the world, reserving one's considerations entirely to the inner and spiritual dimensions, which alone can lead one to the purely spiritual essence of God.

And what is more, in this you are taught to abandon and despise your own self—following the teaching of Christ in the Gospel, where He said: "*Si quis vult venire post me, abneget semetipsum; tollat crucem suam et sequatur me.*" That is: "Whoever would come after me, let him forsake himself, let him bear his cross and follow me."[a] As if He said thus to your understanding regarding our issue: "Whoever will come humbly—not *with* me but *after* me—to the bliss of heaven or to the mount of perfection...."[b] For Christ went ahead by his divine nature, and we come after Him by grace. His divine nature is more excellent than grace, and grace is more excellent than our human nature. And in this He lets us know without a doubt that we may in no way follow Him to the mount of perfection—as would ordinarily happen to us in the exercise of this Work—unless we are moved and led by grace alone.

And that is the complete truth.[c] For you must understand right well—and all like you who might either hear or read this writing—that although I urge you thus clearly and thus boldly to dedicate yourself to this Work, nevertheless I am still entirely certain without error or doubt that Almighty God with his grace must always be the chief mover and worker (either with an intermediary or without) and that you or any other like you only consent and submit—saving that this consent and this submission shall, during this Work, be actually receptive[d] and qualified[e] for this Work in purity of spirit, and properly borne up to your Master, so you can be taught by experience in the mystical revelation of your spirit.[f]

And since it is true that God of his goodness moves and touches diverse souls in diverse ways—some with an intermediary and some without—who then dares to say that God will not move you (or any like you that shall either read or hear) through this writing, with only myself as instrument[g]—though I am unworthy—reserving,[h] of course, His honorable will that pleases Him to do as He likes? I suppose it shall be thus: the Work shall bear witness when you have experienced the Working.[i] And therefore, I beg you, prepare yourself to receive the grace of your Lord, and hear what He says: "Whoever will come after me" (in the manner said above) "let him forsake himself." I beg you, how can a person forsake himself and the world and despise himself and the world more than by refusing[j] to give a thought to any attribute of their beings?[k]

a. The ME has *as for*—"in place of" or "in favor of." I have "in exchange for" from Butcher (201).

b. The translation is exact: *that God is thy being*. It is one of the hardest concepts of the author's ontology to grasp. If I can express the basic premise in inadequately metaphorical terms, it is that in creation God poured out something of the Divine Being itself to provide the necessary spiritual "being" for human beings, to give humans their "essence." In that sense God is, in fact, a human's "being" or "essence"—an understanding of being "in the image of God."

c. A strong and powerful ME word *gnawe*—literally, "bite," "chew," or "gnaw" (Mayhew, 102). The author knows that the sorting out of one's "naked blind being" from all the familiar and usual descriptive overt attributes of that being is no easy task. Part of the paradox of this Work is that even while one "gnaws" at one's own being, one must always maintain a consciousness of God.

d. The author is taking his protégé step-by-step toward the abandonment of self by developing an awareness of the self (the ego) before one is called to reject and abandon that aspect in favor of total engagement with God alone.

e. Colossians 3:10: "Do not lie to one another: but strip yourselves of the old man with his deeds, and put on the new man, who is restored to knowledge in harmony with the image of him who created him." Notice that this Vulgate version places emphasis on the *restoration* of one's original knowledge of one's self as in "the image of God."

f. The ME has *unbilappid*—an early (and more visually acute and faithful) form of the word "enveloped" (Bradley, 642).

g. This is an enormously penetrating and definitive sentence—a summary of one of the three or four principal teachings of the author—offered here in an almost poetic form.

h. A short reiteration of the previous determination: No one can comprehend the true experience of the contemplative revelation unless one has experienced it.

THE EIGHTH CHAPTER

That one must forget one's own being in order to be aware
of the being of God; and of the pain involved in this effort.

For, indeed, consider well that although I bade you forget all things
except the blind awareness of your own naked being, yet nonetheless my
wish is (and my intent has been from the beginning) that you should forget
even the awareness of your own being in exchange for[a] the awareness of
God's being. And for this reason I demonstrated to you in the beginning
that God *is* your being.[b] But because I thought that you were not yet able
precipitously to be raised up to the spiritual awareness of God's own being
(because your spiritual awareness was still so unformed) therefore, so that
you might climb to that by degrees, I bade you first gnaw[c] on the naked
blind awareness of your own being until the time when you might be made
amenable to a high awareness of God by spiritual persistence in this secret
Work. For your intent and your desire should always be to be conscious
of God in this Work.[d] For although I bade you in the beginning—because
of your coarseness and your spiritual immaturity—to wrap and enfold the
awareness of your God in the awareness of yourself, yet afterward—when by
persistence you are made wiser in purity of spirit—disrobe and completely
strip yourself of every kind of self-consciousness, so that you are able to be
clothed with the grace-filled awareness of God's Self.[e]

And this is the true character of a perfect lover—only and utterly to strip
oneself of one's self for the sake of what one loves, and not allow or permit
oneself to be clothed excepting only in what one loves—and that not only
for a time, but to be enveloped[f] in it endlessly in full and final abandonment
of one's self.[g] This is the Work of love that none may know except one who
has felt it.[h] This is the lesson of our Lord when He says: "Whoever will love
me, let him abandon himself"; as if to say: "Strip yourself of your own self

a. The ME has *side*—literally, "wide," "ample," or "far" (Bradley, 546).

b. A reminder of Galatians 3:27: "For whoever is baptized into Christ has put on Christ."

c. The ME has *that neuer schal eende.* I chose "never wear out" based on the garment image in Hebrews 1:11–12: "[The earth and heavens] shall perish, but you shall continue: and they all shall grow old like a garment, and as a garment you shall change them and they shall be changed; but you are the same and your years shall not fail."

d. The ME has *venym*—literally, "snake venom" (Bradley, 659).

e. The counsel to abandon and scorn one's self is the ultimate countercultural charge in a world in which even the most religious counsel commonly calls for great concern with the well-being of the self. The true contemplative way that requires the repudiation of self is not commonly popular.

f. The ME itself has the rare *unbe.* To wish to cancel one's being would be an offense against the God who created that very being.

g. The ME has *prees*—literally, "press" or "push" (Bradley, 707).

h. Notice the progression: from awareness of one's attributes, to an awareness of one's essence, and then to an awareness of God's essence. A basic contemplative reality: that the greatest impediment to union with God is the undisciplined ego that has been conditioned to place itself ahead of all else.

i. Curiously, the ME shows no quotation marks after "follow me"—but obviously the conclusion of the sentence (i.e., "my love in holy awareness of my self") is meant to signify the words of the Lord. With "Lo!" I think the author returns to his own persona.

j. The ME has *desire*—literally, of course, "desire," which can be said to lead to a choice—but the desire itself is not mournful or sorrowful; it is the choice that makes the difference. Hence my decision to use "choice."

if you would be truly clothed in me—for I am the ample[a] garment of love[b] that will never wear out."[c]

And therefore, whenever you consider your Working, and you become aware that it is yourself that you are sensing and not God, then shall you grieve earnestly and wholeheartedly long for the sensing of God, evermore desiring without ceasing to forgo the dismal knowledge and the foul awareness of your own blind being, and yearn to flee from yourself as from poison.[d] And then abandon yourself and scorn yourself harshly, as the Lord bids you.[e]

And then, when you long directly, not wishing to "un-be"[f]—for that would be madness and disrespect to God—but to relinquish the consciousness and the awareness of your own being (which must always occur if God's love is to be as perfectly experienced as much as it can be here on earth), you will see and feel that in no way can you attain your purpose, because a naked sense of your blind being will always follow and accompany your actions, no matter how occupied you are (unless it is some infrequent short moment when God would let you feel Himself in abundance of love). This naked awareness of your own blind existence will always push forward[g] above you, between yourself and your God (as occurred in the beginning with the attributes of your being between you and your self), and then will you consider that self to be an extremely heavy and very painful burden. Yea! May Jesus help you then, for then you need it—for all the woe that may be without that is not a drop compared to that. For then you are yourself a cross to your self.[h] And this is true Working and the way to our Lord, as He Himself says: "Let him bear his cross"—first in his own pain—and then "follow me"—into bliss or into the mount of perfection, "tasting the tenderness of my love in holy awareness of my self."[i] Lo! Here you can see that you must mournfully choose[j] to abandon the awareness of your self and painfully bear the burden of your self as a cross, before you can be one-ed to God and spiritually conscious of God's Self, which is perfect charity.

And here you can see somewhat, and feel in part—all after you are touched and spiritually marked with this grace—the excellence of this Work above all others.

a. The ME has *faire wise*—translated variously as "good means" (Spearing, 122); "best reasoning" (Butcher, 204); "native intelligence" (Wolters, 185). Following MED, I have chosen "pleasing ways."

b. The ME has *queinte*—literally, "famous," "well-known," "clever," "neat," or "elegant" (Bradley, 128).

c. The "Joys of Our Lady" were frequent subjects for meditation (and are still so in recitation of the Rosary). They are the Annunciation, the Nativity, the Resurrection, the Ascension, and Mary's assumption into heaven.

d. The ME has *sotilte*—literally, "subtlety." MED provides "expertise."

e. Early in *The Cloud* the author enumerates good and valid points for meditation: one's sins, the passion of Christ, the lives and works of the saints, the ministry of angels—but he points out that these must be dropped when one has begun the Work.

f. The author leaps in quickly to clarify what may cause confusion: that the meditations he debased in the previous paragraph (and in *The Cloud*, chapter 7) are—in themselves—very good. Indeed, they are essential as a beginning place and are even more essential to bring one to the point of undertaking contemplative practice.

g. The author may have had in mind Saint Paul's comment that he had both suffered and celebrated, that "I know both how to be abased and I know how to abound ... and both to be full and to be hungry, both to abound and to suffer need" (Phil. 4:12).

h. The ME has *trewly*—literally, "truly." MED provides the option "genuinely."

i. "St. Augustine wrote that many who think they are inside are outside, but also vice versa" (Halik, Thomas; *Patience With God* [Random House, New York; 2009], 69); and 1 Cor. 10:12: "Therefore, let those who think they are standing take heed lest they fall."

j. The ME has *prees*—literally, "striving" or "effort" (MED).

k. The ME has *deseert*—literally, "desert" or "merit" (MED).

THE NINTH CHAPTER

That this Work does not lie in busy meditations; and that, nevertheless, meditation on Christ our Lord is the true and only door to the Work.

And, I ask you, how could you accomplish this Work by the use of your wits? Surely, never—not even by your pleasing ways,[a] your subtle, and your fancy[b] imaginations and meditations—yea, even though they are about your sinful life, the Passion of Christ, the Joys of Our Lady,[c] or about all the saints and angels of heaven, or even of any attribute or expertise[d] or circumstance that is related to your own being or that of God.[e] Surely I would rather have such a naked blind awareness of my self (as I touched on before—not of my *deeds*, but of my *self*). Many call their deeds their *selves*, and it is not so, for I who *do* those deeds am one, and my deeds that *are done* are separate. And the same is true of God: for He *is one thing* in Himself, and His *works* are another. And better that it should break my heart in tears because I lack a sense of God and because of the painful burden of my self and that it should kindle my desire in love and longing for the feeling of God, more than all the subtle and the clever imaginations or meditations that a person can tell or can find written in a book, no matter how holy they are, nor how much they appear beautiful to the subtle eyes of your ingenious wit.

Nevertheless, these pleasing meditations are still the truest way by which a sinner can make a beginning of a spiritual awareness of himself and of God.[f] And I would think it were impossible to human understanding—although God can do what He wills—that a sinner could come to be peaceful in the spiritual awareness of himself and of God, unless he first saw and felt by imagination and meditation the bodily actions of himself and of God, and was then saddened by what made for sorrow, and rejoiced for what made for joy.[g] And whoever does not come in by this way, does not come genuinely,[h] and therefore he must stand *outside*, and does so even when he believes that he is entirely *inside*. For many believe that they are within the spiritual door, while they are still standing outside (and must do so until the time that they seek the door humbly).[i] And some there are who find the door quickly, and come in sooner than others, and that is the business of the doorkeeper plainly, without effort[j] or merit[k] of their own.

a. Ephesians 2:19:"Now therefore you are no more strangers and foreigners, but fellow citizens with the saints in the household of God."

b. John 10:9 in the Vulgate Bible: "*Ego sum ostium. Per me si quis introierit, salvabitur: et ingredietur, et egredietur, et pascua inveniet*"—"I am the door. If anyone enters in through me, he will be saved, and he shall enter and go out, and find pasture." Note: The author added the words *sine* and *sive* that do not change the meaning but are not present in the Vulgate text itself.

c. John 10:1 in the Vulgate Bible: "*qui non intrat per ostium in ovile ovium, sed ascendit aliunde, ille fur est et latro*"—"He who does not enter through the door into the sheepfold, but climbs up some other way, he is a thief and a robber." Note: The author added the word *vero*.

d. The author has this often charming way of putting words into Jesus's mouth in his efforts to make biblical passages apply to his unique situation. Often his rewording of Jesus's sayings is quite fine and reasonably accurate, but there are times (such as these present two) when he considerably stretches the biblical text to make it fit his purposes. This last contends that the purpose of the Incarnation was to provide the widest possible access to the heavenly sheepfold—a nice, but dubious, sentiment.

e. The author provides an extensive defense of the practice of meditation on the Passion with emphasis on one's sins compared to the sinlessness of Jesus, and of the glories of his divinity and the agony of his humanity. Critics of *The Cloud* often point to the relative absence of Christological ascetics in the book, but the fact is that *The Cloud* deals with the ascetic steps that are intended to *follow* and *succeed* a solidly Christ-centered meditation (as per this chapter). The Cloud *presumes* a significant traditional Christian ascetical background.

f. It seems that in the face of the author's exhaustive condemnations here, there may be no further denouncing vocabulary possible! The author leaves no doubts about his opinion of those who avoid serious spiritual development and try to dive immediately—unprepared and uncalled—into the depths of contemplation.

g. The ME has *skulker*—literally, "skulker," "loiterer," or "one hiding" (Bradley, 538). Spearing (124) has "pilferer"; Wolters has "thief" (187); Butcher has "pickpocket"; McCann has "day-skulker." But the MED has "vagabond," "predator," and "thief."

h. The ME has *pikith*—literally, "picks" or "hoes" (Bradley, 475). MED has "choose," "steal," "take," or "acquire."

This is a wonderful household[a] and spirituality because the Lord is not only the doorkeeper Himself, but He is also the door. He is the doorkeeper because of his Divinity, and He is the door because of His humanity. Thus He says Himself in the Gospel: "*Ego sum ostium. Per me si quis introierit, salvabitur; et* sine *egredietur* sive *ingredietur, pascua invenient.*[b] *Qui* vero *non intrat per ostium sed assendit aliunde, ipse fur est et latro.*"[c] That is to your understanding as if He said thus to our issue: "I that am Almighty by my Divinity and can lawfully as doorkeeper let in whomever I will (and by whatever way I will) yet because I will that there be a plain communal way and an open entry to all who wish to come in (so that none can be excused by ignorance of the way) I have clothed myself in ordinary human nature and made myself so open that I am the door by way of my humanity, and whoever enters through me, will be saved."[d]

They enter by the door who, in meditating on the Passion of Christ, lament over their wickedness which was the cause of that Passion, with bitter reproving of themselves, who deserved it but did not suffer, and with pity and compassion for that worthy Lord who so vilely suffered and deserved nothing; and afterward they lift up their hearts to the love and the goodness of His Divinity, in which He consented to make Himself so low in our mortal humanity.[e] All these enter by the door, and they shall be saved. And whether they go in (in meditating on the love and the goodness of His Divinity), or go out (meditating on the agony of His humanity), they will find enough spiritual food for devotion, sufficient and abounding for the help and salvation of their souls, even though they never come any further inward in this earthly life.

And whoever does not enter by this door, but climbs up other ways to perfection by the subtle snooping and ingenious bizarre activity of his undisciplined reckless wits,[f] forsaking the plain universal entry (touched on above) and the true counsel of spiritual fathers, he, whatever else he is, is not only a thief by night but a predator[g] by day. He is a thief by night because he works in the darkness of sin, depending more on his presumption of the uniqueness of his own wit and will than on any proper counsel or on this plain communal way touched on above. He is a predator by day because, under cover of clear spiritual living, secretly he acquires[h] the outward signs and words of contemplation and has not the fruit. And

a. The ME has *colour*—literally, "color" in the obsolete sense of "semblance," or "pretext," or "outside show" (ODEE, 192).

b. The danger presented by a young man following "the ferocity of his desire" seems an ageless caution.

c. The author tends to be an ascetic elitist, but with good cause—the low-level spiritual life of the ordinary Christian may not be splendid and glorious, but it is good in itself and is a safe and virtuous path—but to aim higher without the prerequisite development, practice, inspiration, and counsel is massively dangerous spiritually. It is reminiscent of Peter's words in Acts 8:18–24 when Simon tries to buy divine healing power: "You have neither part nor lot in this matter: for your heart is not right in the sight of God … I see that you are in the gall of bitterness, and in the bond of iniquity."

d. The ME has *Bot now forthe*—literally, "But now, forward."

e. It is as though the author recognizes he has been on a tangent in the last chapters and now says, "All right, now let's get back to talking about contemplatives." Johnston (177) has "But now let us return to our subject."

f. The ME has *the grete rust of his boistous bodelynes*—"rust" is a strong and frequent metaphor for the gradual accumulated incrustation of the self by coarse bodily sins. Sins to the soul are like barnacles to a ship's hull.

g. The ME has *techyng*—literally, "teaching," but that seemed too "professorial" in this context, so I used "advice," "counsel," or "guidance."

h. The ME has *the spirit of God*—Spearing has "the Holy Spirit"; Butcher, Johnston, and Griffiths all have "God's Spirit"; Wolters keeps (but capitalizes) "the Spirit of God." I follow the ME exactly although all the other options seem valid.

i. There is an old religious saw that says, "Waiting never destroyed a calling." The author here recommends not undertaking contemplation too quickly or too easily, but waiting until there is a very clear call to undertake the Work itself. He then proceeds to describe such a call.

j. It is significant that the author chooses to use the word "touching" to describe God's gentle nudging toward one's undertaking a contemplative vocation. There should be no expectation of a Road-to-Damascus event, but a "gentle growing desire." The author is not a Charismatic.

k. It should be noted that the author includes all devout Christians in "salvation," but only contemplatives in "Perfection" (which the reader will remember is the highest of the author's four steps in spiritual development: Common, Special, Singular, and Perfect).

thus, because he sometimes feels within himself a pleasant longing (as small as it is) to come near God, therefore, blinded under the pretext[a] of this, he believes that all that he does is good enough when, in fact, it is the most dangerous rationale possible[b]—a young man to follow the ferocity of his desire, ungoverned by counsel—and especially when he is prepared to climb without aid into lofty things that are not only above himself but above the plain common path of Christian people[c] (as touched on before) which I call, by way of the teaching of Christ, the door of devotion and the most genuine entry into contemplation that is possible in this life.

THE TENTH CHAPTER

That one ought always to follow one's own call, without judging others or seeking to coerce God; and that this Work is not ruled by human wisdom, but by the high wisdom of God through the secret inspirations of His Spirit.

But now, leading on,[d] in our matter that especially in this book is relevant to you and to all others like you in that contemplative disposition only.[e] What if this contemplation is the door? Should one then when one has found the door remain standing at it, or within it, and come no further in? I answer for you, and I say that it is good for one to continue to stand there, until the great rust of his coarse fleshliness[f] is in great part rubbed away, with his advisor and his conscience bearing witness—and especially until one is called further in by the secret guidance[g] of the spirit of God,[h] which teaching is the most astute and the surest witness that can be had in this life of the calling and drawing of a soul further into a more special function of grace.[i]

A person may have evidence of this touching in this way: if one feels in one's continuing devout practice something like a gentle growing desire to come near God in this life—perhaps by a special spiritual sense as one hears others speak of or else finds about written in books.[j] For let one who does not feel moved in hearing and reading of spiritual work—and especially in one's everyday devotional exercise by a growing desire to come near God—remain standing at the door, as one called to salvation but not yet to perfection.[k]

a.   The author makes a firm and important point that it is not for any person to judge the vocation (or lack of vocation) of anyone else. Such a matter is deeply private and utterly personal.

b.   Almost with a tongue-in-cheek air, the author punctures the presumption of anyone who tries to tell God his business or who presumes to know better than God what is best for whom.

c.   The ME has *getyn*—literally, "gotten." But the MED provides a rare translation of "guided" (in the sense of "taken and led").

d.   John 15:5c: "*sine me nihil potestis facere*"—"Without me, you can do nothing."

e.   Again the author expands on the biblical translation. Spearing (156 n. 38) has: "Just as in medieval cosmology God as 'first mover' was understood to impart motion to the physical universe, so it is he who must set going the process by which a human being moves towards him in spirit."

f.   The ME has *kynde & degree*—literally, "nature and degree." By "degree" is meant "rank" or "class." The author refers to ordinary practice in both a natural state and a social status—i.e., in the fourteenth century, "nature" would rank man over woman; "degree" would rank noble over yeoman.

g.   The ME has *eelde*—literally, "full age" or "maturity" (Mayhew, 72).

h.   The ME has *compleccyon*—in the fourteenth century, literally, "habit of mind" (ODEE, 198).

i.   The ME has *kunnyng*—literally, "experience," "skill," or "knowledge" (Bradley, 145).

j.   The ME has *stuffid*—literally, "furnished," "provisioned," or "reinforced" (MED).

And of one thing I warn you: whoever you are that shall either read or hear this book—and especially in this place where I distinguish between one called to salvation and one called to perfection—of whichever part you feel is your calling, see to it that you neither judge nor debate the deeds of God or of man, beyond yourself alone—concerning whom He moves and calls to perfection or whom He does not call, or of the length of time involved, or why He calls this one rather than that one. If you would avoid error, see that you do not make judgment, but only hear and understand.[a] If you are called, give praise to God and pray that you do not fall. If you are *not* yet called, pray humbly to God that He may call you when it is His will. But do not teach God what to do. Leave Him alone. He is powerful, wise, and knows well how to do the best for you and all who love Him.[b]

Keep peace with whatever is your own lot. No matter which of the two you have, you need not bemoan yourself, for they are both precious gifts. The first is good and is always necessary. The second is better—get it whoever can—or, as I should more accurately say, whoever by grace is guided[c] and called to it by our Lord.

We may press forward with pride and stumble at the end, but surely without Him what we do is nothing, as He has said: "*Sine me nichil potestatis facere.*"[d] That is to your understanding: "Without me as initiator and first mover, and you alone only consenting and submitting, you can do nothing that is wholly pleasing to me,"[e] which is as it should be in the kind of Work in this book.

And I say all this to confute the erroneous presumption of those who—in the eccentricity of their book-learning or their natural wit—always want to be the primary principal actors themselves, with God only submitting or only consenting, when actually the opposite is true in contemplative matters, for only in them are all ingenious arguments of book-learning or of natural intelligence pushed far back so that God is foremost. Nevertheless, in matters legitimate and active, one's book-learning and natural intelligence shall work with God in due order, only by his consent in spirit, approved by these three witnesses: Scripture, counsel, and common practice in nature and status,[f] maturity,[g] and custom.[h] Therefore in "active" matters, one must not follow the guiding of one's own spirit—no matter how pleasant it seems or how holy—unless it falls properly within the scope of one's own learning and natural ability,[i] regardless of how strongly reinforced[j] it may be by all

a.   It is interesting that the author sees the Work as a kind of "profession," requiring a certain natural inclination, some education, and innate ability. Even if one feels "the guiding of his spirit," one must still take into consideration one's own capabilities and learning. For instance, given his prejudices, the author would probably not suggest that an uneducated farmhand undertake the contemplative way.

b.   "Prelacy" refers to a high ecclesiastical rank, notably bishop, archbishop, cardinal, or pope.

c.   The ME has *the office of that cure*—literally, "the duties [ODEE, 64] of the position" (ODEE, 236).

d.   The ME has *abounde*—literally, "overflow" or "flow over" (Bradley, 3) or "be plentiful" or "possess" (ODEE, 4). Spearing (126) suggests "predominate."

e.   The ME has *suffering*—literally, "enduring," "tolerating," or "allowing" (ODEE, 883).

f.   The author seems actually to overstate his case in this paragraph by repetition—promoting the fairly simple understanding that without God one can do nothing or go nowhere spiritually. The human "degrees" and the way God relates to them are of some interest: (1) tolerating sin—i.e., allowing humans to choose sin with their free wills—but not giving any divine consent; (2) both allowing and agreeing to the devotional life of the ordinary Christian active; (3) actually taking over as prime worker for contemplatives, in this case leaving it up to contemplatives to tolerate, allow, and accept God's principal role in their devotion.

g.   The ME has *sentence*—literally, "opinion," "doctrine," "judgment," "practice," "authority," or "significance" (MED).

or by any of these three witnesses mentioned above.[a] And truly it is only reasonable that a person should be more than his own works. For this is so by the statute and the ordinance of Holy Church: there shall no person be admitted to the prelacy[b] (which is the highest degree in active life) unless the duties of that position[c] fall within one's ability as testified to by true examination. So that in matters active, one's learning and natural ability shall principally dominate[d] as far as devotion is concerned, God graciously consenting, and with the approval of these three witnesses. And, reasonably so, for all active matters are subordinate and subservient to human wisdom. But in matters contemplative, the highest wisdom that is possible in a human (as such) is lessened so that God may be primary in the Work and the human only the one who consents and submits.

And this is how I understand this word of the Gospel: "*Sine me nichil potestis facere*"—that is, "Without me you can do nothing"—in one way for actives and in another for contemplatives. In actives, God must be present— either tolerating[e] or consenting or both—if anything is to be accomplished (depending on whether it is legitimate and pleasing to Him or not); in contemplatives, God must be present as the primary worker Himself, asking of them nothing else except only their submission and consent. So, in order generally to understand: in all our doings, lawful and unlawful, active or contemplative, without God we can do nothing. He is with us in sin (only by toleration and not by consent) to our ultimate damnation unless we humbly amend ourselves. In deeds that are active and lawful He is with us both by toleration and consent, to our reproof—if we go backward—and to our great reward—if we go forward. In activities that are contemplative He is with us, leading us as primary mover and worker, and we by only submitting and consenting—to our great fulfillment and the spiritual one- ing of our soul to Him in perfect charity. And since all in this life can be divided into three: sinners, actives, and contemplatives, therefore, generally regarding the whole world, this word of our Lord may be spoken to all: "Without me . . . "—only tolerating and not consenting in sinners, or else both tolerating and consenting in actives, or (what is more than all this) as primary mover and worker in contemplatives—" . . . you can do nothing."[f]

Lo! Here are many words and little significance![g] Nevertheless, I have said all this to let you know in which things you should expend the effort

a. The system is now very plain: in *active* spirituality, the person acts and God accepts and consents—in *contemplative* spirituality, God acts and the person accepts and consents.

b. The ME has *going*—literally, "going," or "walking," or "journeying," or "entering" (MED).

c. The ME has *rathest*—literally, "soonest," "most easily," or "principally" (MED).

d. The ME has *without errour*.

e. The ME has *grace*—literally, "grace," "gift," "favor," "fortune," "lot," or "providence" (MED). *Grace* is so frequently used in these writings that one finds the meaning tends to change considerably depending on the context.

f. The ME has *entre*—literally, "entry," or "admittance," or "beginning" (MED).

g. The ME has *febely*—literally, "feebly" or "weakly," but with the rarer meaning of "delicately" or "carefully" (MED). The word has stymied most translators here, who try some construct of "feeble," "weak," or "pathetic."

h. The ME has *blynde*—literally, "deprived of discernment" (MED). Once again, some form of the word *blynde* is used so frequently that its meanings must shift somewhat depending on the context—from "blind" to "blinded" to "unseeing" to "invisible" to "simple" to "plain" or to "imageless" (Spearing, 156 n. 39).

of your wits, and in which not; and how God is with you in one work and how in another.[a] And yet, perhaps by this knowledge you may avoid deceptions into which you might have fallen had this not been explained. And therefore, since it is said, let it be, although only slightly relevant to our issue. But now, forward[b] to our subject.

THE ELEVENTH CHAPTER

Of two specific tokens by which a person can discern the call of God to this Work.

But you may ask me this question: "By what one sign or more—if you please—can I most easily[c] know for certain[d] whether this growing desire that I feel in my everyday devotions and this pleasant stirring that I have in reading and hearing of this contemplative matter is truly a calling of God to a more special activity of providence[e] (as is the subject of this book); or if it is nourishment and sustenance of my spirit to remain still and to continue devotions in my ordinary lot in what you call the door and the common beginning place[f] of all Christian men?

To this I answer as carefully[g] as I can: you see well here that in this book I laid down for you two kinds of signs by which you could test your spiritual calling from God regarding this contemplative Work—one inward, and one outward. Of these two neither can suffice fully in this case, as I see it, without the other. But where they are both united and in accord, then your evidence is full enough without anything lacking.

The first of these two signs (which is within) is this growing desire that you feel in your daily devotions. And you should know this about this desire: that although the desire is a work of the un-seeing[h] soul itself—for the desire is as proper for the soul as touching and walking are for the body (and you know well yourself that both touching and walking are unconscious activities of the body)—yet no matter how blind the action of this desire, it is accompanied and followed by a kind of spiritual insight which is partly its cause and partly a means of furthering this desire. Look carefully, then, at what your daily devotions actually are—and if they involve a recollection of your wretchedness, the Passion of Christ, or any such that is part of the

a. First, it is an evidence of the author's authentic commitment to the contemplative way that he doesn't hesitate to advise *against* beginning contemplation if there is the slightest sign that the person is not ready. Second, it should be noted that the author does not criticize the questioner for meditating on his sins, or the Passion of Christ, or "any such that is part of the ordinary devotions of Christian people." There is nothing spiritually incorrect, improper, or inadequate with those meditations, but they may also be precedents and prefaces to contemplation itself. *All* Christians should be paying attention to these things in their devotional lives—indeed, these things should define true devotion for most Christians for their entire lives. Some few, however, are specifically called "beyond" these matters to the heights of the contemplative way.

b. The author is dealing, of course, with "tokens" or "signs" of a contemplative vocation—premised on the understanding that the source of such a vocation is the spiritual influence of God, rather than one's own will. And, although the author speaks about the contemplative way specifically, his "tokens" and "signs" are relevant for the discernment of *any* vocation—the deep and constant inward dissatisfaction and growing desire for "something else" or "something more"—and the subtle interest and quiet enjoyment when one hears or reads about a particular way of living (or praying).

c. "Just as the five senses are the mind's window on the world, the individual mind's reasoning capacity must be for each one of us the final interpreter of the extraordinarily diverse and often confusing data that the senses supply us with" (Cahill, n.p.).

d. Once again the author doesn't hesitate to advise even very devout practicing Christians that their feelings and desires may not be strong enough or long-lived enough to suggest a calling to the contemplative way. He is driven *not* to try to steer people in the contemplative direction who are not truly called to it. He is not trying to drum up business for the contemplative way.

e. The ME has *thou wost never what*—literally, "you know never what."

ordinary devotions of Christian people (as referred to before), if it turns out to be the case that this spiritual vision that accompanies and follows your blind desire arises from these ordinary visions, certainly then it is a sign to me that the growth of this desire is only a nourishing and encouraging of your spirit to remain still and to continue devotions in your ordinary fortune, and no calling or stirring of God to any more special favor.[a]

Now, furthermore, the other second and outward sign is a pleasant stirring that you feel in reading or hearing of this contemplative matter.[b] I call this sign "outward" because it comes from outside through the windows of your bodily senses[c]—such as by hearing and seeing when you are reading. Now regarding this second sign, if it happens that this pleasant stirring (which you feel in hearing and reading of this contemplative matter) lasts or continues with you no longer than the duration of your reading or hearing, but then ceases (or else soon afterward) so that you neither wake nor sleep in it or with it, and especially that it does not follow you into your daily devotions—as it were, entering[a] and thrusting itself between you and your devotions, stirring and guiding your desire—then it is a true sign, in my opinion, that this pleasant stirring that you feel in hearing and reading of this contemplative matter is only a natural gladness that every Christian soul has in hearing or reading of the truth (and specifically that which touches sweetly and declares truly the properties of perfection that are most in accord with the human soul and particularly with the perfection of God) and no spiritual touching of grace, no calling of God to any other special working of grace than that which is the door and common beginning place for all Christians.[d]

But if it happens that this pleasant stirring that you feel in reading and hearing of the contemplative way is so abundant in itself that it goes with you to bed, rises with you in the morning, follows you forth all day long in all that you do, plucks you from the ordinary daily activity and gets between it and you, accompanies and follows your longings so closely that you think it must be all only one desire or you-know-not-what,[e] alters your movements, and makes you well-behaved, and while it lasts everything seems to comfort you and nothing can trouble you. You would run a thousand miles to meet and talk with someone whom you know had felt this same thing; and yet, when you arrived there, you can say nothing—no matter how well you can

a. The "four-f's" alliteration is in the original Middle English—a frequent rhetorical feature of the author's prose.

b. The author knows from experience that a contemplative's language is foreign to non-contemplatives—and frequently seen as folly or heresy or error. A mystic's language is incomprehensible to anyone else, and in writing about it, one runs a serious risk of condemnation and serious judgment.

c. The ME has *speedful*—literally, "beneficial," "advantageous," "effective," "favorable," or "logical" (MED).

d. The ME has *pride*—literally, "unreasonable self-esteem," "vanity," "arrogance," "ostentation," "glory," and "honor" (MED). It is unusual that the word should have alternative translations that seem to be in direct conflict with each other.

e. There is much controversy over the exact meaning of this sentence since it appears in varied forms in different manuscripts. Hodgson (213) examines all options and concludes that this translation is the most accurate: "thy delight is pleasure in playing with a child."

f. The words *contemplation* and *solitude* are virtually inseparable. Even within the community of a Carthusian monastery, individual solitude is maintained strictly and absolutely. And any practicing contemplative can witness that while rare and occasional "corporate contemplation" can be enriching, ultimately the contemplative way is one that is walked in solitude and seclusion.

g. This preceding paragraph is surely one of the author's finest literary efforts—the breadth and beauty of his catalog of evidences of a contemplative calling is both poetically and practically splendid. It includes (in the ME) some ten examples of alliteration, most of which are sadly lost in translation.

h. The ME has *fautours*—usually "followers," or "adherents," or "abettors" (MED). I made the decision to convey that sense in this context as "indicators."

i. The ME has *bareyn*—literally, "barren" or "deprived of possessions" (MED).

j. I have used the odd constructions of "bodiliness" and "spiritualness" to maintain the literary parallels with the ME *bodelines* and *goostlines*.

k. The ME has *gete*—literally "get," "earn," "obtain," "catch, "conquer," "fetch," or "manage." (MED)

speak—because you do not want to speak about anything except this. Your words are few, but full of fruit and fire.[a] A short word from your mouth contains a world full of wisdom, yet it seems to be only folly to those who dwell in their senses.[b] Your silence is sweet; your speech beneficial;[c] your prayer is private; your honor[d] is pure; your manners humble; your mirth mild; your delight is the enjoyment of playing with a child.[e] You love to be alone and sit by yourself;[f] others would get in your way, you think, unless they were contemplating with you. You are not pleased to read or hear a book unless it is about contemplation, so that both your inward and outward evidence are in accord and woven together as one.[g]

THE TWELFTH CHAPTER

Of desolation and of consolation, and why God sends them; with the conclusion about the tokens.

Yea! and if both these evidences, with all their indicators[h] (now written down here—for you have had them all or some of them), cease for a time, and you are left as if you were destitute,[i] you think, as well without the feeling of this new fervor as well as without the old familiar exercises, so that you think you have fallen between the two evidences, never having either one but lacking them both. Do not be too despondent about this, but accept it humbly and await patiently the will of our Lord. For now, it seems to me, you are on the spiritual sea, sailing across from bodiliness to spiritualness.[j]

Many great storms and temptations probably shall arise during this time, and you will not know where you should run for help. Everything is missing from your feelings—both ordinary grace and special blessings. Do not be too fearful (although you think you have reason to be afraid) but have a love-trust in our Lord—however much you can manage[k] for the moment— for He is not far off. He shall look up—possibly very soon—and touch you again with a more fervent stirring of that same grace than any you have ever felt before. Then you are completely restored and all well enough,

a. The ME has *last while it laste may*—literally, "last while it can last."

b. The ME has *blundryng*—literally, "blundering" or "moving blindly" (ODEE, 102). The word is "frequently used in Middle English to signify the uncertain movement of a blind person" (Hodgson, 214).

c. The ME has *behote*—literally, (as *bihoten*) "promise," "pledge," "assure," or "demand" (MED).

d. The ME has *pleying*—literally, "playing" (Mayhew, 174) or "fitting" (Bradley, 478). Spearing (130 n.) suggests "pliant."

e. The ME has *roon*—probably "roan" (i.e., soft sheepskin leather). Possibly *rone*: "a kind of leather cured in a method originating in Rouen" (MED).

f. The ME has *worche*—literally, "work," "mold," "carve," or "shape" (MED).

g. The ME has *propirly*—literally. "properly," "completely," or "thoroughly" (ODEE, 716).

h. The ME has *never the rather*—literally, "none the more" or "not at all" (MED).

i. Julian of Norwich echoes our author: "I was … left to myself in such sadness and weariness of my life, and annoyance with myself that scarcely was I able to have patience to live. There was no comfort nor any ease…. And immediately after this, our Blessed Lord gave me again the comfort and the rest in my soul, in delight and in security so blissful and so powerful that no fear, no sorrow, no bodily pain that could be suffered would have distressed me. And then the pain showed again to my feeling, and then the joy and the delight, and now the one, and now the other, various times—I suppose about twenty times…. This vision was shown me, for my understanding, that it is advantageous for some souls to feel this way—sometimes to be in comfort, and sometimes to fail and to be left by themselves" (I Julian, 113–14).

j. Note that in this sentence the first person plural ("we," "our," "us") is used for the first and only time in the letter. It is the only direct indication that the author speaks from his own specific experience (a point missed by most commentators).

k. The ME has *bygyng*—translated as "establishing" (Hodgson, 214).

l. The ME has *worscheping*—in Middle English it is a good example of a false cognate, meaning "honoring," not "worshipping" (Mayhew, 261).

m. The ME has *sensible*—literally, "able to be sensed." I have used "sentient" to translate *sensible* because its cognate modern meaning is inaccurate.

as you think—let it last while it can.[a] For suddenly, before you know it, everything is gone, and you are left destitute in the boat, blown blindly,[b] now here, now there—you do not know where from or where to. Yet do not be confounded, for He will come, I swear to[c] you, very soon, when He wishes to relieve you and valiantly deliver you from all your grief, far more admirably than He ever did before. Yea! and if He goes again, He will come back again, and each time if you conduct yourself with humble deference, He will come more gloriously and joyfully than before. And all this He does because He wishes to have you made as pliant[d] to his spiritual will as a soft leather[e] glove is to your bodily hand.

And if He sometimes goes and sometimes comes, therefore in this double work of His, He will secretly test you and your own work in both ways, and shape[f] you to His own work. By the withdrawing of your fervor (which you consider His departure, although it is not so) He will thoroughly[g] test your patience. For know right well that though God sometimes withdraws these sentient sweetnesses, these fervent feelings, and these burning desires, nevertheless, He never ever[h] withdraws His grace from within His chosen.[i] For surely I cannot believe that His special favor can ever be withdrawn from His chosen ones who have once been touched by it—unless mortal sin were the cause. But all these sentient sweetnesses, these fervent feelings, and these burning desires (which in themselves are not grace, but signs of grace) are often withdrawn in testing our patience, and often for many other spiritual benefits for us—more than we could hope for. For grace in itself is so high, so pure, and so spiritual, that it cannot be felt in our senses.[j] The *signs* of it can, but not grace itself. And thus sometimes our Lord will withdraw your sentient fervors both in establishing[k] and testing your patience, and not only for this reason, but for many others which I will not recount here at this time. But onward to our subject.

By the distinction, the frequency, and the progression of these sentient feelings mentioned above (which you consider His arrival, although that is not so) He will nourish and sustain your spirit to endure and to live in love and honor[l] of Him. So that thus—by patience in the absence of sentient[m] feelings, the signs of grace, and by that life-giving nourishment and that loving sustenance of your spirit in their presence—He will make you in both together so gladly submissive and so pleasingly pliant to the perfection

a. In his *Epistle on Prayer*, our author wrote: "A chaste love is such that when you ask of God neither relief from pain, nor increase of wealth, nor even the sweetness of his love in this life … you ask of God nothing but Himself. And neither anticipate for nor consider whether you shall be in pain or in bliss, as long as you have Him whom you love" (ME from Hodgson, 199; my translation).

b. The ME has *felist hym*—literally, "feel him," but the author is not talking about the sense of touch ("feeling") or the emotion ("feeling"), but the "sense of presence," so I have used the more rare "commune with" translation (MED).

c. The ME has *blyndely*—literally, "blindly," or "secretly," but also, rarely, "dimly" (ODEE, 100).

d. Being "clothed with God" reminds one of Saint Paul's words: "we shall be changed. For this corruptible must put on incorruption, and this mortal shall put on immortality. And when this mortal shall have put on immortality, then shall come to pass the saying that is written: Death is swallowed up in victory" (1 Cor. 15:53–54).

e. The ME has *fall toe*—literally, "come" or "happen" (MED).

f. The ME has *felyng*—literally, "feeling." See note "b" above.

g. "This is the Unitive Life when the mind has lost all consciousness of the separation between itself and God" (Hodgson, 214).

h. "If I am to know God directly, 'I' must become completely 'He' and 'He' 'I'; so that this 'He' and 'I' become and are one 'I'" (Meister Eckhart, Sermon 94, cited by II Underhill, 420).

i. The author's ultimate threefold test for a true calling to the contemplative way, once one has perceived the indicated signs or tokens: (1) Scripture—that is, one must have examined the Bible and found nothing in it that seems contrary to or discredits one's calling; (2) counsel—the essential element of a spiritual director, one who is familiar with both the character and the spiritual growth of the seeker; and (3) conscience—which has always been understood to be the "quiet voice of God" in one's mind and soul.

and the spiritual one-ness with His own will (which one-ing is perfect love) that you shall be as glad and as joyful to forgo such sentient feelings at His will, as to enjoy them and feel them continually all your lifetime.

And in this time your love becomes both chaste and complete.[a] Now you both gaze upon your God and your love, and nakedly commune with[b] Him also by spiritual one-ing to His love in the supreme pinnacle of your spirit, just as He is in Himself (though dimly[c] as is possible here), utterly stripped of your self and nakedly clothed in Him[d] just as He is, not clothed and cloaked in any of the sentient feelings (no matter how sweet or how holy) that can take place[e] in this life, but in purity of spirit He is perceived properly and perfectly and sensed as He is in Himself—far distant from any delusion or false opinion that may be present in this life.

This vision and this sense[f] of God—thus in Himself, just as He is—can no more be distinguished from God as He is in Himself[g] (in your understanding of what you feel and what you see) than can God Himself be distinguished from His own being with which He is solely one both in essence and also in nature. So that just as God cannot exist separate from His own being because of their one-ness in nature, so the soul that sees and feels this way cannot be separated from the thing that it sees and feels because of their one-ness in grace.[h]

Lo, thus and by these signs you can to some degree sense and partially test the manner and the distinction of your calling and the stirring of grace in your inward spiritual devotions and in your outward reading or hearing of this matter. And then, from the time that you, or any other like you in spirit, have had true experience of all these signs (or of any of them)—for at the beginning there are only very few that are so specially touched and marked with this grace that they can rapidly or instantly have in true experience the proof of all of the signs; nevertheless, it is enough to have some one or two, though no one has all of them immediately—and therefore if you feel that you have true experience of one or two signs, proven by true examination of Scripture and of counsel and of conscience,[i] then it is beneficial for you at that time to cease from the peculiar meditations and the bizarre imaginations about the properties of your being and of God's, and of the works of yourself and of God (in which your senses have been fed and with which you have been led from worldliness and physicality to that current

a. Although the author tends to belittle the earlier meditations and imaginations, he recognizes that they were necessary stepping-stones that provided spiritual nourishment until his protégé would be ready to engage in the Work of contemplation.

b. John 16:7: "But I tell you the truth: it is expedient for you that I go; for if I do not depart, the Comforter will not come to you—but if I depart, I will send him to you." Note: The Latin Vulgate word for "depart"—*abiero*—can also properly be translated as "disappear." As usual, the author has slightly adapted Scripture without changing its basic meaning by adding "bodily" to make his point.

c. The ME word *doctor*—literally, "doctor"—in the fourteenth century described a person with the authority and the capability of serving as a teacher. "Doctor" comes from the Latin *doceo* meaning "to teach." We still use it in that sense when we speak of a "doctor's degree" (e.g., PhD) as a prerequisite for a professorship.

d. Almost certainly a reference to Saint Augustine: "By his divinity he is always with us, but unless he departed from us in body, we would always see only his fleshly body, and we would never believe spiritually" (Augustine, *Sermon* 93.4).

e. The ME has *taast*—literally, "taste"—a beautiful metaphor: "taste a bit of God's love"! And it reminds one of Psalm 33:9 [34:8]: "Taste and see that the Lord is pleasant; blessed is the man who trusts in him."

f. The author stresses the significance of remaining aware of one's true "self"—not the false self or persona one often adopts in the world—so one can offer that unimpeded and "naked" self to God.

capacity for grace),ᵃ in order to learn how you should be occupied spiritually with awareness of yourself and of God, about whom you have learned to know so well previously by your actions of thinking and imagining.

THE THIRTEENTH CHAPTER

That our Lord Himself teaches this contemplative Work; and that the contemplative should persevere in humility and in love.

Christ showed an example of this in this life. For if it had been that there were no higher perfection in this life than in beholding and in loving Christ's *Humanity*, I believe that He would not then have ascended into heaven while this world still survived, nor withdrawn His bodily presence from His special lovers on earth, except because there was a higher perfection that humanity could attain in this life (that is to say, a pure spiritual sensation of love of His *Divinity*); therefore He said to His disciples—who begrudged having to forgo His bodily presence (as you begrudge in part and in a way having to forgo your bizarre meditations and your peculiar devious perceptions)—that it was beneficial for them that He went away bodily from them:"*Expedit vobis ut ego vadam*"—that is,"It is beneficial to you that I go bodily from you."ᵇ About this word the Doctorᶜ said thus:"That unless the shape of his manhood is withdrawn from our bodily eyes, the love of his Godhead cannot be fixed in our spiritual eyes,"ᵈ and so I say to you that it is beneficial sometimes to leave off your bizarre laboring in your wits and in your *spiritual* awareness learn to tasteᵉ something of the love of your God.

And this awareness will come to you by the way I tell you (through the help of grace leading you) and that is that you always without ceasing rely on the naked awareness of your very self, always offering your being to God as the most precious offering that you can make.ᶠ But see to it, as I have often said, that it be *naked*—for fear of falseness. If the awareness is naked then in the beginning, it will be very painful for you to remain in it for any length of time; and that is, as I said before, because your senses find no food for them in it. But no matter that, for then I would love it the better. Let those senses fast awhile, I beg you, from their natural delight in their own knowledge; for, as it is well said, a person naturally desires to

a. "All men by nature desire to know"—the first words of Aristotle's *The Metaphysics* (Clarendon Press, Oxford: 1924).

b. 1 Corinthians 8:1b: "Knowledge puffs up; love truly builds up."

c. A short summary of the author's anti-rationalist bias. The thirteenth-century Christian scholars put reason and intellect at the summit and would claim they were the only true routes to union with God. Our author consistently denies those premises and claims that intuition, feeling (i.e., "sensing"), affect, and love are beyond knowing and finally will provide the only *true* way to one-ness with God.

d. The ME has *batayle*—literally, "battle." The conflict is not only a mild upset.

e. The ME has *my wittys wolden haue me awey*—literally, "my wits would have me away"—often translated as "my intelligence would have me stop."

f. There is a hint of Saint Paul: "For I do not do the good I want to do; but the evil I do not want to do, that I do" (Rom. 7:19).

g. We must remember that this statement has been put in the mouth of his protégé by the author himself—in order to set himself up for the answer he wishes to give.

h. The author does not sugarcoat the issue and claim that there is no pain or conflict in contemplation, but that the benefits of a certain knowledge of what must be done and the confidence that the soul will not go far astray are worth the price.

i. This last paragraph was not present in the original manuscripts. It first appears in a 1677 manuscript (Ampleforth, 42) attributed to the Carthusian monk Maurice Chauncey († 1581), and several translators have chosen not to include it. Since without this paragraph the ending seems abnormally abrupt, Walsh has suggested that the original epistle may not have been finished or may have originally had a cover letter (II Walsh, 283). The paragraph is nonetheless true to the author's style and is a singularly appropriate conclusion.

know;[a] but surely he cannot taste of spiritual awareness in God except by grace alone, no matter how much knowledge one has from book-learning or from the natural world. Therefore, I beg you, seek more for awareness than for knowledge, for knowledge often deceives with pride, but humble loving awareness cannot beguile. *Scientia inflat, karitas edificat.*[b] In knowledge is trouble, in affection is rest.[c]

But now you may say: "What is this rest that you speak of? For I think that it is struggle, suffering, and not rest. For when I set myself to do as you say, I find there pain and conflict[d] on all sides. On the one hand, my wits would have me away,[e] and I will not; and on the other hand, I want to feel God and avoid feeling myself, and I cannot[f]—so conflict and pain are on all sides and I think this is a deceitful kind of rest that you speak of."[g]

To this I answer and say: that you are not used to this Work, and therefore it is more painful to you. But if you were used to it and knew by experience what benefit lay therein, you would not willingly leave it in exchange for all the bodily joy and rest in the world.[h] And yet it is great pain and great struggle also, but nonetheless I call it "rest," because the soul is not in doubt what it ought to do, and also because a soul is guaranteed (I mean in the time of this action) that it shall not greatly err.

And[i] therefore go forth with humility and fervent desire in this Work, which begins in this life and shall never have an end in the life everlasting. To which I beseech almighty Jesus to bring all those whom He has bought with His precious blood. Amen.

NOTES FOR THE
TRANSLATOR'S INTRODUCTION

1   Butler, Dom Edward Cuthbert; *Western Mysticism* (Constable, London: 1927), 3–4.

2   *Oxford English Dictionary*, s.v. "mystic."

3   It is important to recognize that contemplative prayer is not merely a skill one decides to develop, but that it is ultimately a calling—a gift of God's grace—offered, perhaps, to many but characteristically embraced by only a few. While it tends to be elevated above all other practices by its advocates, it is not *morally* superior to a simple life of virtue and sincere devotion.

4   By the fourteenth century, the practice of hesychastic prayer in the East came eventually to be virtually identified with the repetitive use of the Jesus Prayer as a mantra.

5   Giles Fraser, "Loose Canon," *The Guardian*, February 29, 2014.

6   This concept is not as obtuse as it seems, since there are many situations in human experience where words fail us and are ineffective. Consider these challenges: (a) find words that perfectly describe the odor of a rose; (b) describe the color blue to a blind person; (c) define "time"; (d) explain exactly the experience of love. In these instances we are driven to use metaphors because *literal* description is virtually impossible—so, too, with God in the *via negativa*.

7   The converse is kataphatic prayer (sometimes spelled "cataphatic"): that is, prayer that exults in the created world, in outward forms, in the beauty of nature, in the lives of the saints and in the life and passion of Christ, and in statues, crucifixes, icons, and the like.

8   We should be aware that in classical Christian theology love has nothing to do with emotions, feelings, sexual attraction, or passions. "Christian love" is a matter of *choice*—an act of the *will* (which Aquinas calls "the rational appetite")—and, as Aquinas defines it, love is "willing the good for another" (*Summa Theologica* 6.4).

9   Hodgson, lxvi.

10   All translations are my own from the Latin Vulgate.

11   One uses the word *gnostic* here advisedly, recognizing that a clear distinction needs to be made between this "Christian gnosticism" and the heretical Gnostic movement among some early Christians, which taught that there was a secret

knowledge (*gnosis*) that would be imparted only to initiates and that alone would lead one to God (referred to in 1 Tim. 6:20 as "knowledge falsely so-called") and that the world and all material things were irredeemably evil and were created not by God but by a semidivine demiurge. The movement began in the second century and continues in isolated instances today.

12   In Gosset, Thierry; *Women Mystics of the Contemporary Era* (Staten Island, NY; 2003), cited in *The Tablet*, December 14, 2013.

13   See http://en.wikipedia.org/wiki/Thomas_Merton.

14   Cited in James V. Schall, SJ, "The Pope Chats with an Atheist," *The Catholic World Report*, October 4, 2013.

15   Cited in Cropper, Margaret, *The Life of Evelyn Underhill: An Intimate Portrait of the Groundbreaking Author of Mysticism* (Skylight Paths Publishing, Woodstock, VT; 2002), x (reprint of Harper 1958 edition).

16   Cited in Fanous, Samuel and Gillespie, Vincent, eds., *The Cambridge Companion to Medieval English Mysticism* (Cambridge Univ. Press; Cambridge; 2011), 6.

17   Rahner, Karl; *The Practice of Faith*, trans. and ed. by Karl Lehmann and Alvert Raffelt (Crossroad, New York; 1986), 69–77.

18   In a February 4, 2014 e-mail from Ann Fontaine; quoted with permission.

19   Additional writings generally accepted as by the same author include *The Letter of Privy Counsel* (included in this volume), *The Epistle on Prayer, The Epistle of Discretion*, translations of *Denis Hid Divinity* and *Benjamin Minor*, and the paraphrase of two sermons of Saint Bernard entitled *Of the Discerning of Spirits*.

20   Evelyn Underhill thought that he was a monk of some indeterminate order, but definitely not a Carthusian; Harvey Egan spoke without hesitation of him as "the anonymous Carthusian"; Pollard spoke of "his possibly Carthusian world." René Trixier said that the treatises "point towards a Carthusian origin"; Justin McCann believed the author was a secular East Anglian priest; Phyllis Hodgson recognized him as a hermit of some sort; Helen Gardner concluded that he was an anchorite; Julia Holloway identified him as Adam Easton and his protégé as female, possibly Julian of Norwich; Aubrey Gwynn named him an Austin Hermit Friar (like Walter Hilton); Jonathan Hughes suggested that he was (or had been) a Dominican.

21   See the prayer that precedes the Prologue to *The Cloud* and the note on it.

22   See the last paragraph of chapter 75 of *The Cloud*.

23   " . . . those prayers that are ordained by Holy Church, for they that are true laborers in this Work honor no prayer so much as those, and therefore they do them in the form and under the procedures that were ordained by the holy fathers before us" (*The Cloud*, chapter 37).

24   Notably in Gardner, Helen, in *Medium Aevum* 16 (1947): 40–41.

25 "The resemblances between the two in doctrine and language are certainly very striking and imply some kind of relationship" (I Knowles, 68).

26 "The advanced form of prayer which he advocates ... and which it seems certain he practised himself, points to his having led a life of strict retirement" (Hodgson, lxxxiv).

27 It is possible that Grimlaicus's "Rule for Solitaries" (ca. 900) may have been an influence on Bruno's founding of the Carthusians. (Thanks to Sara Ward for this reminder.)

28 *Consuetudines* 1.1, accessed at http://www.statcrux.co.uk/ocart/cl1.htm.

29 Some describe the levels of these cells in reverse: with the workshop, etc., on the second level.

30 In the *Consuetudines* of Guido I. This remains "the most complete contemporary record of bookmaking supplies available to modern codicologists, and is often used as the exemplary description of medieval scribal materials" (Brantley, 47).

31 "Beauvale Charterhouse," 2014 brochure from the website.

32 *Consuetudines* 14.

33 Thurston, 35.

34 In fact, the Carthusians were seen to be so devout that some prominent "protestant" Lollards—who generally despised monasticism for its impropriety, hypocrisy, and duplicity—actually defected from their puritanical movement and joined a Charterhouse (Catto, 147–48).

35 Davies, 50.

36 Both Augustine Baker and David Knowles hold that "the author had, of set purpose, taken pains to remain anonymous" (Hodgson, lxxxii).

37 It is impossible, as has been claimed by one commentator, that the recipient could have been a woman. See chapter 12: "... though you were to cut away your private parts"—an unlikely statement to make to a woman. (See I Clark, introduction, 20.)

38 *The Cloud*, chapter 1.

39 There were several sets of workers affiliated with the monastery, who were not monks proper: *conversi* (lay brothers under vows with separate housing, dining, and liturgy); *redditi* (administrators not under vows—often in charge of business affairs—occasionally ordained); *donati* (lay brothers who did not take vows); *prebendarii* (brothers whose support was prepaid by family—often sons of gentry); and *mercenarii* (virtually, hired hands). (I am indebted for most of these definitions to Canon Michael McLean of Norwich Cathedral.) Guido I stipulated sixteen lay brothers for every thirteen monks (Brantley, 39).

40 It is important to realize that the *conversi*—lay brothers—were not merely secular servants, but were devout monastics themselves, living pious celibate lives under

vows, wearing a habit almost exactly like that of the monks. Indeed, in modern Charterhouses, they are much more fully integrated with the Cloister Monks.

41 Brantley, 39.

42 In fourteenth-century England, the normal minimal age for ordination was twenty-four. In 1348 the Bishop of Norwich was granted papal permission to ordain at the age of twenty-one, because so many priests in Norwich had died of the plague that year that there was a shortage of priests (Blomefield, Francis; *A Topographical History of Norfolk*, vol. 3, published in 1739).

43 Hodgson, xlix–l; an opinion shared by I Knowles, 70; Hughes, 102; Wolters, 13; and I Walsh, 8.

44 "The earliest of the seventeen manuscripts of *The Cloud of Unknowing* ... are written in an East Midlands dialect.... On this basis the editor of The Cloud had concluded that the original works were written by someone from the north-east Midlands, in the region of Nottinghamshire" (I Knowles, 70, and see Hughes, 103).

45 It is interesting that Beauvale is only twenty miles from Thurgarten in Lincolnshire where the author's fellow mystic, Walter Hilton, lived as a hermit. A close friend of Hilton's, Adam Horseley, joined the Beauvale Charterhouse, and Hilton considered it but ended up joining the Augustinian Canons Regular at Thurgarten and eventually living as a solitary hermit.

46 In the fourteenth century in England there were also Carthusian Priories at Witham (founded 1178 in Somerset), Hinton (founded 1221 in Somerset), Hull (founded 1369 in Yorkshire), London (founded 1370), Coventry (founded 1381 in Warwickshire), Axholme (founded 1396 in Lincolnshire), and Mount Grace (founded 1398 in Yorkshire).

47 Doubleday, 83–86.

48 Complete details can be found in I Knowles, 181–82, and II Thompson, 207–14. Note that in Dugdale, in the records of Haugham (ca. 1540) is listed income from a *firma rectoris* ("farm of the rector"), and the title "rector" meant a Carthusian superior living where the full Rule could not be followed, such as in a grange (Hendriks, 40)—so we know that in the sixteenth century there was one Carthusian monk at Haugham, and we can reliably presume that had been the case since the fourteenth century as well.

49 "Granges were established on demesne land held by the charterhouse. Although worked by servants, Carthusian granges may have accommodated the cell of a monk-supervisor" (*English Heritage*, s.v. "granger," accessed at http://www.eng-h .gov.uk/mpp/mcd/sub/court1.htm).

50 When a monk of the Hull Charterhouse applied for permission to leave the monastery and enter an anchorhold, his request was denied (Brantley, 42).

51 "A Rector ... is the superior of a Charterhouse in which for some reason the rule cannot be observed in its entirety" (Hendriks, 40). We also know that in later records (Roll 31 Hen.VIII) a "Rector" is mentioned at Haugham Priory.

52 Paper was not generally available in England until the fifteenth century, and even then it was extremely expensive and was called "cloth parchment" (Smith, 45) In fact, the Church initially banned paper, calling it a "pagan art" unworthy of carrying the Sacred Word (Fuller, n.p.). In the fourteenth century, a parchment book like *The Cloud* could have cost about as much as a semester's tuition at Oxford, a year's salary for a master carpenter, or 20 pigs (Dyer, 77 and Hodges).

53 See, for instance, the last sentence in chapter 1 and first sentence of chapter 2.

54 Hodgson, i–xcii, and II and III Clark.

55 Gallacher, Patrick J. *The Cloud of Unknowing* (TEAMS, Medieval Institute Publications: Kalamazoo, MI; 1997).

56 "For at one time people thought it humility to say nothing out of their own heads unless they affirmed it by Scripture and sayings of the Fathers—and now this practice has turned into idiosyncrasy and the flaunting of cleverness. You do not need it and therefore I do not do it" (*Cloud*, chapter 70).

57 In Acts 17:33–34: "So Paul departed from among them. But certain men followed him, and believed: among which was Dionysius the Areopagite."

58 II Julian, chapters 7, 26, 31, 71, and throughout.

59 *The Book of Common Prayer*, 336.

60 1 Jn. 4:12b–13: Clementine Vulgate, my translation.

61 Darwin, Charles; *Descent of Man* (John Murray; London; 1871), 2:405.

62 *Privy Counsel*, chapter 7.

63 *The Cloud*, chapter 2.

64 It should be noted that on the basis of the doctrine of creation ex nihilo, the Council of Nicaea "denies the soul's natural kinship with the divine and affirms an uncrossable ontological gap between the creator and created human nature" (Gallacher, 3).

65 Gallacher, 10.

66 *The Cloud*, chapter 29.

67 *The Cloud*, chapter 67. Also note: The word "God" in this sentence is capitalized in both Hodgson's and Gallacher's transcriptions.

68 2 Pet. 1:4.

69 Saint Athanasius, *On the Incarnation of the Word* 54.3.

70 Saint Augustine, Sermon 166.8.

71 Thomas Aquinas, *Opusculum 57, in festo Corpus Christi*, Sermon 1.4.

72 Mayne, Michael, *This Sunrise of Wonder* (London: Darton, Longman & Todd, 2008), 53.

73 Buechner, Frederick, *The Alphabet of Grace* (HarperCollins; New York; 2009), 8.

74 Alison, James; *Undergoing God* (Continuum; New York; 2006), 18.

75 Cited in Arends, Carolyn; "Knowing God Means More Than Describing Him," *Christianity Today*, April 4, 2014.

76 See chapter 4 for evidence of the author's deep commitment to Jesus.

77 Karl Heinz Steinmetz in Jones, 135.

78 *Deus Absconditus* is merely from the Latin Vulgate in Isa. 45:15: "*Vere tu es Deus absconditus, Deus Israël salvator*"—"Truly you are a <u>hidden God</u>, O God of Israel, the Savior."

79 I Clark, 27–28.

80 Hodgson, lxv.

81 In the preface to I Walsh.

82 1 Cor. 8:1b–3 (my translation).

83 Ruysbroeck, Jan van; trans. by Dom, C. A. Wynschenk, *The Adornment of The Spiritual Marriage: The Sparkling Stone and The Book of Supreme Truth,* (London: J. M. Dent; 1916), 203–4.

APPENDICES

APPENDIX I

Following is a portion of a recorded first-person account by a contemplative who has practiced the Work of *The Cloud* for several years and has requested anonymity:

The first time, it was truly frightening. I mean you have tried to give up all of the ideas about your "self" that you have developed over a lifetime—you know, to assure yourself that you are important, and worthwhile, and intelligent, and safe, and secure. And suddenly that is all swept away, and you're like a stranger even to yourself. And then it seems like you are lost—sort of dangling in empty space (although that's too physical a picture) and there's nothing there except this driving mind-hunger for whatever God is. And it's like being in a spiritual fog—for me the metaphor is more like an all-enveloping London fog than a cloud—and there's this odd sense of "presence" in the hazy spiritual invisible landscape. (That's a paradox, isn't it? But it's the way it was. But I don't mean I *saw* anything—with my eyes—it was more like a dream.) And then—only once in a while (only four times since I started the practice a while ago)—there is this staggering split-second spiritual surge—like a sudden eruption or an outburst. And then you're changed. And when you are aware of things again, it seems like you've been away for a long time—even though you've been in contemplation for only ten or twenty minutes.

APPENDIX 2

Following is a poem by Saint John of the Cross (1542—1591) that demonstrates the same spiritual realities discussed in *The Cloud* two hundred years later. (The translation is my own.)

"Coplas hechas sobre un Èxtasis de harta contemplaciôn"
(Verses Made about an Ecstasy of Contemplation)

I entered into unknowing
and dwelt there unknowing
beyond all comprehension.

I did not know the way
but when I found myself there,
not knowing where I was,
I learned things immeasurable,
but what I felt I cannot say,
for I dwelt in unknowing,
beyond all comprehension.

It was the perfect place
of peace and holiness.
In hidden solitude
I found the path:
a secret wisdom won
that I was stammering and stunned,
beyond all comprehension.

I passed so far within,
so overcome and carried off,
my senses swept away and drowned,
my feelings gone and stolen.

My soul had come upon a truer way:
a knowledge of unknowing,
beyond all comprehension.

And he who comes in truth
Is lost as in a sleep,
for all that once he knew
now seems a wretched thing,
and thus does knowledge flee and melt away
that he remains unknowing,
beyond all comprehension.

The higher he ascends
the dimmer is the world;
it is the shadowed cloud
that purifies the dark,
and so the soul who understood
continues ever in unknowing,
beyond all comprehension.

This knowledge by unknowing
is such a towering might
that scholars' efforts strive
and find no victory but loss
Whose intellect surrenders in the trial
to understand unknowing,
beyond all comprehension.

This seems a sovereign wisdom
rising to a splendid height;
the best of reason soaring then
falls crumbling in the dark;
but one who can override the night
by wisdom of unknowing
beyond all comprehension.

And if you wish to know
The way to highest wonder,
to an exalted sense
of God's most holy Self;
then from his mercy comes his grace:
to keep us all unknowing,
beyond all comprehension.

The great Benedictine and champion of contemplation John Main wrote that through the practice of contemplative prayer "you will eventually be unhooked from your ideas, your concepts, your words, your thoughts, all that amalgam of distraction that is going on in your mind most of the time, and you will come, with patience and fidelity, to clarity of consciousness" (quoted in Miller, 11).

I am now going to take a great presumptuous leap and step beyond what the author of *The Cloud* describes as the functions and workings of the contemplative way and build upon the author's methods by mentioning briefly some results and effects that appear to be fairly common among those who attempt to live a serious continuing contemplative life in the contemporary world.

There are dozens of how-to manuals on beginning contemplative prayer— and our author gives some splendid pointers and clues for beginners as well. And it must be said that the vast majority of contemplatives today live and pray contentedly and productively at the "Singular" level, often following the lead of the teachings of Dom John Main, osb, or Father Thomas Keating, ocso. If one is satisfied and fulfilled with this character of contemplation and does not sense a "stirring" or longing for more, there is no need to feel inadequate, incomplete, or lacking.

And there are some fairly universal results from the practice of the contemplative way that might be noted.

As one begins the process of emptying oneself of distractions, future plans, and past memories, it is quite common that there occurs a great, almost overwhelming flood of reminiscence of sins one has committed in the past—sins that were long ago absolved and have been utterly forgotten for years or decades—and often the memories are of temptations and sins of a sexual nature. I have known those who have been so frightened by these memories that they have fled and forsaken further meditation. It seems that this may be God's way of reminding us that we are sinners and unworthy in and of ourselves to approach God. It helps us develop a sense of helplessness, vulnerability, and dependency—the essential first steps on the contemplative way.

As one becomes more and more adept at the "Work," a sense of elemental union begins to build almost unnoticeably—the dissolution of apparent barriers and obstacles between oneself and other persons—and between oneself and animals and plants and even inanimate things such as rocks, waters, and skies. There is a subtle melding that seems to discover hitherto imperceptible and inconceivable commonalities between oneself and everything that exists. (An exercise: gaze uninterruptedly at a rock or tree or a cloud for twenty minutes, holding the single thought in your mind: "Teach me." And be ready to be surprised.)

A gradual satisfaction begins to grow with one's present state and condition. Social ambition seems gradually to evaporate, and a kind of contentment or satisfaction begins to take its place. One grows less and less driven to accomplish or achieve great feats that were once of singular importance. "Winning" or "gaining" begin to slide toward irrelevance.

Slowly one's own erstwhile certainties begin to fade, and the search for such certainties dissolves. Dogmatic certitudes (for which one may once have done battle) slip slowly into external insignificance. It is not that beliefs are abandoned, but they seem to be internalized, quietly, without contest or strife.

All thoughts of petitioning God for *anything* simply disappear. One feels wrapped in a caring that provides all one's needs without a single entreaty.

And, be warned, often one can spend a very long time in contemplative prayer with *no* noticeable results at all. To my mind, this is simply God asking, "Are you with me because you seek some sweet reward—or because you want only to be with me?"

Almost all other prayer may go on through one's life but is extinguished by death, but the prayer of contemplation is endless and eternal—it is the prayer of heaven. Indeed, it is "the Beatific Vision" itself.

BIBLIOGRAPHY

MANUSCRIPTS OF *THE CLOUD OF UNKNOWING* AND *THE LETTER OF PRIVY COUNSEL*

An estimate of the date of each manuscript is bracketed (Hodgson, ix–xviii).

British Library

MS Harleian 674 (includes *A Book of Contemplacyon the whiche is clepyd the Clowde if Vnknowyng* and *The Book of Priue Counseling*) [early 15th c.]. Gallacher's transcription of this MS is the copy text for this *Cloud*; Hodgson's transcription of this MS is the copy text for this *Privy Counsel*.

MS Harleian 959 (contains only *The Clowde of Vnknowyng*) [mid-15th c.]

MS Harleian 2373 (includes *The Cloude of Vnknowyng* and *A Tretyse of Priue Counseile*) [late 15th c.]

MS Royal 17 C xxvi (contains only *The Diuyne Clowde of Vnknowynge*) [mid 15th c.]

MS Royal 17 C xxvii (contains only *The Diuyne Clowde of Vnknowing*) [late 16th c.]

MS Royal 17 D v (includes *The Diuine Clowde of Unknowyng*) [late 15th c.]

Cambridge University Library

MS Ff. vi. 41 (includes *An Epistle of Priuate Counsell* and *The Divine Cloude of Vnknowing*) [17th c.]

MS Ii. vi. 31 (includes *The Pystle of Pryuate Cownsell*) [15th c.]

MS Ii. vi. 39 (contains only *The Clowde of Vnkowyng*) [15th c.]

MS Kk. vi. 26 (includes *A Boke of Contemplacion the whiche is called the Cloude of Vnknowynge* and *A Tretyse of Pryuey Conseylle*) [late 15th c.]

Pembroke College, Cambridge

MS 221 (includes *Caligo Ignorancie*—Latin translation of *The Cloud* by Richard Methley) [late 15th c.]

Bodleian Library, Oxford

MS Douce 262 (includes *The Dyuyne Cloude of Vnknowyng* and *The Pystelle of Priuat Councelle*) [ca. AD 1500]

MS Bodleian 576 (includes *The Boke of the Deuyne Clowde of Vnknowynge* and *The Pystell of Pryvate Cownsell*) [early 16th c.]

MS Bodleian 856 (includes *Nubes Ignorandi*—Latin translation of *The Cloud*) [mid 15th c.]

University College, Oxford

MS 14 (includes *The Cloude of Contemplasion* called at the end of the text *The Clowde of Onknowynge*) [mid 15th c.]

Trinity College, Dublin

MS 122 (includes *The Cloude of Unknowyng* and *A Treatyse of Pryve Conseille*) [15th c.]

St. Hugh's Charterhouse

Parkminster MS D 176 (includes *The Dyuyne Clowde of Vnknowing* and *The Pistle of Pryuate Cownsell*) [early 16th c.]

MODERN TRANSCRIPTIONS OF *THE CLOUD OF UNKNOWING* AND *THE LETTER OF PRIVY COUNSEL* IN MIDDLE ENGLISH

Gallacher, Patrick, ed.; *The Cloud of Unknowing*; TEAMS Middle English Text Series at Medieval Institute Publications; Kalamazoo, MI; 1997. (Available online at http://www.lib.rochester.edu/camelot/teams/cloud.htm)

Hodgson, Phyllis; *The Cloud of Unknowing and the Book of Privy Counselling edited from the Manuscripts with Introduction and Notes*; (Early English Text Society, orig. ser. no. 218); Oxford Univ. Press; London; 1944 (reprint 1958).

THE CLOUD OF UNKNOWING AND THE LETTER OF PRIVY COUNSEL IN MODERN ENGLISH

Anonymous, ed.; *The Cloud of Unknowing*; Benediction Classics; Oxford; 2010.

Anonymous, ed.; *The Cloud of Unknowing*; Abingdon Press; Nashville, TN; 1997.

Anonymous, ed.; *The Cloud of Unknowing*; Aziloth Books; 2011.

Backhouse, Halcyon; *The Cloud of Unknowing: A New Paraphrase*; Hodder & Stoughton; London; 1985, 1987, 2009.

Baker, Augustine (Collins, Henry, ed.); *The Divine Cloud*; with notes and preface by Fr. Augustine Baker; Thomas Richardson & Son; London; 1871.

Baker, Augustine; *The Cloud of Unknowing*; Burns & Oates; London; 1924.

Bangley, Bernard; *The Cloud of Unknowing*; Paraclete Press; Orleans, MA; 2009 (e-book and Kindle, 2010).

Bose, Mishtooni; *The Cloud of Unknowing*; Wordsworth Editions Limited; London; 2000, 2001, 2004.

Brinton, Howard H., ed.; *The Cloud of Unknowing: A Version in Modern English of a Fourteenth Century Classic* (Little Gold-Jacketed Series); Harper; New York and London; 1948.

Butcher, Carmen Acevedo; *The Cloud of Unknowing with the Book of Privy Counsel*; Shambhala Publications; Boston; 2009 (Kindle, 2009).

Celiz, Edward; *A Cloud of Unknowing: A Personal Survey of the Great Issues of Religion*; Vantage; New York; 1991.

Clark, John P. H., ed.; *The Cloud of Unknowing: An Introduction*; vols. 1–3; Analecta Cartusiana 119:4–6. Salzburg Institut für Anglistik und Amerikanistik; Universität; Salzburg; 1995–96.

Cowan, Douglas E.; *A Nakid Entent Vnto God: A Source/Commentary on* The Cloud of Unknowing; Longwood Academic; Westfield, NH; 1991.

Dernler, Susan, ed.; *The Cloud of Unknowing*; eChristian, Inc.; Escondido, CA; 2007. (Audio)

Farrington, Tim, and Griffin, Emilie eds.; *The Cloud of Unknowing*; HarperCollins; New York; 2004 (Kindle, 2004).

Freeman, Lawrence; *The Cloud of Unknowing*; Element Books; Rockport, MA; 1997.

Griffiths, John, tr.; *A Letter of Private Direction*; Crossroad; New York; 1981.

I Hodgson, Phyllis; *The Cloud of Unknowing and the Book of Privy Counselling*; Early English Text Society, vol. 218; Oxford; 1944, 1958, 1973, 1981.

Hodgson, Phyllis; *The Cloud of Unknowing and Related Treatises*; Analecta Cartusiana 3; Salzburg Institut für Anglistik und Amerikanistik; Universität; Salzburg; 1982.

Johnston, William, sj; *The Cloud of Unknowing and the Book of Privy Counseling*; Doubleday Image; New York; 1973, 1996, 2005 (reprints: Sourcebooks; Naperville, IL; 1992. Fordham Univ. Press; Bronx, NY; 2000. Doubleday eBook, 2012. Ebsco Publishing E-book. St. Anthony Messenger Press Audio, 2008. Kindle, 2012).

McCann, Justin; *The Cloud of Unknowing and Other Treatises by an English Mystic of the Fourteenth Century, with a Commentary on the Cloud by Father Augustine Baker*; Burns Oates & Washbourne; London; 1924, 1936, 1942, 1943, 1947. (Revised 1952: Newman Press; Westminster, MD; 1952. Burns & Oates; London; 1960, 1964. Templegate; 1964.)

Methley, Richard (Clark, John P. H., ed.); *Divina Caligo Ignorancie: A Latin Glossed Version of the Cloud of Unknowing*; Salzburg Institut für Anglistik und Amerikanistik; Universität; Salzburg; 2009.

Obbard, Elizabeth Ruth; *The Cloud of Unknowing: For Everyone*; New City Press; London; 2007 (reprint: New City Press; Hyde Park, New York; 2008 (e-book, 2008).

Progoff, Ira; *The Cloud of Unknowing: A New Translation of the Classic 14th Century Guide to the Spiritual Experience*; Harper; New York and London; 1948 (reprints: Rider & Sons; London; 1959. Julian Press; New York; 1957. Dell; New York; 1957, 1973, 1983. Crown; New York; 1963. Random House; New York; 1983, 1989).

Smith, Huston; *The Cloud of Unknowing and the Book of Privy Counselling*; CD; St. Anthony Messenger; Cincinnati, OH; 2008.

Spearing, Anthony Colin; *The Cloud of Unknowing and Other Works*; Penguin Books; London; 2001 (Kindle, 2002).

I Underhill, Evelyn; *A Book of Contemplation the Which Is Called The Cloud of Unknowing, in the Which a Soul Is Oned with God*; John M. Watkins; London; 1912, 1922, 1934, 1946, 1950, 1956, 1970, 1998 (reprints: HarperCollins; 1997, 2003. Vega Books; 2003. Dover; 2003.

Digireads E-book; 2004, 2011. Kessinger; 2004, 2007, 2010. Cosimo; 2007. BiblioBazaar; 2007. Lamp Post, Inc.; 2009. Kindle; 2010. E-book Dover; 2012. Bottom of the Hill Publishing; 2012. Jazzybee Verlag; 2012. Limovia.net; 2012. Lulu; 2013. 1922 edition online at Christian Classics Ethereal Library. Theophania; 2013. Audio version, LibriVox (David Barnes, reader); 2008).

I Walsh, James; *The Cloud of Unknowing*; Paulist Press; New York; 1981. (HarperCollins; 2004; Abridged Audiobook; 1998).

Way, Robert; *The Cloud of Unknowing*; Anthony Clarke; London; 1986; and Sourcebooks; Naperville, IL; 1994.

Wolters, Clifton; *The Cloud of Unknowing and Other Works*; Penguin Classics; Baltimore and Harmondsworth, UK; 1961, 1967, 1977, 1978, 2002.

Wyatt, Thomas; *The Cloud of Unknowing*; Penguin Group; New York; 1977, 1978.

NON-ENGLISH TRANSLATIONS OF *THE CLOUD OF UNKNOWING*

Canon, Maria Pauls, and Walsh, James; *La Nube del no Saber/The Cloud of Unknowing*; Editorial Bonum; Argentina; 2009.

Clark, John P. H.; *Introduction and Notes for* Nubes Ignorandi, *the Latin Version of* The Cloud of Unknowing *in Bodleian Library, Oxford*; Salzburg Institut für Anglistik und Amerikanistik; Universität; Salzburg; 1989.

Clark, John P. H.; *The Latin Versions of the Cloud of Unknowing: Nubes Ignorandi, MS Bodley 856*; Analecta Cartusiana 119, no. 1); Salzburg Institut für Anglistik und Amerikanistik; Universität; Salzburg; 1989; and Edwin Mellen Press; Lewiston, New York; 1999.

Durel, Bernard, tr.; *Le Nuage de L'inconnaissance: Une Mystique Pour Notre Temps*; Editions Albin Michel; Paris; 2009.

Hogg, James, ed., Methley, Richard: *Diuina Caligo Ignorancie* from the Pembroke College MS 221; Analecta Cartusiana 119:3; 1995.

Guerne, Armel, tr.; *Le Nuage d'inconnaissance*; Editions des Cahiers du Sud; Paris; 1953. (New edition: Paris Seuil; 1977.)

Massa, Willi, and Willems, Georga; *Die Wolke des Nichtwissens;* Matthias-Grünewald-Verlag; 1975, 1978.

Noetinger, Dom M., OSB, tr.; *Le Nuage de l'Inconnaissance et les Épîtres qui s'y Rattachent*; Alfred Mame & Fils; Tours; 1924. (Newer editions: Solesmes; 1925, 1977.)

Okuda, Heihachiro, tr.; *The Cloud of Unknowing*; Classic Library; Gendaischicho; Tokyo; 1977. (Translation into Japanese.)

Renaudin, Paul, ed. (Bénédictins de Solesmes, trs.); *Mystiques Anglai: Richard Rolle, Juliane de Norwich, Le Nuage de L'inconnaissance, Walter Hilton*; Aubier; Paris; 1954, 1957.

Riehle, Wolfgang, ed.; *Die Wolke des Nichtwissens*; Johannes-Verlag; Einsiedeln, Switzerland; 1980, 1983, 1984, 1991.

Sainte-Marie, Alain; *Le Nuage de l'Inconnaissance*; Les Éditions du Cerf; Paris; 2004.

Strakosch, Elizabeth, tr.; *Die Wolke des Nichtwissens: Ein Anonymes Englisches Werk des 14 Jahrhunderts*; Johannes Verlang; Einsiedeln, Switzerland; 1958.

Von Ivanka, E., ed.; *Die Wolke des Nichtwissens*; Johannes Verlang; Einsiedeln, Switzerland; 1958.

SELECTIONS, ANTHOLOGIES, AND ABRIDGEMENTS OF *THE CLOUD* AND *PRIVY COUNSEL*

Anonymous, ed.; *Selections from the Cloud of Unknowing*; Upper Room Books; Nashville, TN; 1959, 1961.

Anonymous, ed.; *The Cloud of Unknowing and the Jefferson Bible*; Limitless Press; Jupiter, FL; 2011.

Braybrooke, Neville; *A Partridge in a Pear Tree: A Celebration for Christmas*; Darton, Longman & Todd; London; 1960; and Newman Press; 1965. (A massive collection of Christmas material including "To Men of Good Will" from *The Cloud of Unknowing*.)

Clark, John P. H.; "The Cloud of Unknowing," in *An Introduction to the Medieval Mystics of Europe*; Szarmach, Paul E., ed.; State Univ. of New York Press; Albany; 1984; pp. 273–91.

de Jaegher, Paul, ed.; *Christian Mystics of the Middle Ages: An Anthology of Writings*; Courier Dover Publications; North Chelmsford, MA; 2004.

Denaker, Susan, narrator; *The Cloud of Unknowing*; Cassette; Abridged; Audio Literature; Los Angeles; 1995. (EBSCO Publishing E-book, n.d.)

Fleming, David A., ed.; *The Fire and the Cloud: An Anthology of Catholic Spirituality*; Paulist Press; New York; 1978.

Grant, Patrick; *A Dazzling Darkness: An Anthology of Western Mysticism*; Eerdmans; Grand Rapids, MI; 1985.

Hansen, Gary Neal, ed.; *Kneeling with Giants: Learning to Pray with History's Best Teachers*; InterVarsity Press; Westmont, IL; 2012.

Holt, Bradley P.; *The Wisdom of the Cloud of Unknowing*; Lion Hudson PLC; Oxford, UK; n.d.

Kirvan, John; *Where Only Love Can Go: A Journey of the Soul into the Cloud of Unknowing*; Ave Maria Press; Notre Dame, IN; 1996, 2004, 2009.

Kline, Meredith G.; *Images of the Spirit*; Wipf & Stock; Eugene, OR; 1999.

Llewelyn, Robert; *The Dart of Longing Love: Daily Readings from the Cloud of Unknowing*; Templegate; Springfield, IL; 1982, 1986; and Darton, Longman & Todd; London; 1983, 2004.

Miller, Gordon L.; *The Way of the English Mystics*; Burns & Oates; Tunbridge Wells, Kent; 1996.

Wolters, Clifton; *A Study of Wisdom: Three Tracts by the Author of The Cloud of Unknowing*; SLG Press; Oxford; 1980.

Studies and Commentaries on *The Cloud* and *Privy Counsel*

Anonymous; *Articles on 14th-Century Christian Texts, including: Divine Comedy, the Cloud of Unknowing, Purgatorio, Wyclif's Bible, Codex Cumanicus, Vatican Croat*; Hephaestus Books (BiblioBazaar); 2011.

Anonymous; *The Cloud of Unknowing and the Jefferson Bible: Contrasting and Complimentary Ways to Know God*; Limitless Press LLC; Jupiter, FL; 2011.

Armstrong, Karen; *Visions of God: Four Medieval Mystics and Their Writings*; Tandem Library; Minneapolis, MN; 1994.

Ball, Robert Edward; *The Law and the Cloud of Unknowing*; Arthur H. Stockwell; London; 1976.

Bancroft, Anne; *The Luminous Vision: Six Medieval Mystics and Their Teachings*; George Allen & Unwin; London; 1982.

Boa, Kenneth; *Faconnés à Son Image*; Editions Farel; Croissy Beaubourg, France; 2004.

Boenig, Robert; Greenspan, Kate; and Giles, Mary, eds.; *Studia Mystica,*vol. 16; Edwin Mellen Press; Lewiston, New York; 1995.

Burrow, J. A. "Fantasy and Language in *The Cloud of Unknowing*"; *Essays in Criticism* 12 (1977); reprinted in Burrow, J. A.; *Essays on Medieval Literature*; Clarendon Press; Oxford; 1984.

Butler, Dom Edward Cuthbert; *Western Mysticism: The Teaching of SS. Augustine, Gregory and Bernard on Contemplation and the Contemplative Life: Neglected Chapters in the History of Religion*; E.P. Dutton; New York; 1923; and Constable; London; 2nd ed., 1927 and 3rd ed., 1967 (reprints: Arrow Books; 1960; London; 1967; Courier Dover; 2003; Routledge; 2012).

Celiz, Edward; *A Cloud of Unknowing: A Personal Survey of the Great Issues of Religion*;Vantage; Springfield, MA; 1991.

Clark, John P. H. et al., eds.; *Introduction and Notes for* Nubes Ignorandi, *the Latin Version of The Cloud of Unknowing in Bodleian Library, Oxford, MS Bodely 856*; Analecta Cartusiana 278; Salzburg Institut für Anglistik und Amerikanistik; Universität; Salzburg; 2009.

I Clark, John P. H.; *The Cloud of Unknowing: An Introduction*, vol. 1; Introduction; Analecta Cartusiana 119.4; Salzburg Institut für Anglistik und Amerikanistik; Universität; Salzburg; 1995.

II Clark, John P. H.; *The Cloud of Unknowing: An Introduction*, vol. 2; Notes on *The Cloud of Unknowing*; Analecta Cartusiana 119.5; Salzburg Institut für Anglistik und Amerikanistik; Universität; Salzburg; 1996.

III Clark, John P. H.; *The Cloud of Unknowing: An Introduction*, vol. 3; Notes on *The Book of Privy Counselling*; Analecta Cartusiana 119.6; Salzburg Institut für Anglistik und Amerikanistik; Universität; Salzburg; 1995.

Coleman, Thomas W.; *English Mystics of the Fourteenth Century*; Epworth Press; London; 1938; and Greenwood Press; Westport, CT; 1971 (reprint: Kessinger; 2013).

Cooper, Austin; *The Cloud: On the Cloud of Unknowing*; St. Pauls/Alba House; Staten Island, New York; 1990.

Cooper, Austin; *The Cloud of Unknowing: Reflections on Selected Texts*; Burns & Oates; London; 1991; and Search Press;Tunbridge Wells, Kent; 1994.

Cowan, Douglas E.; *A Nakid Entent unto God: A Source-Commentary on the Cloud of Unknowing*; Hollowbrook Publishing; Wakefield, NH; 1991.

Curran, Thomas M.; *An Introduction to "The Cloud of Unknowing"*; Carmelite Centre of Spirituality; Dublin; 1978.

Davis, Carmel Bendon; *Mysticism and Space: Space and Spatiality in the Works of Richard Rolle, the Cloud of Unknowing Author, and Julian of Norwich*; Catholic Univ. of America Press; Washington, DC; 2008.

Davis, Charles, ed.; *English Spiritual Writers from Eelfric of Eynsham to Ronald Knox*; Burns & Oates; London; 1961.

Elwin, Harry Verrier; *Christian Dhyåana, or Prayer of Loving Regard: A Study of "The Cloud of Unknowing"*; SPCK; London; and Macmillan, New York; 1930.

Englert, Robert William; *Scattering and Oneing: A Study of Conflict in the Works of the Author of "The Cloud of Unknowing"*; Salzburg Institut für Anglistik und Amerikanistik; Universität; Salzburg; 1983.

Gardner, Helen L.; *Walter Hilton and the Authorship of the Cloud of Unknowing*; Sidgwick & Jackson; London; 1933. (The most significant work totally disproving the earlier belief that Walter Hilton authored *The Cloud*.)

Gatta, Julia; *Three Spiritual Directors for Our Time: Julian of Norwich, the Cloud of Unknowing, Walter Hilton*; Cowley; Cambridge, MA; 1987. (Reissued as *The Pastoral Art of the English Mystics*; Wipf & Stock; Eugene, OR; 2004.)

Gibbard, Mark; *Guides to Hidden Springs: A History of Christian Spirituality Through the Lives of Some of Its Witnesses*; SCM Press; London; 1979.

Graff, Eric; *The Transmission and Reception of "The Cloud of Unknowing" and the "Cloud" Corpus*; ProQuest; Ann Arbor, MI; 2006.

Griffiths, John; *A Letter of Private Direction*; Crossroad; New York; 1981.

Gwynn, Aubrey; *The English Austin Friars in the Time of Wyclif*; Oxford Univ. Press; London; 1940.

Harrison, Edward; "The Cloud of Unknowing" in *Masks of the Universe*; Macmillan; New York; 1985.

Hilditch, J.; "*The Cloud of Unknowing*: Its Inheritance and Its Inheritors"; unpublished thesis; Univ. of Saint Andrews; Fife; 1987.

Hilton, Walter (Dalgrains, Rev. J. B., ed.); *The Scale of Perfection*; John Philip; London; 1870.

Hodgson, Phyllis, ed.; *The Book of Vices and Virtues: A Fourteenth Century English Deonise Hid Diuinite and other Treatises on Contemplative Prayer Related to the Cloud of Unknowing*; Oxford Univ. Press; London; 1958.

Hodgson, Phyllis; *Three 14th Century English Mystics*; Longmans; London; 1967.

Holt, Bradley, ed.; *The Wisdom of the Cloud of Unknowing*; Lion Hudson; Oxford; 1999.

Hort, Greta; *Sense and Thought: A Study in Mysticism*; George Allen & Unwin; London; 1936.

Hundley, Laura Starr; *A Linguistic and Stylistic Comparison of the Cloud of Unknowing, Julian of Norwich's Revelations and William Langland's Piers the Plowman*; Harvard Univ. Press; Cambridge, MA; 1989.

Jefferson, Thomas; *The Cloud of Unknowing and the Jefferson Bible: Contrasting Ways to Know God*; Limitless Press; Jupiter, FL; 2011 (E-book, 2011).

Johnston, William; *The Mysticism of the Cloud of Unknowing; A Modern Interpretation*; Desclée; New York; 1965, 1967 (reprints: Fordham Univ. Press, 1967, 2000. Anthony Clarke; 1974, 1978. Abbey Press; 1975. SourceBooks; 1992, 1988, 2000; EBSCO; E-book, 2000).

Keating, Thomas; *The Contemplative Journey*, 2 vols.; Cassette; Audio Literature; Los Angeles, CA; 2002.

Kendall, Edith; *A City Not Forsaken: English Masters of the Spiritual Life*; Faith Press; London; 1962.

Kivan, John J.; *There Is a God, There Is No God: A Companion for the Journey of Unknowing*; Sorin Books; Notre Dame, IN; 2003.

Knight, Hilary; *The Apophatic Experience with Special Reference to the Cloud of Unknowing*; Univ. of Wales; Lampeter; 2003.

Knowles, Barbara Damrosh; "Language and Spiritual Action in *The Cloud of Unknowing*"; unpublished Master's thesis; Columbia University; New York; 1966.

I Knowles, David; *The English Mystical Tradition*; Burns & Oates; London; and Harpers; New York; 1961.

Knowles, David; *The English Mystics*; Benziger Brothers; New York; 1927.

Knowles, David; and Hadcock, R. N.; *Medieval Religious Houses: England and Wales*; Longmans; London; 1953.

Lock, C.; "The Cloud of Unknowing: Apophatic Discourse and Vernacular Anxieties," in Borch, Marianne, ed.; *Text and Voice: The Rhetoric of Authority in the Middle Ages*; Univ. Press of Southern Denmark; Odense; 2004.

MacKinnon, Effie; *Studies in Fourteenth Century English Mysticism: Richard Rolle, Walter Hilton, Juliana of Norwich, the Cloud of Unknowing*; (PhD dissertation at Univ. of Illinois; 1934); Kessinger; 2007.

McGinn, Bernard; *The Foundations of Mysticism*, vol. 1 of *The Presence of God: A History of Western Christian Mysticism*; Crossroad; New York; 1991.

McGinn, Bernard; *The Varieties of Vernacular Mysticism (1350–1550)*, vol. 5 of *The Presence of God: A History of Western Christian Mysticism*; Crossroad; New York; 2012.

McIntyre, D. M.; "The Cloud of Unknowing" in *The Expositor*, ser. 7, vol. 4; 1907.

Mariconda, Joseph E.; *The Cloud of Unknowing Annotated: The Art of Contemplative Prayer*; e-book http://christianmystics.com/Ebooks/The_Cloud_Unknowing/Cloud_of_U_Annotated.pdf.

Melillo, Elizabeth G.; *Gloriana's Court*; http://www.gloriana.nu/cloud.html.

Meninger, William A.; *The Loving Search for God: Contemplative Prayer and the Cloud of Unknowing*; Continuum; New York; 1988, 1994, 2007.

Moore, Hastings, and Moore, Gary W. (eds.); *The Neighborhood of IS, Approaches to the Inner Solitude, a Thematic Anthology: Plotinus, Dionysius the Areopagite, the Cloud of Unknowing, the Book of Privy Counseling, Meister Eckhart*; Univ. Press of America/Rowman & Littlefield; Lanham, MD; 1984.

Nieva, Constantino Sarmiento; *The Transcending God: The Teaching of the Author of "The Cloud of Unknowing"*; Mitre Press; London; 1971.

Norquist, Bruce M.; "Prayer: Our Participation in the Triune Life of God: An Analytical Interpretation of the Theology of the Cloud of Unknowing"; unpublished thesis; Univ. of Aberdeen; 1992.

Peers, E. Allison; *Behind the Wall*; SCM Press; London; 1947.

Prokup, Nicholas R.; "Words Made Flesh: Imagery and Incarnation in The Cloud of Unknowing"; unpublished senior honors thesis; Eastern Michigan Univ.; Ypsilanti, MI; 2009.

Riehle, Wolfgang (Standving, Bernard, tr.); *The Middle English Mystics*; Routledge & Kegan Paul; London; 1981.

Rissanen, Paavo; "The Prayer of Being in *The Cloud of Unknowing*"; *Mystics Quarterly 13* (1987).

Sanchez, Celeste D.; "A Study of the Cloud of Unknowing from the Perspective of the Psychology of Consciousness"; unpublished PhD dissertation. n.d.

Sawyer, Michael E., ed.; *A Bibliographical Index of Five English Mystics: Richard Rolle, Julian of Norwich, The Author of the Cloud of Unknowing, Walter Hilton, Margery Kempe*; Clifford E. Barbour Library; Pittsburgh Theological Seminary; 1978.

Steinmetz, Karl-Heinz; *Mystische Erfahrung und mystisches Wissen in den mittelenglischen Cloud-Texten*; Akademie Verlag; Berlin; 2005.

Tixier, René; "'this louely blinde werk': Contemplation in *The Cloud of Unknowing* and Related Treatises," in Pollard, William F., and Boenig, Robert, eds.; *Mysticism and Spirituality in Medieval England*; Boydell & Brewer; Woodbridge, Suffolk; 1997.

Tixier, René; *Mystique et Pédagogie dans "The Cloud of Unknowing"*; ANRT; Univ. of Lille, France; 1990.

Turner, Denys; *The Darkness of God: Negativity in Christian Mysticism*; Cambridge Univ. Press; Cambridge; 1998.

Van Cleef, Jabez L.; *The Song of the Cloud of Unknowing: A Manual in Verse for Teaching the Contemplative Life and a Help for Guided Meditation*; CreateSpace Independent Publishing; 2008.

II Walsh, James; *The Pursuit of Wisdom and Other Works by the Author of the Cloud of Unknowing*; Paulist Press; Mahwah, NJ; 1988.

Watson, Graeme; *Strike the Cloud: Understanding and Practicing the Teaching of the Cloud of Unknowing*; SPCK; London; 2011.

Watson, Katharine; "Friends of God: A Study of the Relationship between Teacher and Disciple in *The Cloud of Unknowing* and Other Medieval English Letters of Spiritual Instruction"; unpublished PhD dissertation; University College; Cardiff, Wales; 1987.

Wiebe, Linda Tiessen; *Questions on the Cloud*; Watershed Online; http://watershedonline.ca/index.shtml.

BACKGROUND AND INFORMATION

Anson, Peter; *The Quest of Solitude*; J. M. Dent & Sons; London; 1932.

Aquinas, Thomas; *Summa Theologica*; Cambridge Univ. Press, Cambridge; 2006.

Augustine of Hippo; *The City of God*; Random House; New York; 2010.

Avrin, Leila; *Scribes, Script, and Books*; American Library Association; Chicago; 2010.

Blans, Bert; "Cloud of Unknowing: An Orientation in Negative Theology from Dionysius the Areopagite, Eckhart, and John of the Cross to Modernity," in Bulhof, Ilse Nina, and ten Kate, Laurens; *Flight of the Gods*; Fordham Univ. Press; Bronx, NY; 2000.

Brantley, Jessica; *Reading in the Wilderness: Private Devotion and Public Performance in Late Medieval England*; Univ. of Chicago Press; Chicago; 2007.

Butler, Dom Edward Cuthbert; *Western Mysticism*; Kegan Paul International; London; 2000.

Cahill, Thomas; *Mysteries of the Middle Ages: And the Beginning of the Modern World*; Random House; New York; 2010.

Chidester, David; *Word and Light: Seeing, Hearing and Religious Discourse*; Univ. of Illinois Press; Urbana, IL; 1992.

Clay, Rotha Mary; *The Hermits and Anchorites of England*; HardPress; Stockbridge, MA (reprint: 2012).

Clément, Olivier; *The Roots of Christian Mysticism: Texts from the Patristic Era with Commentary*; New City Press; New York; 1993.

Colledge, Eric (Brother Edmund); *The Medieval Mystics of England*; Murray; London; 1962.

Connor, Steven; "Towards a New Demonology," in *Becoming Human: New Perspectives on the Inhuman Condition* (ed. Paul Sheehan); Praeger; Westport, CT, and London; 2003.

Corèdon, Christopher, and Williams, Ann; *A Dictionary of Medieval Terms and Phrases*; D. S. Brewer; Cambridge; 2004.

Curtiss, Frank Horner; *The Mystic Life*; Order of Christian Mystics; Philadelphia; 1936.

Davies, Gerald S.; *Charterhouse in London: Monastery, Mansion, Hospital and School*; John Murray; London; 1921.

de Besse, Ludovic; *The Science of Prayer*; Burns, Oates & Washbourne; London; 1925.

de Sales, Francis (Fr. John-Julian, ojn, tr.); *The Complete Introduction to the Devout Life*; Paraclete Press; Orleans, MA; 2013.

De Voragine, Jacobus (Graesse, J. G. Th., ed.); *Legenda Aurea*; Arnoldiana Library; Leipzig; 1801.

Dimon, Theodore, Jr.; *The Body in Motion: Its Evolution and Design*; North Atlantic Books; Berkeley, CA; 2011.

Doubleday, Herbert Arthur, ed.; "Houses of Carthusian Monks: Priory of St. Anne, Coventry," in *The Victoria History of the County of Warwick*, vol. 2; A. Constable; Edinburgh; 1908.

Dugdale, Sir William (Caley, John; Ellis, Henry; Bandinel, Bulkley, trs.); *Monasticum Anglicanum: A History of the Abbies and Other Monasteries ...*; James Bohn; London; 1846.

Dupré, Louis K., and Wiseman, James A.; *Light from Light: An Anthology of Christian Mysticism*; Paulist Press; Mahwah, NJ; 2001.

Dunion, Paul; *Path of the Novice Mystic*; River Grove Books; Austin, TX; 2014.

Dyer, Christopher; *Standards of Living in the Later Middle Ages: Social Change in England c. 1200–1520*; Cambridge Univ. Press; Cambridge; 1989.

Earle, Mary C., ed.; *Celtic Christian Spirituality: Essential Writings—Annotated and Explained*; SPCK; London; 2012.

Egan, Harvey; "The Devout Christian of the Future Will Be a 'Mystic': Mysticism and Karl Rahner's Theology," in *Theology and Discovery: Essays in Honor of Karl Rahner* (Kelly, William J., ed.); Marquette Univ. Press; Milwaukee, WI; 1980.

Fanous, Samuel, and Gillespie, Vincent, eds.; *The Cambridge Companion to Medieval English Mysticism*; Cambridge Univ. Press; Cambridge; 2011.

Fosbroke, Thomas Dudley; *British Monachism or Manners and Customs of the Monks and Nuns of England*; M. A. Nattali; London; 1843.

Fox, George; *A Collection of Many Select and Christian Epistles, Letters, and Testimonies...*, vol. 1 (*The Works of George Fox*, vol. 7); Marcus T. C. Gould; Philadelphia; 1831.

Fraser Papers; *A History of Paper;* Fraser Paper, Ltd.; New York; 1962.

Fry, Timothy, OSB, ed.; *RB 1980: The Rule of St. Benedict in Latin and English with Notes;* Liturgical Press; Collegeville, MN; 1981.

Fuentes Litúrgicas; Ordo Missae Carthussiensis*; Centro de Estudios Filosóficos Medievales; Universidad Nacional de Cuyo;* Mendoza, Spain; 2004.

Fuller, Neathery Batsell; *A Brief History of Paper;* St. Louis Community College; St. Louis, MO; 2002.

Gardiner, Edmund G., ed.; *The Cell of Self-Knowledge: Seven Early English Mystical Treatises printed by Henry Pepwell MDXXI;* Chatto & Windus; London; 1910.

Glasscoe, Marion; *The Medieval Mystical Tradition in England;* Boydell & Brewer; Woodbridge, Suffolk; 1992.

Gossip, Arthur John; *In the Secret Place of the Most High: Being Some Studies in Prayer;* Charles Scribner's Sons; New York; 1947.

Grant, Patrick; *A Dazzling Darkness: An Anthology of Western Mysticism;* Eerdmans; Grand Rapids, MI; 1985.

Green, John D.; *A Strange Tongue: Tradition, Language, and the Appropriation of Mystical Experience in Late Fourteenth-Century England and Sixteenth-Century Spain;* Peeters Publishers; Leuven, Belgium; 2002.

Gregory of Nyssa (Danielou, Jean, ed.); *From Glory to Glory: Texts from Gregory of Nyssa's Mystical Writings;* St. Vladimir's Seminary Press; Yonkers, New York; 1997.

Grimlaicus (Thornton, Andrew, tr.); *Rule for Solitaries;* Liturgical Press; Collegeville, MN; 2011.

Hall, Christopher A., and Boyer, Steven D.; *The Mystery of God: Theology for Knowing the Unknowable;* Baker Academic; Ada, MI; 2012.

Harper, John, ed.; *The Forms and Orders of Western Liturgy from the Tenth to the Eighteenth Century…;* Oxford Univ. Press; London; 1991.

Harper-Bill, Christopher, ed.; *Medieval East Anglia;* Boydell Press; Woodbridge, Suffolk; 2005.

Harrison, Edward R.; *Masks of the Universe: Worlds in the Making; The Heart Divine; The Cloud of Unknowing;* Macmillan; New York; 1986 (reprints: Cambridge Univ. Press; Cambridge; 2003, 2011).

Hendriks, Lawrence; *The London Charterhouse: Its Monks and Its Martyrs, With a Short Account of the English Carthusians After the Dissolution;* Kegan, Paul, Trench & Co.; London; 1889 (reprint: HardPress; Miami, FL; 2013).

Hines, Brian; *Return to the One: Plotinus's Guide to God-Realization*; Adrasteia Publishing; Salem, OR; 2004.

Hodges, Kenneth; *Internet Medieval Sourcebook*; Fordham University; Bronx, NY; 2011; fordham.edu/halsall/source/medievalprices.html

Hogg, James; "Life in an English Charterhouse in the Fifteenth Century: Discipline and Daily Affairs," in Luxford, Julian M., ed.; *Studies in Carthusian Monasticism in the Late Middle Ages*; Brepois; Turnhout, Belgium; 2008.

Holt, Bradley P.; *Thirsty for God: A Brief History of Christian Spirituality*; Augsburg Fortress; Minneapolis, MN; 1993.

Hopkins, Jasper; *Hugh of Balma on Mystical Theology*; Arthur J. Banning Press; Loveland, CO; 2002.

Hughes, Jonathan; *Pastors and Visionaries: Religion and Secular Life in Late Medieval Yorkshire*; Boydell & Brewer; Woodbridge, Suffolk; 1988.

Ingram, Daniel M.; *Mastering the Core Teaching of the Buddha*; Aeon Books; London; 2008.

John of the Cross (Kavanaugh, Kieran, tr.) *John of the Cross: Selected Writings*; Paulist Press; Mahwah, NJ; 1987.

Johnston, William; *Mystical Journey: An Autobiography*; Orbis Books; Maryknoll, NY; 2006.

Jones, R. M.; *The Flowering of Mysticism: The Friends of God in the Fourteenth Century*; Macmillan; New York; 1939.

I Julian of Norwich (Fr. John-Julian, OJN, ed.); *The Complete Julian of Norwich*; Paraclete Press; Orleans, MA; 2009.

II Julian of Norwich (Marion Glasscoe, ed.); *Julian of Norwich: A Revelation of Love*; Univ. of Exeter Press; Exeter, UK; revised ed. 1993.

Kelsey, Morton; *The Other Side of Silence: A Guide to Christian Meditation*; Paulist Press; New York; 1976.

Kerr, Julia; *Life in the Medieval Cloister*; Bloomsbury; London; 2009.

Knowles, David, et al.; *The Heads of Religious Houses: England and Wales, 1377–1540*; Cambridge Univ. Press; Cambridge; 2008; 3:181–82.

Lacoste, Jean Yves; *Experience and the Absolute: Disputed Questions on the Humanity of Man*; Fordham Univ. Press; Bronx, NY; 2004.

Laird, Martin; *Into the Silent Land: A Guide to the Christian Practice of Contemplation*; Oxford Univ. Press; New York; 2000.

Lane, George A.; *Christian Spirituality: A Historical Sketch*; Loyola Press; Chicago; 2010.

Lewis, Clive Staples; *The Allegory of Love*; Oxford Univ. Press; Oxford; 1959.

Lewis, Clive Staples; *The Complete C. S. Lewis Signature Classics*; HarperCollins; New York; 2007.

Llewelyn, Robert; *With Pity Not With Blame: Reflections on the Writings of Julian of Norwich and on the Cloud of Unknowing*; Darton, Longman & Todd; London; 1984, 1989.

Louth, Andrew; *The Origins of the Christian Mystical Tradition: From Plato to Denys*; Oxford Univ. Press; Oxford; 1983.

Macguire, Nancy Klein; *An Infinity of Little Hours: Five Young Men and Their Trial of Faith in the Western World's Most Austere Monastic Order*; Public Affairs (Perseus Books Group); New York; 2006.

MacKendrick, Karmen; *Immemorial Silence*; State Univ. of New York Press; Albany, NY; 2001.

Main, John; *Christian Mediation: The Gethsemani Talks*; Bloomsbury Publishing; New York; 1999.

Main, John (Freeman, Laurence, ed.); *Word Into Silence: A Manual for Christian Mediation*; Canterbury Press; Norwich, UK; 2006.

Main, John (Freeman, Laurence, ed.); *Essential Writings*; Orbis Books; Maryknoll, NY; 2002.

Main, John; *Moment of Christ: The Path of Meditation*; Bloomsbury Publishing; New York; 1998.

Main, John (Freeman, Laurence, ed.); *Monastery Without Walls: The Spiritual Letters of John Main*; Canterbury Press; Norwich, UK; 2006.

Main, John; *The Way of Unknowing: Expanding Spiritual Horizons Through Meditation*; Canterbury Press; Norwich, UK; 2012.

Main, John; *Word Made Flesh: Recovering a Sense of the Sacred Through Prayer*; Canterbury Press; Norwich, UK; 2009.

Maréchal, Joseph, SJ (Thorold, Algar, tr.); *Studies in the Psychology of the Mystics*; Magi Books; Albany, NY; 1964.

Martin, Dennis D.; *Fifteenth Century Carthusian Reform: The World of Nicholas Kempf*; Brill; Leiden, Netherlands; 1992.

Maskell, William; *The Ancient Liturgy of the Church of England According to the Uses of Sarum, York, Hereford, and Bangor...*; Clarendon Press; Oxford; 1882.

McColman, Carl; *Answering the Contemplative Call: First Steps on the Mystical Path*; Hampton Roads; Newburyport, MA; 2013.

McColman, Carl; *The Aspiring Mystic: Practical Steps for Spiritual Seekers*; Adams Media; Fairfield, OH; 2000.

McColman, Carl; *The Big Book of Christian Mysticism: The Essential Guide to Contemplative Spirituality*; Hampton Roads; Newburyport, MA; 2010.

McColman, Carl; *Spirituality: Where Body and Soul Encounter the Sacred*; North Star; Medina, OH; 1997.

McEvoy, J. J., tr.; *Mystical Theology: The Glosses of Thomas Gallus and the Commentary of Robert Grosseteste on* De Mystica Theologia; Peeters Publishers; Leuven, Belgium; 2003.

McGinn, Bernard; *The Essential Writings of Christian Mysticism*; Random House; New York; 2006.

Merton, Thomas; *Contemplative Prayer*; Doubleday; Garden City, NY; 1969.

Merton, Thomas; *Thoughts in Solitude*; Macmillan; New York; 2011.

Montealegre, David; *El Deus Absconditus en Lutero:* Portal Koinonia; http://servicioskoinonia.org/relat/384.htm. (English by Google Translation: *The* Deus Absconditus *in Luther: Contributions to a Theology of Religious Pluralism*.)

Mortimer, Ian; *The Time Traveler's Guide to Medieval England*; Simon & Schuster; New York; 2008.

Mursell, Gordon; *English Spirituality: From Earliest Times to 1700*; Westminster John Knox Press; Louisville, KY; 2001.

Neilson, Eric Robert; *Beyond God's Veil: A True Story of Piercing the Cloud of Unknowing*; MGTG Productions; Port Hueneme, CA; 2012.

Netton, Ian Richard; *Islam, Christianity and the Mystic Journey: A Comparative Exploration*; Edinburgh Univ. Press; Edinburgh; 2011.

Nicholas of Cusa; *The Vision of God*; Dutton; New York; 1928 (reprint: Frederick Unger; New York; 1978).

Oakley, Francis; *The Western Church in the Later Middle Ages*; Cornell Univ. Press; Ithaca, NY; 1985.

Pepler, Conrad; *The English Religious Heritage*; Blackfriars; London; 1958.

Plotinus (O'Brien, Elmer, tr.); *The Essential Plotinus*; Hackett; Cambridge, MA; 1975.

Porter, Stephen; *The London Charterhouse*; Amberley; Stroud, UK; 2009.

Rahner, Karl (Kidder, Annemarie S., tr.); *The Mystical Way in Everyday Life: Sermons, Prayers, and Essays*; Orbis Books; Maryknoll, NY; 2010.

Richard of St. Victor (Zinn, Grover A., tr.); *Twelve Patriarchs, Mystical Ark, Book Three of the Trinity*; Paulist Press; New York and Toronto; 1979.

Roberts, M.; *The Story of Beauvale Priory and the Martyrs*; privately published; n.d.

Rudman, Mark; *Realm of Unknowing: Mediations on Art, Suicide, and Other Transformations*; Wesleyan Univ. Press; Middletown, CT; 1995.

Saudreau, Auguste (D.M.B., tr.); *The Mystical State: Its Nature and Phases*; Burns, Oates, & Washbourne; London; 1924.

Sells, Michael A.; *Mystical Languages of Unsaying*; Univ. of Chicago Press; Chicago; 1994.

Simmons, Thomas Frederick, and Nolloth, Henry Edward, eds.; *The Lay Folks' Catechism*; E.E.T.S.; Kegan Paul, Trench, Trübner; London; 1991.

Smith, Joseph Edward Adams; *A History of Paper: Its Genesis and its Revelations, ...*; Clark W. Bryan & Co.; Holyoke, MA; 1882.

Steinmetz, Karl Heinz; "Thiself a cros to thiself," in Jones, Edward Alexander, ed.; *The Medieval Mystical Tradition in England*; Exeter Symposium 7; D. S. Brewer; Woodbridge, Suffolk; 2004.

Stoeber, Michael; *Evil and the Mystics' God: Towards a Mystical Theodicy*; Univ. of Toronto Press; Toronto; 1992.

Stroumsa, Gedaliahu; *Hidden Wisdom: Esoteric Traditions and the Roots of Christian Mysticism*; Brill; Leiden, Netherlands; 2005.

Tauler, Johannes (Shrady, Maria, tr.); *Johannes Tauler: Sermons*; Paulist Press; New York; 1985.

Taylor, William Frederick; *The Charterhouse of London: Monastery, Palace, and Thomas Sutton's Foundation*; J. M. Dent & Sons; London; 1912.

Temple, William; *Nature, Man and God*; Macmillan; London; 1960.

Tennyson, Hallam; *Alfred Lord Tennyson: A Memoir by his Son*; Macmillan; New York; 1897.

I Thompson, Ethel Margaret; *A History of the Somerset Carthusians*; John Hodges; London; 1895.

II Thompson, Ethel Margaret; *The Carthusian Order in England*; SPCK; London; 1930.

Thurston, Herbert; *The Life of Saint Hugh of Lincoln*; Burns & Oates; London; 1898.

Tollington, Richard Bateman; *Clement of Alexandria: A Study in Christian Liberalism*, vol. 2; London; 1914. (reprint: Gorgias Press; Piscataway, NJ; 2010.)

Tuoti, Frank X.; *Why not Be a Mystic?*; Crossroad; New York; 1995.

II Underhill, Evelyn; *Mysticism*; Meridian Books; New York; 1957.

Vaughan, Henry (Chambers, E. K., ed.); "The Night" in *The Poems of Henry Vaughan, Silurist*, vol. 1; Lawrence & Bullen; London; 1896.

Voeglin, Eric; *Anamnesis: On the Theory of History and Politics*, vol. 6: Univ. of Missouri Press; Columbia, MO; 2002.

Ward, Benedicta; *Miracles and the Medieval Mind*; Univ. of Pennsylvania Press; Philadelphia; 1987.

Way, Robert E.; *The Wisdom of the English Mystics*; Sheldon Press; London; 1978.

Wells, John Edwin; *A Manual of the Writings in Middle English, 1050–1400*; Connecticut Academy of Arts and Sciences; New Haven, CT; 1919.

Windeatt, Barry A.; *English Mystics of the Middle Ages*; Cambridge Univ. Press; Cambridge; 1994.

REFERENCE

Bradley, Henry, ed; Stratman, Francis Henry; *A Middle-English Dictionary*; Oxford Univ. Press; New York; 1995.

Burrow, J.A. and Turville-Petre, Thorlac; *A Book of Middle English*; Blackwell; Cambridge, MA; 1992.

Gesenius (Tregelles, Samuel Prideaux, ed.); *Hebrew and Chaldee Lexicon of the Old Testament*; Eerdmans; Grand Rapids, MI; 1954.

Hachett, Marion J.; *Commentary on the American Prayer Book*; The Seabury Press; New York; 1981.

Mayhew, A. L., and Skeat, Walter W.; *A Concise Dictionary of Middle English*; Clarendon Press; Oxford; 1888.

Mossé, Fernand (Walker, James A., tr.); *A Handbook of Middle English*; Johns Hopkins Univ. Press; Baltimore; 1968.

Onions, C.T., et al, ed.; *The Oxford Dictionary of English Etymology*; Oxford Univ. Press; New York; 1966.

MUSIC, POETRY, FILM, ART, BLOGS

Adams, John Luther; *Clouds of Forgetting, Clouds of Unknowing*; Apollo Chamber Orchestra, JoAnn Fallerra, conductor; New World Records; 1997. (Orchestral work.)

Anonymous; "A Nekid Entente unto God"; http://throughother.wordpress.com/.

Blackshaw, James; *The Cloud of Unknowing*; CD; Tompkins Square label; 2007. (Folk album.)

Claudia Quintet; *I, Claudia*; Cuneiform Records; Silver Spring, MD; 2004. (Contains a track called "The Cloud of Unknowing.")

Cohen, Leonard; "The Window" on *Field Commander Cohen* album; Columbia/Legacy; 2001.

Current 93; David Tibet, composer; *Of Ruine or Some Blazing Starre*; Durto label; 1994. (Contains a track labeled "The Cloud of Unknowing.")

Douglas, James, composer; *Cloud of Unknowing*; Caritas Records; 2001. (Includes the 2nd Movement of "The Cloud of Unknowing" Symphony for Organ.)

Garbarek, Jan; *In Praise of Dreams*; ECM Music Group; 2004. (Includes a track called "The Cloud of Unknowing.")

Geller, Dorothy; *Caught in Unknowing*; CD; Quagmire Records; Santa Cruz, CA; 2013.

Gorillaz; *The Cloud of Unknowing* on the album *Plastic Beach*; Parlophone and Virgin Records; 2010. (Featuring Bobby Womack and Sinfonia VIVA.)

Finch, John R.; *Cloud of Unknowing* song at https://www.youtube.com/watch?v=8scOhgrTfjI.

Fullbright, William; *The Cloud of Unknowing: An Apophatic Retreat—allowing God's Indefinable Presence via Contemplation*; blog: http://fullbrightit.com/thecloudofunknowing.

Harrison, Mike; *The Cloud of Unknowing*; MP3 Download of "progressive rock music" on "Mike Harrison Label"; 2010.

Herrstrom, David Sten; *The Book of Unknowing: A Poet's Response to the Gospel of John*; Wipf & Stock; Eugene, OR; 2012.

Ho Tzu Nyen's performance piece "The Cloud of Unknowing" showed at the Cannes International Film Festival, 2009; the 54th Venice Biennale 2011; the Mori Art Museum, Japan 2012; St. Paul Street Gallery, Auckland, NZ, 2013.

Jenkinson, Megan, artist; *The Cloud of Unknowing*; Art Works; showing at Jonathan Smart Gallery; Christchurch, NZ; 2000; and Book ("a series of images in book form"); self-published; 2004.

Jones, Rickie Lee; *Cloud of Unknowing*; CD; Reprise Recording; 1997.

Laramee, Guy, sculptor: "Fogs and clouds erase everything we know, everything we think we are. After 30 years of practice, the only thing I still wish my art to do is this: to project us into this thick 'cloud of unknowing.'" http://www.guylaramee.com/index.php/intro/.

Lay, Keith, composer; *The Cloud of Unknowing for Orchestra*; 1985. (Performed by the Univ. of Akron Orchestra conducted by Richard Duncan.)

Levertov, Denise; *This Great Unknowing: Last Poems*; New Directions; New York; 2000.

Mehldau, Brad; American jazz pianist refers to *The Cloud* in an interview on a CD sleeve. (Cited in Cook, Vivian; *It's All in a Word: History, Meaning and the Sheer Joy of Words*; Profile Books; London; 2010; p. 225)

Newman, Barbara; *Contemplating the Trinity: Text, Image, and the Origins of the Rothchild Canticles*; Univ. of Chicago Press; Chicago; 2013; (Original medieval miniature in Beinecke Rare Book and Manuscript Library; Yale University; New Haven, CT.)

Omnium Gatherum; "The Unknowing T-Shirt" featuring cover art from the Thomas Cook novel; also a T-shirt with the statement: "We the unwilling, led by the unknowing; are doing the impossible; for the ungrateful." (Attributed to Konstantin Josef Jireček, 1881.)

Pike, Lionel; "God Unto Whom All Hearts Are Open"; Anthem: text from *The Cloud of Unknowing*; Lynwood Music; West Hagsley, UK; 1995.

Pott, Francis; *The Cloud of Unknowing* by Jeremy Filsell; CD; Signum UK label; 2007.

Roach, Steve; *The Magnificent Void*; Fathom Records; 1996. (Includes a track named "The Cloud of Unknowing.")

Rundgren, Todd; *Nearly Human*; Warner Bros. Records; 1989. (Refers to *The Cloud of Unknowing* in the song "The Waiting Game.")

Sylvarnes, Richard, writer, director, editor; *The Cloud of Unknowing*; True Fiction Pictures film; 2002.

Vanderveen, Ad; *The Cloud of Unknowing*; CD; Binky Records label; 2007.

Yarborough, Randal, director and writer; *The Unknowing*; Film; Roundpen Productions; 2009.

ABOUT PARACLETE PRESS

WHO WE ARE

Paraclete Press is a publisher of books, recordings, and DVDs on Christian spirituality. Our publishing represents a full expression of Christian belief and practice—from Catholic to Evangelical, from Protestant to Orthodox.

We are the publishing arm of the Community of Jesus, an ecumenical monastic community in the Benedictine tradition. As such, we are uniquely positioned in the marketplace without connection to a large corporation and with informal relationships to many branches and denominations of faith.

WHAT WE ARE DOING

PARACLETE PRESS BOOKS | Paraclete publishes books that show the richness and depth of what it means to be Christian. Although Benedictine spirituality is at the heart of all that we do, we publish books that reflect the Christian experience across many cultures, time periods, and houses of worship. We publish books that nourish the vibrant life of the church and its people.

We have several different series, including the best-selling Paraclete Essentials and Paraclete Giants series of classic texts in contemporary English; Voices from the Monastery—men and women monastics writing about living a spiritual life today; award-winning poetry; best-selling gift books for children on the occasions of baptism and first communion; and the Active Prayer Series that brings creativity and liveliness to any life of prayer.

MOUNT TABOR BOOKS | Paraclete's newest series, Mount Tabor Books, focuses on liturgical worship, art and art history, ecumenism, and the first millennium church; and was created in conjunction with the Mount Tabor Ecumenical Centre for Art and Spirituality in Barga, Italy.

PARACLETE RECORDINGS | From Gregorian chant to contemporary American choral works, our recordings celebrate the best of sacred choral music composed through the centuries that create a space for heaven and earth to intersect. Paraclete Recordings is the record label representing the internationally acclaimed choir Gloriæ Dei Cantores, praised for their "rapt and fathomless spiritual intensity" by *American Record Guide*, the Gloriæ Dei Cantores Schola, specializing in the study and performance of Gregorian chant; and the other instrumental artists of the Gloriæ Dei Artes Foundation.

Paraclete Press is also privileged to be the exclusive North American distributor of the recordings of the Monastic Choir of St. Peter's Abbey in Solesmes, France, long considered to be a leading authority on Gregorian chant.

PARACLETE VIDEO | Our DVDs offer spiritual help, healing, and biblical guidance for a broad range of life issues including grief and loss, marriage, forgiveness, facing death, bullying, addictions, Alzheimer's, and spiritual formation.

Learn more about us at our website:
www.paracletepress.com or phone us
toll-free at 1.800.451.5006

SCAN
TO
READ
MORE